The Psyche Exposed

Inner Structures, How They Impact Reality and
How Philosophers, Scientists and Religionists
Misconstrue Both

Mike!
Aha - here to
delve into! Distract this
will add to understanding and
big benefit as well...

My best...

First published by O-Books, 2011
O-Books is an imprint of John Hunt Publishing Ltd., Laurel House, Station Approach,
Alresford, Hants, SO24 9JH, UK
office1@o-books.net
www.o-books.com

For distributor details and how to order please visit the 'Ordering' section on our website.

Text copyright: Thomas Daniel Nehrer 2010

ISBN: 978 1 84694 743 8

A CIP catalogue record for this book is available from the British Library.

Design: Stuart Davies

Printed in the UK by CPI Antony Rowe
Printed in the USA by Offset Paperback Mfrs, Inc

We operate a distinctive and ethical publishing philosophy in all
areas of our business, from our global network of authors to
production and worldwide distribution.

The Psyche Exposed

Inner Structures, How They Impact Reality and
How Philosophers, Scientists and Religionists
Misconstrue Both

Thomas Daniel Nehrer

Cover Image and Original Artwork By
Abraham Mathias Nehrer

BOOKS

Winchester, UK
Washington, USA

A Note to the Reader:

What can I do for you?

Actually, I might be able to answer that question better than you at the moment. There is one purpose to the 110,000 words coming up – one single gist to all the illustrations, verbal and pictorial, one point to all the Angles, sections, paragraphs, analogies, metaphors and subtle implications: understanding how life works.

Clearly there's **something** going on here: you find yourself embedded inside a body, sensing a surrounding world. But all the old explanations you've heard just don't describe it accurately.

If you sincerely seek understanding, yearn to see beyond the dim distortion that religion and science have presented and suspect that your core nature far exceeds what you currently grasp, indeed I can help. I have many an insight to share, key realizations to further your quest and benefit your very life – all points of clarity I've gained through my long journey, all integral to improving my life and peace of mind.

If, though, you feel you are well along an esoteric trail toward grand enlightenment, having grasped the key message of a trusted teacher, guru, mystic or Ph.D. of philosophy, that's a different story. Firm adherence to that source as the final, ultimate answer inhibits your ability to absorb anything I have to offer.

Worse, should you stumble upon these passages, totally convinced of your god or your formulae, attached to a philosophical stance or advanced spiritual truth, wanting to show off your status, argue your philosophy, or promote your discipline, yogi, religion, favorite author, healing technique or commercial enterprise based on any of those, then – as an old high school teacher of mine used to say – ah, **you've got the wrong pool hall.**

I suggest you quietly close this book and return to your vaunted truths. If you feel you and your source of expertise have all the answers, you can scarcely benefit from my accounts, for I will likely refute your sacred certainty, **whatever it is**. And you won't appreciate that. Your closed-minded assuredness, blind adherence to whatever notion, will preclude real grasp of my message.

My purpose is never to convince you of anything, nor to argue, prove or persuade. My goal is never to attract you as follower, to convert you to my point of view or impress you with my status. My single purpose is to share insights into life I have personally gained through my long journey. Quite simply: if you are open to them you will benefit greatly. If you aren't, you won't.

That's what I can do for you.

Table of Contents

Preface   1
Begin...   10
Introduction:
  My Role and Your Life   13
  How I Got To Where I Am   14

Angle One: How Life Works   18
  Structured Beliefs   21
  On Brain Function and Gravity   24
  On Action and Being   30
  On This Expression   34
  Being an Unteacher   38
  On Open-Minded and Closed-Minded People   43
  The Illusion of an Objective Reality   49
  And While We're At It   53
  Paradigms and the Psyche   55

Angle Two: Your Journey   60
  Turn to the Right   61
  The Subconscious   74
  Delving Inward   79
  Core Components of the Psyche   86
  Mechanisms of Mind   91
  Conscious-Subconscious Divide   101
  Inner Storage of Information   103
  Important Points   113
  Inner Structures   121
    Projections of Power to "Real" Things   121
    Projections of Power to Conceptualized Things   126
    Planning-Action Projectors of Power   135

Localized Focus: Authority Figures and Limits
    to Scope   136
Supplanting Fantasy for Reality   141
Self-Image   150
World View   159
Truth   160
Compressed Effects at Birth   163
Generated External Forces   168
Automatic Projection of Power   172
Active, Conscious Projection of Power   179
Direct Mother-Related Elements   189
PUFF the Magic Curtailment   209
Separation   211
Vulnerability   213
Behold, The Psyche!   214
Angle Two Wrap   217

Angle Three: Your Path   220
The Lord's Prayer   221
Insurance   230
Relaxation Technique   232

Angle Four: Previous Teachings   235
Man's Long Quest for Understanding   241
The Background   247
From the East   252
From Western Thinking   259
From Clear Awareness   263
Point One: The Nature of the Universe   266
Point Two: Man's Place in the Universe   318
Point Three: What are Good and Evil?   324
Point Four: The Nature of God   331
Point Five: Fate vs. Free Will   338
Point Six: The Soul and Immortality   347

Point Seven: Man and the State 354

Point Eight: Man and Education 362

Point Nine: Mind and Matter 364

Point Ten: Ideas and Thinking 372

Philosophical Regard 377

Conclusion: The End of Text 386

Bibliography 388

Spiritual? What Isn't?

Often enough, seeking great insight into the nature of being, esoteric disciplines attempt to look beyond the mundane for purer, higher spiritual revelations. They may seek altered states of consciousness or contact with advanced spirits to uncover hidden truths from higher planes.

My focus here is much more immediate and direct: I regard life itself. For life must be understood in its entirety, not severed into portions: a pristine spiritual up there and a miserable, problem-laced mess down here. Seeking idealistic, exotic other realms or fancy, mind-blowing special effects, **when you don't yet understand this reality and the standard-state mind that encounters it is** *pure folly*. The real world experienced daily and the psyche, this conscious Self, engaging it – that's what you are looking to understand.

Precisely that is what I illustrate here.

In a brief epiphany on the Greek island of Corfu during a year spent traveling around Europe, I could see clearly that I wasn't one thing, separate and apart from the rocks, trees, water and hills I was viewing – but that I was a **Oneness**, the totality of all things perceiving itself from **within** its own being.

At that point I'd long since abandoned the religion handed me as a child. So I didn't interpret that clarity of vision with imposed notions of winged glory and chanting heavenly host, my perception inflated by convictions of divine grandeur. Nor was the experience an incidental thought, a conclusion or theory, some precept popping out of my rational store of previously heard ideas – and certainly not a hallucination enhanced by Greek ouzo.

Rather, it was a simple, clear recognition of **my core nature**, an intimate awareness spawned as the many beliefs I still held then – scientific tenets, residual religious dogma and other philosophical speculation – seemed to part like heavy curtains that otherwise concealed the simplicity of conscious existence.

That lucid vision passed. But my journey over many years – significantly aided by an inborn ability to recognize fallacious explanations whenever I hear them – led me back to that clarity of perception. Using techniques laid out in the coming pages, I found and eliminated inner roots to outer problems, thus improving my life at each turn as I became ever more aware and confident of the intrinsic tie between Self and the real world. Also, in the process, I scoured my psyche of all synthetic, fallacious notions as to causality – illusory forces and sources that seem to drive life, but which really only respond to one's own propensities.

That journey, then, yielded not only enormous improvement in my life – health, relationships, accomplishment, success, etc. – but a return to that mystic awareness first glimpsed on Corfu. Only unlike that fleeting moment, my clarity of perceiving the Oneness through which life unfolds is ongoing: my normal daily state of awareness – not mystic anymore, simply clear and untainted.

So the unique insights I would share here illustrate in depth the Self **which you are**. They don't highlight a spiritual aspect of life, white-robed and incense-burning, apart from the mundane, but regard all existence consciousness encounters. They look inward to intimate, core aspects of the psyche and connect those intangible elements of mind with real effects manifested in daily events and relationships.

These insights come not from philosophical conclusions I've studied, not from heavenly revelation, not from eastern yogic tradition nor from any age-old or new-age healing technique or spiritual discipline. My unique perspective comes from having spent decades clearing away all the beliefs, conceptualizations, definitions and underlying assumptions that distort the mind's perception of reality.

So I don't illustrate occult othernesses, realms beyond perception and seemingly beyond commonplace grasp. I illustrate *how life works*, how your psyche is embedded every moment of every day in a reality that reflects its own nature. I show from many angles, how Consciousness and Reality, appearing to be separate, related but different, are indeed **intimately connected**.

Thus, understanding life for its myriad of meaningful offerings – creative ventures, child rearing, artistic expression, building of civilizations, travel, music and thousands of other potentials – I see far less value in seeking **escape** from this realm in search of higher planes than in coming to purely perceive how **this one** works. Having arrived at that clarity, you understand that the principal characteristic of **all such encountered realities** remains the same: the manifestation of held values as real encounters. (Life being as brief as it is, we'll both have plenty of time to explore other realms soon enough!)

So for me, the goal had always been – before and after mystic experience – to understand **what I am** and **how life works**. Having come to see that with unique clarity, my purpose here is to share insights leading toward that end.

The purpose of engaging this lifetime is not to duck out on it, to bypass it for other realms, but to come to understand it.

Some Background

The perspectives presented here build upon the core message presented in my first book, *The Essence of Reality* (*EoR*), and my longstanding website of that same name. Those sources and this message illustrate a process in life, a flow which is taking place at all times within your unfolding experience, one wherein real events and relationships are tied directly to your nature.

You may not be particularly aware of that inherent connection between Self and the quality of experienced reality. Much of current humanity isn't, rather ascribing causality of effects in their lives not to themselves but to forces "out there" in the real world – or to intangible sources in an imagined one.

Like them, you learned to see and interpret reality as your parents and culture taught you. At an early age, while learning to communicate and hearing many stories and explanations, you absorbed common cultural notions for what is happening here – beliefs and definitions woven into all you encountered.

These shared beliefs and common religious and scientific concepts were, to a degree, openly incorporated into early lessons, passing along to you quite consciously a defined world view. But more significantly – i.e., with an even greater impact on your life – your parents' world view and societal stance motivated their social behavior and conduct towards you, so that many subtle notions and underlying assumptions were ingrained into your psyche through your treatment, the family's economic status and imposed behavioral standards.

More than that, even, ideas come packaged within language: preset notions, principally of separation between you and the world around you, comprise grammatical structures and the overall gist of language as it breaks Reality into objective pieces **by the very act of word formation**.

The problem is that the preponderance of notions you absorbed – along with their underlying assumptions – were and are at all levels no more than conceptualizations, ideas, synthetic mental constructs that were then and remain even now fundamentally inaccurate and thus fallacious; they are correspondingly damaging.

Because your inner realm, the value content of your psyche, lies at the root of manifested, real experience, imagining that creative power lies outside your Self in real or intangible external forces builds powerlessness into your own self-image, generates fear in your regard for life and results in mistrust of your own ability vs. those external determiners. Because Consciousness and Reality are inherently connected, **inner fallacy** *invariably* **generates outer problems.**

Intensifying that situation are corresponding illusions formed by misunderstanding. The mind embraces held beliefs and pre-accepted tenets. It interprets experience with innate bias towards its favored definitions, such that *any beliefs and definitions you hold seem valid,* regardless of what they are. If you believe in a god, **it seems to be there,** however implausible its depicted nature; if you feature luck, fate or chance as cornerstone processes of life, real experience appears consistent with those archaic notions.

Awareness is *never* **enhanced** by beliefs and definitions held as true; rather, perception is invariably distorted by them. You, as millions of others who have scurried about the face of this planet, do not perceive yourself as the core instigator of real life experience so long as you believe in, consistent with common world views, an array of forces that dictate your life. You can't clearly see the inner-outer connection while attributing causality to sources "out there" which you learned to be causal at an early age.

To avoid the natural shortcoming of the mind – its utter gullibility – the means to gain awareness of life's flow and thus dominion over it, is decidedly **not** to grasp at yet another set of definitions, even seemingly esoteric, spiritual ones, even notions that fairly well depict the inner-outer connection. The psyche can hold many ideas as true, even those in direct conflict with each other – and **all** of them **appear valid**. New understanding presented here, if stacked upon currently held ideas without explicit elimination of those older, invalid ones simply adds to the muddle, resulting in more inner conflict and confusion.

5

No, the solution to clarifying awareness of life's flow requires not acceptance of a newer, greater paradigm, but conscious removal of *all the old ones*, of archaic, fallacious, imaginary notions as to how life works.

Thus, each and every illustration provided here is intended to enhance your awareness of life's inner-outer flow. But it does so, not by building up a new paradigm, but by exposing old fallacy, revealing entrenched illusions and clarifying negating elements held in the psyche. I provide techniques through which you can delve inward into your own mindset to explore, evaluate and spur change, experiencing directly in the process how the real world responds to inner change.

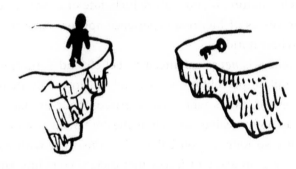

The intention is never to build a new religion or construct a new paradigm, but to get rid of the old ones.

The singular ultimate purpose in exposing psychic functionality from my unique viewpoint is to improve mankind, one reader at a time – because all man's problems lie rooted in age-old misunderstanding of the nature of his own being. And those problems will not abate until man outgrows the old thinking by which he creates and sustains them.

The Exposition
In *EoR*, I looked at life from Four Angles, first divulging illusions formed by common notions then illustrating techniques to delve inward to explore unconscious elements of the psyche – then

clarifying what to look for within. In the Third Angle, I discussed impediments on Your Path toward what I always term "Clear Awareness" – seeing Reality and your Self without the distorting veil of beliefs and definitions. Finally I regarded elements of the western mindset – conceptual roots in religious and scientific tenets common to our time and doubtless woven into your mindset – and past teachings regarding life, pointing out value and exposing fallacy wherever either is apparent.

Here, I delve deeper and look farther.

Expanding on each Angle, I first present here additional perspectives on How Life Works, further exposing illusions native to western thinking – necessary precursors to later illustrations.

The Second Angle regards "Your Journey", for real inner change requires an extensive inward venture from one way of thinking to another. Where *EoR* illustrates Mechanisms of Mind as explicit building blocks that form inner structures at the root of problems in your life, *Psyche* explores much deeper. Here I expose larger scale structures, principally negating elements, which I encountered within my own mindset that restricted quality of life and personal ability to accomplish my goals – until I eliminated them. Some of these you likely harbor as well, for they are embedded in common cultural attitudes. But, whether or not you hold similar inner hindrances, illustration of the complex structures and how to eliminate them reveals the process involved in clearing away inner restrictions.

All such perspectives illustrating the psyche are presented from first-hand experience. My intimate inner view was gained not from academic absorption of knowledge, nor from some guru, ancient visionary or discarnate spirit, but from delving deeply into my own psyche. Having first glimpsed the inner-outer connection in that mystic experience during my twenties, I regained that intimate perception somewhat into my thirties, then proceeded for another quarter of a century to clear away inner limitations to health, quality relationships and success. The message embodied in Angle Two, while highly practical when applied, is unique and unparalleled in its intimate view of the integrated Oneness of Consciousness/Reality.

Angle Three, pointing out hindrances along Your Path, covers three brief (but significant) topics that block progress.

Likewise, Angle Four features extensive new perspectives as I delve into the trail of Western Philosophy. Where my previous writings focus on religion and science as principal influences on the western mindset, here I review historic contributions of philosophers in evolving cultural notions we all received via shared heritage.

For clarity and continuity, each section of this book includes a cursory review of points illustrated in depth in *EoR*. Each reader would benefit by reading *The Essence of Reality* and applying its basics prior to delving into *The Psyche Exposed* – those who have are better prepared for making use of these perspectives. However, that may not be the case. Thus, a brief recap of background material serves a dual purpose: to newcomers, it sets the stage for this deeper look; for those familiar with my approach, it provides a useful review.

But I can only strongly emphasize this point, **critical to your progress** toward seeing life's function and flow more clearly: just reading my perspectives, while of considerable value in overt and subtle ways, will not get you nearly as far along the path as *personally delving into your own psyche*, via techniques illustrated here and in *EoR*.

The inner realm is always causal to the outer. By finding and dispelling, through personal inner excursions, psychological roots to outer problems – core elements of mind which *always* underlie life's difficulties – you, the reader, not only improve all facets of your life, but become, with each step, more clearly aware of the process: an integrated Oneness in which elements of Self become manifested in Reality. And only with that direct exposure to inner-outer flow, can you realize your own power to direct the course of life – a course that improves in quality at each step.

Begin...

In ancient lore, Psyche was the embodiment of beauty, a girl so attractive that even Venus became jealous of the attention she attracted. Venus' plan was to have her son Cupid poke Psyche with one of his arrows so that she would fall in love with a monster – presumably **that** would fix **her**, getting her out of circulation!

But Cupid was so caught up with the beauty of his target that he ended up inadvertently pricking *himself* with his arrow, and, ZAP, he fell in love with **her**. (Apparently even gods then were caught up in external causality.)

Anyway, Cupid and Psyche, with many more twists provided by Venus, became quite the couple – still are, I suppose, as Psyche was eventually granted immortality by Jupiter. So they must be around somewhere – chateau on Mt. Olympus, I suppose.

From Greek times, with Eros and Aphrodite playing the supporting roles, the beautiful Psykhe had been the personification of spirit, breath and life itself – that core initiating entity that inhabits and drives the body. The root word survived in common usage through many language iterations: *psyche* came to refer rather synonymously to the "soul" or "spirit", even "mind" – thus lending its reference to qualities of consciousness from psychological to psychic. But the difficulty of pinning down the exact meaning in this reference equates to that posed by the assignment of quantification by all words: just what part of Reality does it include?

The difficulty of all such words referring to consciousness and its – i.e., your and my – nature is that they try to objectify, to quantify and carve out of apparent reality something that isn't reducible. The soul, spirit, psyche or mind – these are references to the first-person stance each of us takes in the engagement of any reality, waking, sleeping, current or post-death. The Self is, in essence, the totality of what you are, not a limited quantity, set apart by boundaries, a **thing** possessed by something else.

If I could adequately picture that totality here, right now, by a smooth and convincing set of other words, we could save me a lot of writing and you the equivalent amount of reading. But totalities aren't easily pictured by words, as each verbal expression forms subtle boundaries around set quantities comprised by their definitions. So when soul is defined, it becomes some **Thing**, in and of itself, set apart from what surrounds it. The spirit becomes a wispy item, flashing sneakily out of the body at death rather than a reference to the core, focused being of the Self. The mind seems a **possession** of consciousness rather than a functional characteristic of its very incarnated nature.

When I discuss the **psyche**, then, I do so without venturing to solidify the definition of it, because it isn't an "it" at all, but is experienced by you as the Self you perceive – though I may perhaps strip away artificial notions of physical being you might carry within the content of your mindset. Your mind is timeless and extant, your essence superimposed on this real-seeming universe, transfixed within a body and structured to peer out of its eyes at a dynamic, interactive realm.

So the psyche is not something you **have**; it's the functional, cognitive aspect of *what you are*. And that psychological, psychic essence stands embedded in a flowing, interconnected reality that is, in meaning that plays out daily, equally its essence. That is, the meaning displayed by and embodied in real events and relationships is a manifestation of the same meaning held in the complex of the psyche, yours – or more accurately, you, as **it is what you are**, not something you own.

When you come to see that personally, my explanation will make much more sense. But by then, you won't need my depiction anymore..

I wonder if the name of the mythical Psyche came to refer to the deep, seemingly unfathomable essence of being of the beautiful female perceived through the eyes of ancient males wending their myth from such mysteries as they tried to fathom her wiles and whims. Perhaps. But upon understanding your own conscious functionality, piercing prior mysteries of your own mind, you will much less need to play the "away" game of having to analyze the psyche of others.

My Role and Your Life

First Person Singular

The vast majority of people who would elucidate how life works do so in exchange for money. Every preacher, priest, rabbi, self-help expert, imam, avatar, psychologist, scientist, evangelist, prophet, new-age practitioner, financial adviser and bartender is happy to explain the nature of being to you – but please pay as you go, or, in the case of the bartender, leave a tip. It seems, indeed, that anybody currently who gains a shred of enlightenment quickly tries to cash in on whatever discipline got him/her there. (Of all the above experts, only the bartender offers some substance in return for your investment.)

My website, read worldwide, and my many talks internationally are always done for free. Book sales contribute to expenses I encounter in travel but don't profit me personally: any income derived from readers/viewers/listeners beyond expenses will be preserved to assure my message continues after my exit. My purpose in speaking extensively, writing books and maintaining a website is not to make money, but to communicate valued insights I've gained throughout my lifetime.

I neither want nor need anything from anybody.

Indeed, when you come to see life clearly, *you never need to extract money from those who ostensibly don't*. Consider **that** when you evaluate your next favorite spiritual leader.

This arrangement is "right" from other angles as well. Because I don't seek money or acceptance, I keep my message absolutely pure, never compromising my point of view to appeal to potential followers. In fact, I don't want any followers, including you.

To maintain clarity of understanding, you must trust and rely on **yourself** and see things clearly personally. Following anybody, however vaunted and apparently spiritually superior, only limits your own stance, creating in the process detrimental aspects of your self-image.

As a conscious entity engaged in a real environment, you have all the status and personified existential quality necessary within your core nature *right now*. No other being, currently incarnated or in any spiritual realm, has any inherent advantage over you, any intrinsic qualities you lack or any powers beyond your own. What some may have to a greater degree than you is a simple, yet intimate, **awareness** – a recognition of their own nature.

But awareness is not a quality to be gained! It need only be freed by scraping away hindering beliefs and definitions that diminish it, not developed by building up some capability you lack. Intensifying your psychic abilities is unnecessary – you already have them in perfectly functioning condition. You only need to become more aware of your intimate connection to reality. You need not nurture any special spiritual orientation. All of life is spiritual in basis – you only need to recognize clearly that the basis of all human endeavor is **meaning** oriented, not fantasy skewed with idealistic persona and mythical figures. Thus bowing to worship any entity anywhere is likewise unnecessary. You only need to recognize that the rich, deep and multi-faceted qualities of creativity, love and personal expression you hold, so also do others – neither more nor less than you in quantity, only different in current quality.

How I Got To Where I Am

And Where I Am

My unique path to this stage of presenting deep insights into the function of the psyche entails several key elements. It behooves you to recognize my standpoint, as it would to know that of any person you listen to.

First and foremost of these, absolutely critical to my journey, has been that uncompromising, independent nature, a self trust which has allowed me to explore the world of explanations and the inner realm of meaning with a clear reference to reality – not to some fantasy attribution of a religious bent or scientifically tainted description.

I could always evaluate an explanation, a proposed paradigm, and judge clearly whether it could actually apply to how Reality functions. Indeed, after many such episodes, it became clear that *no paradigm* did – or even *could* – adequately explain what was going on here. The propensity of the mind to camouflage input to suit preconceived notions eliminated in my case that common human frailty of diving mind-first into any fragrant vat of religious notions – never noticing that the fragrance was a synthetic aroma covering the real smell of decayed ideas.

So that freedom of mind got me through religious brain-washing already at an early age.

(I clearly recall lying in bed one night as a child, saying my prayers, when I realized that **there wasn't anybody on the other end listening to me!** I had often prayed for certain toys or events, requesting as my mother had taught me for God – the conceptualized Christian one with a capital "G" – to grant my wish. But mostly I never got those things. It didn't take overwhelming wisdom to figure out that that particular paradigm just didn't work.)

Eliminating science as the Great Answer took a while longer – being somewhat trickier to discern in its fallacious nature.

(Science, as a field of inquiry, proudly deems itself to be the ultimate objective look at reality, with two functional short-comings: first, science itself isn't objective, but rather money-biased and predisposed to maintain established notions in which older, entrenched scientists have invested their careers; and second, this Reality is not an objective realm, but subjective – a nature impossible to comprehend through an objective model.)

Science died away as the foundation to my understanding it had been through my teen years (that period when one has all the answers) only through a process of several stages covering many years...

First, I'd left chemical engineering to travel extensively throughout Europe and across the US, the former hitchhiking, the latter with my VW Beetle. During a year of European adventure, covering Ireland to Morocco, Greece to Scandinavia, with intimate exposure to real people via hitchhiking, I began to recognize the effect of how commonly accepted beliefs and definitions affect perception: every culture, widely diverse in belief and general outlook, worked just fine, none much better than the other, only different.

And along the way, I had the mystic experience – something like, looking back on it, the cosmic equivalent of being told the ending of a movie before you've seen much of it.

So for me, that epiphany left a memory of a mindset that was attainable, a psychological perspective very desirable to recapture – but with little clue as to how to get back there.

Return, I would. And the path, while taking more than a decade, included a two-fold view of consciousness: one from the outside, the other from within.

For a time during my thirties I gave psychic readings, able to access intimate information for open-minded subjects who came seeking it – meaningful information pertinent to their lives, not fluff and groping generalities. At the same time, I was developing various techniques for delving into my own subconscious – to be detailed shortly here – seeking inner roots to various real problems I was continuously encountering. In both endeavors, I had begun to explore the unbounded, intangible, yet discernable, realm of the subconscious mind, a vast repository of specific information indicative of, personal to and a critical part of the individual, whether me or any other.

By my late thirties I had regained the immediate Clear Awareness experienced on Corfu – a direct recognition of the intimate Oneness of Self with Reality. Only from then onwards, it was ongoing awareness, not a fleeting glimpse.

It remained the task of another two decades and more, however, to fully utilize that "Clear Awareness" to shed inner restrictions to the realization of my desire. That process involved extensive inner scouring of negating mind mechanisms and limiting conceptualizations – predominant elements of which are illustrated in Angle Two where I expose the function of the **psyche**.

At this point, I am very healthy, never needing recourse to medications, vitamins or any other artificially applied, rationally concocted gesture to make my body be healthier. I have wonderful relationships in my friendships and meet many exceptional people while traveling widely to present my unique perspectives. And I am succeeding in my life's venture – a gesture embodied in this book as well as other outlets of expression – to communicate beneficial insights into life on a widespread scale.

And it only gets better!

So, as I illustrate the functional Oneness of life from Four Angles, understand that I personify my own message: the techniques I discuss, I have used to improve my life **in all aspects**. The mechanisms and greater psychic structures I explain I have worked with in great depth within my own psyche for decades. And the perspectives I offer have been garnered through my own inner journey, neither blindly accepted through an academic learning procedure, ascribed to or copied from a vaunted master nor accepted in idealistic faith from any traditional discipline.

ANGLE ONE: HOW LIFE WORKS

Oneness with Reality

You bring a great deal into a lifetime. Stepping back, conceptually, and regarding your own nature, you notice various qualities unique to your Self that aren't displayed in just that blend by others, even close siblings who share environmental and family traits.

You have unique tastes in music and clothes, talents and tendencies, some degree of confidence and some degree of wariness in a custom blend. You have innate abilities in math, or not, interests in sports, the outdoors, gardening, dancing, intellectual pursuits, reading, history, automobiles, travel in general – or you don't. You likely have considerable inquisitive attributes (or you wouldn't be reading this book) that are indelibly you, unique to your being.

While traditional views might ascribe these characteristics to inherited genetic structures or to qualities of nurturing in your environment, neither of these factors is actually causal of anything. Indeed, the consciousness **which you are** entails the particular batch of qualities that constitute your nature, whereas the physical structure as built from genetic attributes along with the environment you incarnate into – all of these qualities *result from* your nature; they don't cause it.

To have come to your current complex state of mind, you would have lived many lifetimes, learned many lessons and grown as a conscious entity in a multitude of ways.

I say that, not because I accept some eastern philosophical basis of reincarnation or buy into various obvious indicators of the continuity of consciousness beyond death: past life regressions via hypnosis, out of body experiences, near-death experiences, etc.

I say that, rather, because I have navigated the complexities of my mindset for decades, clearing away conceptual debris, archaic notions and mechanisms negating and neutralizing of my intent. I have explored elements of self-esteem, self-awareness and my world view, meaningful and interrelated facets of my unique individuality and cornerstone elements of my own personal value structures.

Within the unbounded unconscious realm – made conscious, actually, by virtue of the retrieval of stored and accessible information – I have found such a rich store of interwoven information, meaning and emotional propensity that the integrity of consciousness as **principal essence**, foremost in all of being, is clearly obvious. Thus, my certainty as to continuity of consciousness beyond death stems from **awareness** of a timeless, highly complex mind function far exceeding in depth and richness any simple accumulation of environment-perception during a single lifetime.

To the point, consciousness finds existence in a now-moment realm of its own engagement, its own making – stemming from qualitative proclivities. You exist, not in a flow of time, but only ever in this *Now* moment, experiencing a kaleidoscope of events and relationships that, however it may seem, emanate in value from you yourself. Life's flow manifests not from second to second, season to season, year to year as the earth orbits the star of its show with axis tilted. No, the real flow is one of meaning, of accomplishment and disappointment, of partnering and family rearing, of career and leisure, of roosting and traveling – with all the meaningful ramifications of those and many other aspects, all taking place in this infinitesimally shallow Now moment.

The thrust of my writing is aimed to help break down illusory notions commonly held – and specifically held **by you** – so that you can come to see that flow clearly.

You can never understand the psyche while holding fallacious views regarding your Self and Reality, notions that invariably distort perception of the integrated Oneness which those seemingly separate essences entail. Further, because the psyche is directly connected to Reality, you cannot begin to fathom Reality's function until you grasp mechanisms and structures layered within the psyche's mindset.

Thus, to adequately illustrate the functionality of the psyche – ultimately clarifying the flow of Reality – I have to first clear away some of the debris that inhibits your current view.

And I do that in Angle One by chipping away at illusory pseudo-truths.

Meaning: Meaning What?

Life exudes purpose; its engagement ranges from the Major Purpose – growing toward greater understanding of your core creative nature – to multifold minor purposes woven into many episodes and aspects. Growth of understanding involves coming to see clearly – not just subscribing to a philosophical tenet thereto – how life unfolds in response to your own nature and resulting in the array of meaningful elements lived out daily.

So, in order to perceive that *purpose itself* and its implicit meaning are at the base of conscious existence, it is vital to discard many common notions that depict reality otherwise.

In Angle Two, I lay out specific inner structures of the psyche, illustrating parts of your mind's function that have been going on in the background of your cognizance throughout your lifetime. But to clear away conceptual debris – in the form of archaic cultural notions – I need first to clarify some aspects of the Consciousness/Reality Oneness that will be vital as preparation for later understanding.

Structured Beliefs

What You Are Consists of What You Hold in Mind

Eastern Mystics teach of chakra points, a series of energy foci that run up and down the spinal column and control various aspects of life. Considerable detailed information is put forth describing chakras and how they impact life and health. The odd part of chakras, however, is that if never taught about them, you don't perceive such a thing. This is because chakras don't exist – unless believed in. In that case, they still don't exist, but they **appear to** within the framework of perception...

Long ago the Greeks believed that their crops wouldn't grow without the blessings of Demeter, who, with some complexity, was the goddess of harvest. It's hard to imagine anybody now actually believing that such a frivolous god could, at her whim, dictate the death of crops. But the people of the time, taught such stories since childhood, had a highly superstitious view of Reality – **all** events and outcomes were deemed consequences of divine decree by one or another of their specialized gods. Thus these stories indeed appeared valid. Entire episodes evolved depicting gods interacting as super-human characters. We know these as "myths", but to the Greeks and later the Romans, these  were real stories, embodying cultural truth, such that gods' personalities seemed real.

So Jupiter, as chief among gods, was as vivid to Romans as Zeus had been to Greeks before them. Likewise, Zeus had evolved as a conceptualized god from Indo-European myth prior to the Greek era, seeming just as real to people who believed in him as Odin to the North German tribes or Wotan to

West Germans of the time – and they as real as Re, Nut or Aten to Egyptians, An or Marduk to Mesopotamians and many other gods of different times to many other cultures.

Of course, none were real **for real**, neither then nor now, but they **appeared** to exist to people taught to believe in them, particularly during childhood when the naïve mind is open to such programming.

(Note: "deiwos" is the root name reference of god in proto-Indo-European, the language spoken by a group of people who, having developed agriculture and the wheel, began to spread out from their homeland near the Black Sea some 6000 years ago. As they populated much of Europe, they diversified into the Celts, Greeks, North and West Germans and Goths, Slavs, Baltic peoples, eventually Romans and others whose languages — along with their innate notions – all stem from one original tongue. As they moved south and eastward, often blending in with other ethnic groups, they became tribes speaking Hindi, Urdu, Punjabi and other languages on the Indian subcontinent and various Persian groups: Farsi, Pashto and Kurdish are all Indo-European languages. As these peoples split and differentiated, blending in with local populations, the language separated in different areas – as did original religions and attributed god-figures.)

Most can appreciate those archaic stories about exotic gods as fiction. Our culture has long since outgrown those primitive beliefs: Wotan and Zeus have long since retired. And most westerners don't subscribe to chakras and eastern teaching, so these beliefs are easily acknowledged as artificial, invalid.

But what will happen when I debunk your own beliefs? Will you make the conceptual leap to recognize that your most cherished concepts, learned as an impressionable child, reinforced by cultural agreement, perhaps enhanced by university professors, are actually only artificial mind-images?

Can you even consider that things held as real only appear to be because **you were taught to see things** that way?

Let's give it a try. Because, without regarding personal beliefs critically, you won't progress very far towards understanding **the psyche**...

Do you believe in a god? The Christian god, named "God" (with a capital "G") is an outgrowth of Yahweh, a local deity held by the Hebrews in ancient times. They believed in Yahweh much like neighboring tribes who had their own gods – with the minor exception that Baal and the others were carved images, idols, while Yahweh was a concept. There really isn't much difference.

Over time, this deity's described characteristics evolved considerably from 1000 BCE, when he was considered a vindictive force to be invoked against enemies, until Jesus of Nazareth depicted a loving and forgiving "Heavenly Father" a millennium later. Now the god didn't change, since there never was such a being outside the fervent imagination of the Hebrews. But the **mind-image of him** held in succeeding generations did. Of course, since then the supposed nature of that god has evolved even further – ever adapting to suit the needs of the current priesthood and the mentality, generally fearful, of the believers.

But if you believe in a god, perhaps even the god named God, he may well seem real. So, what is the nature of this deity? Where is he? Is he corporal, shaped like a man – looking like the image on the Sistine Chapel? Does he exist suspended in a real environment somewhere? Does he make events happen in your life, in the whole world, in the entire universe or in many universes? How does he do so, and why? Does this god consume energy from some source to drive Reality? Where did he come from? Does he change as time goes on?

Of course, believing strongly enough in a god, you will have some sort of answer to such questions, regardless of whether that answer pertains to observed reality – or even makes any sense. If your mind balks at the questioning, you may simply avoid the subject, ignore reality and still cling to old beliefs.

Beliefs, as will be implied, noted and illustrated here many times over, **never clarify how reality works;** *they only cloud your perception of it.* The mind grasps tightly at its favored concepts, comparing all sensory data it perceives to the complex structure of beliefs held – a process to a great extent invisible to conscious attention. The mind rapidly filters and interprets experience, accepting that which falls within its pre-structured beliefs as true, rejecting the rest as false or ignoring it altogether. Thus, ongoing, the mind reinforces its beliefs by favoring familiar, trusted notions consistent with established truths.

Beliefs are like foggy, rippled lenses to awareness, yet often, however bizarre the image that comes through those distorted lenses, it is accepted as clear and normal to the conditioned mind. People often wear their beliefs like a banner, proud of them, as though this confidence would actually provide some validity to artificial mental constructs – as though believing something firmly actually made it true.

In the greater scheme of clarity of consciousness, beliefs have no place whatsoever – whether chakras, harvest deities, or culturally favored creator gods. While harboring **any** beliefs, you will not perceive Reality clearly and will compromise not only perception, but, as a consequence, your full being.

On Brain Function and Gravity

Cerebral Illusions of Considerable Density

Were this an objective reality as assumed by science – and ultimately so confirmed to its own satisfaction by its own proofs (the mind invariably verifies its own beliefs) – it should be easy to discern the mechanism behind two of the most fundamental aspects of reality: consciousness and gravity.

Because science attributes causality only to real-world sources and forces, disavowing any metaphysical roots to life's effects, and because, within that model, the brain is pretty well established as the producer of consciousness, it should be quite obvious where memories are stored: in the brain. (As opposed to lymph nodes, hair follicles or knee tendons.)

Memories, as the stored gist of perception, are as critical to awareness as the driveway and road system are to automobiles. With no roadways, cars would sit in the garage, unable for whatever drivability it entails, to go anywhere; in such a setting it would be meaningless.

Likewise, without recollection of what has already happened as context, what is happening **right now** is meaningless, indecipherable with no ongoing accumulation of meaning to reference – like that car with nowhere to go, having been nowhere. Awareness of an unfolding, enveloping environment absolutely requires reference to what has preceded the immediate present. That reference frame we regard as memory, gathered continuously, accumulates added meaning as we proceed.

So memory is utterly vital to consciousness. Yet no physical structure or mechanism is scientifically apparent for memory. For sure, certain parts of the brain seem associated with – somehow connected to – various body parts. Certain specific locations can be stimulated that induce feelings of pleasure, muscle twitches or other responses. Other areas, mildly jolted, might cue the incursion of memories, yearnings or emotions.

But specific memories are **nowhere to be found**. In a purely physical universe, brain cells would have to manufacture some representative formed substance, some symbolic notation of sensory input – specific molecules or electric charges, something real and tangible to represent all the colors, shapes, smells, impressions, sounds, etc., that make up the complex scene encountered every second – and store these someplace in the cranium for future reference. And there would have to be some dedicated physical element for input from each sense organ, plus representations of meaning drawn from experience and other peripheral items as well as abstract thoughts, plus cascading levels to record emotional significance, fearful response, etc.

But there are no molecules, shreds of protoplasm, minute globules of fat or anything else stuck somewhere either within cells or into gaps between neurons, stored there as symbols of real sensory input and physically retrievable for later recall.

Synapses sparking in the brain are highly complex in nature, communicating immediate information between brain cells using hundreds of trillions of intercellular connections. But passage of that information is momentary, fleeting, holding within the physical realm no depth in time for storage of the enormous complex of memory and associated sensory input and derivative meaning that is available for recall throughout life.

Ponder for a moment how many memories and how much associated information is stored...

Normally, much of your life may not seem readily available to recall: by age 28 you will have lived over 10,000 days. Many of them were probably inconsequential, routine and mundane, thus seemingly lost to recall: you've had perhaps 30,000 meals in that time and thousands of episodes, too, of other regular body functions. You've washed your face, put on shoes and walked out the door how many times in that period? Untold thousands. Much of this redundant, commonplace experience seems to be simply not retained.

But wait! Under hypnosis (not a magic spell, but simply uncompromised focus) many people can recall vividly a great deal of their lives, remembering grand visual scenes, smells, tastes, associated thoughts, details regarding objects, feelings, etc., from all times of their lives. Even tasks of apparently lesser consequence can be recalled in exacting detail through concentrated focus. Indeed, except for some difficulty in discerning one dinner from the other, particularly if many were the same, **your whole life** is stored in memory.

Whether or not you are very adept at recalling details is another question – but it's all there to be remembered.

So the question becomes, how **could** the brain store all this info? Every element of every sense experience would have to be somehow translated into symbolic representation in chemical or electric signals and stored for retrieval in a physical system. But that "system" consists only of cells, specialized brain cells. But even they are only tiny units whose primary purpose is to process nutrients and pass off waste and whose secondary chore is to carry out – unknowingly through reactive response – extremely simple tasks of communication via synapse with its neighbor.

Understanding the complexity and demands on computer disk space of storing and recalling a single, large graphic image – whose data representation is orders of magnitude less than a momentary glance at any 3-D visual field – you might picture how huge a capacity any purely physical system, a brain, would need to store a representation of that view. Yet, according to the scientific paradigm, all accumulated data from years of memory would have to be present in the brain for immediate recall. Vast complexes of visual fields interwoven with meaning evaluation, other sensory data of associated smells and touch, plus emotional responses linked with them at the time of experience – all of that would have to be catalogued for storage and linked in meaning, then contained within whatever physical means was storing it. And, adding to the complexity, memory of all such times even includes memory of the thoughts and feelings attached to even earlier memories that were elicited during prior episodes.

Ponder as well the additional enormous latent capacity for

memory storage used by a concert pianist who has memorized hundreds of works containing millions of notes and other critical notation, of lawyers who memorize volumes of statutes, architects who recall detailed plans from years earlier. In ancient times, prior to the development of writing, communities had specialists who learned and could recite the history of people within their clan – thousands of stories concerning all family lines within their tribe over tens, if not hundreds, of generations. The extent of memorization here clearly indicates that, far from filling up "memory banks" as in a physical storage scenario, the mind gets only better at storage the more it is called upon to store.

Given this enormous capacity for memory, one would think that science could identify the mechanism for how the brain – which is regarded as the source of consciousness in this supposedly purely physical realm – stores information for immediate recollection.

But it can't – because there is no such mechanism in the brain, no chemicals tucked into slots for recall, no synapses logging past items, no physical representation holographic or otherwise, for real experience. There couldn't be for the 20,000 days already lived by a 55-year-old, the 320,000 waking hours spent by then, the 19,000,000+ waking minutes, over one billion waking seconds from which to recall episodes – and still allow immediate access to minute detail from any point within that billion seconds. Every day adds to those numbers, yet the conscious mind can sort through it all virtually instantly for details pertinent to specialized subject matter.

Coming to see consciousness as the **basis** of life, you recognize the artificiality and basic unworkable nature of the scientific paradigm for explaining consciousness as a resultant function of brain operation. It's not that a physical mechanism for memory exists but hasn't been deciphered yet by experts. It's that the functional, living brain, while serving as the focal perspective of consciousness during a lifetime, is **not the basis** of consciousness itself. A physical organ could not possibly store memories, let along function cognitively and creatively, imagining great complex buildings, musical compositions, love, desire and all the complexities of man.

Rather, it's the other way around: Consciousness itself is the basis of being. The brain, like the rest of the body's specialized organs – and indeed all aspects of encountered reality – is a consequence of the specific needs for individual consciousness during an incarnation: an *effect*, not a **cause**. The brain is not a computer for data storage, but a communication organ to interface Consciousness with Reality, the Self with its current vessel for living out a lifetime.

Gravity is a similar non sequitur from the scientific paradigm. Science can measure it, relate it to mass and discern other properties associated with the phenomenon. Empiricism allows significant predictions based on this data and associated observation, develop useful and helpful formulae for widespread applications, apply those understandings for developing machinery and advanced technology. But it can't explain gravity: why do all particles, objects, heavenly bodies, star systems and galaxies – objects on any scale observable – attract each other? Why?

How, in an objective world of particles and objects that are perceived to be and always regarded as separate and apart from each other, can all elements of matter be attracted to all other matter, regardless of scale or distance across empty space? Actually they can't. Or rather, "couldn't", hedging toward the subjunctive mode of implied reality, because this is **not an objective realm**, but absolutely *subjective*.

Only if all matter, all sub-atomic particles, all quarks and all of the apparently physical space they inhabit are part of the same Singularity could elements of Reality attract or repel across space – because they are all parts of the same Oneness, the same interdependent, inter-functional Essence.

Generally, science is great answering "how much", "when" and "what", but really meager with "why". However handy a tool for applications and developments, the scientific paradigm is blind to the inter-active Oneness you encounter daily, held tidily on the surface of this planet, able to remember with meaning all that you encounter.

On Action and Being

What Can Be or Be Done

Mankind has produced a broad range of languages during its tens of millennia communicating complex concepts. Each language subtly tints and flavors the experience of reality in unique ways, such that a speaker of one language doesn't see things just as a speaker of another does.

Grammatical constructs among those tongues vary widely: thoughts assembled into one language come out different from identical ideas molded into expressive structures of another. Words, too, have different delineations. Even equivalent cognates in closely related languages can carry different shadings of meaning, and evoke dissimilar mental images. In this regard, a given individual experiences the same situation differently when considering it in thoughts built in different languages.

But one universal similarity among languages involves the limited nature of what is described by linguistic expression. In effect, only two main aspects of reality can be depicted by speech: being and action. Any language can describe *Being*, the nature and status of what is (or was or will be), or depict *Action*, what is happening (or did happen, was happening, or will happen). Slight offshoots of these exist, as some languages deal with what might have been or should be, what could or would have happened in other conditions, etc. But even these are restricted to evaluating those two categories of status and deed.

Action and Being... That's what we are talking about in all the billions of utterances expressed daily. And almost all of that deals with illusory elements of Reality, for it is so easy to build conceptualizations that seem real, but aren't.

News reports, for example, constitute much of daily expression. Yet news, reported as fact, is **purely** a subjective account, with all reports based on initial interpretation by the correspondent closest to the action, revised by bureau chiefs, distorted at each step, and ultimately edited by the final media source that makes it public. That account, not only distorted by perception every step along the way, was likely twisted further by political bias or even the commercial interest of advertisers. What is reported publicly ultimately bears only superficial similarity to original events and their real significance.

Very much of our modern impression of life is derived from this flow of "news" from centralized sources on down, since rapid communications are now so prevalent and reportage dominates the specific world-views of considerable portions of the population. Even on a much more localized scale, impressions of what's happening around you are based on second- and third-hand reports that have passed through others' interpretation.

What you *encounter*, though, is much more significant to the subsequent context of your life than what you simply hear about. The Action and Being encountered directly is a reflection of you, while the reported events and conditions common to media news releases can only affect you if you build fear as a response to those reports, and accept the events as having some power over you.

The ongoing flow of your life unfolds thus: you exist at this moment of emergence, encountering a Reality that responds to your total nature.

What drives personal Reality – your immediate life, not far-removed events and reports of events, and reports of reports of events – is not the Action aspect that language describes as commonly assumed, but the **Being** part. That focus on Being contradicts our usual notion that you need to take Action, rationally contrived and executed Action, manipulating objects and others to accomplish anything.

The overall image embodying **status of Being** held in mind directly determines unfolding events and relationships you encounter. Planned Action, on the other hand, while it often appears to cause accomplished results, actually only sets into motion (or continues) an encountered Reality that resists, negates or fulfills your efforts.

Planning a course of Action in itself exposes a feature of your mindset: the belief that effort and manipulation are necessary to impel the physical realm. It reveals your self-image as to personal power in relation to others and what their powers are to affect you. And as you proceed, it reinforces that imagined relationship within your mind set.

It doesn't matter *in end effect* what Action you decide to take and ultimately do take. The outcome has been preset by your psyche's nature of Being. Any Action, however cleverly planned and expertly executed, is only part of the consequence; it is never causal.

Action, then, takes place within the *context* of Being, not as commonly regarded as though it would causally shape Being through the manipulative action taken.

My point here is reminiscent of Lao Tzu who pointed out in his *Tao de Ching* (see Angle Four) the limitations of taking Action. But, I'm not warning against taking planned Action, suggesting to avoid or limit efforts. *Avoiding* taking action, based on rational decision-making, is the same rational process as planned Action itself!

Indeed the **real** alternative to taking planned action is simply **responding to natural urges**, spontaneous impulses, without overriding them via rational counter-thought. But you were taught – as Angle Two illustrates – at an early age not to trust your impulses!

Given the tie between your psyche and the reality it encounters, the only effective way of proceeding to impact real events and relationships is, first, to recognize their inherent connection to you. Then come to understand the inner mechanisms involved in your creation of those outer manifestations. And finally, exert your innate power to change your own nature inwardly, whereupon the quality of those events and relationships of your life alters in response.

That process, the clearing of inner limitations, is not to be confused with Action taken. Picking up a rock and tossing it into the river is an **act**. Focused awareness to revise inner values and beliefs involves no "act", no rational, externally manipulative gesture. In revising inner elements, you are not taking Action, but rather reiterating your own Being, establishing a more fulfilling quality-state for personal nature.

Stated otherwise: you are only ever a given, specific Essence – a meaningful status comprising an exact, though very complex set of values. As you change inwardly, you remain a specific Essence **now**, in each moment – though the specific nature has changed due to altering of your subconscious store. Newly revised qualities of Self constitute a revision of Being, with no Action having taken place, even though significant change has occurred. (If this point is still unclear, don't worry: you will grasp it better while proceeding through this book!)

And only personal nature, both at the outset **and after** the change, dictates the ongoing, unfolding quality of events and relationships that constitute life, never that contrived Action you learned to take.

On This Expression

An Excruciatingly Simple Message

Illustrations, iconoclastic expositions and unique insights offered here explore aspects of life as seen from an angle unusual in this time, reflecting a clear

perception of the Oneness of all that is in Reality. You will notice a particularly unique quality in my words: that these depictions never offer up definitions of esoteric things or conceptualized entities not immediately encountered. I only ever deal with things you can see or experience.

Other philosophical systems, though, commonly offer defined, esoteric entities. For example, there are eastern philosophies that depict *kundalini* as an energy pictured as a serpent coiling out the base of the spine; *sushumna* is said to be the central channel for this energy, running as a conduit for the kundalini up the spine to the crown of the head. Along this channel are supposed to exist those chakras mentioned previously, which ostensibly govern parts of the body. To improve these parts of the system, one is recommended to meditate on these things and picture them positively.

But try to find kundalini or sushumna. They're nowhere to be seen.

Quite similarly, western religions typically depict a god to which is attributed creation of the entire encountered universe. This grand and glorified entity is thought to be all powerful – and indeed it would have to be to conjure up untold billions of galaxies, scattered across billions of light-years of space, each containing multi-millions of stars and correspondingly more planets – not to mention dark matter. (This vastness was not perceived when most gods were concocted, so they had to be stretched over time – as needed – to fit.)

Go look for that god; he's not to be found in this reality.

Science, on the other hand (and there are lots of such hands) pictures a universe based on gobs of free-floating, yet inter-reacting particles. It describes detailed, observed forces that dictate the flow of such particles. Most things are thought to consist of atoms, with those in turn made up of sub-atomic particles – neutrons, protons and electrons – which are pictured as each being a combination of yet more elemental (and tinier) particles, quarks. Maybe those are made up of strings...

But wait. Where is an electron, for example, to be found? The closer you look for any such particle, the less you see anything material-like. You find only probability valences, minute fields where some fleeting wisp of energy-stuff might be at any given time – hardly the substantial stuff matter appears to be in daily experience. So, looking for a quark – considered in various combinations to be components of sub-atomic particles – you find nothing of substance. String theory, the latest conceptual-ization, proposes yet smaller components of matter – but these like kundalini or the Christian God, are seen only in descriptive statements (in this case mathematical) but never in reality.

(Quick to add: I have no argument with the conceptual-ization of sub-atomic particles – such a view leads to useful technologies, much more so than gods and kundalini. But as hard and fast objects, however tiny, they just don't exist.)

Some spiritual ventures depict realms or dimensions of different densities or vibratory rates. These are said to coexist with ours and can be experienced in alternate states of consciousness. One common reference is the *Astral Plane*, reputedly the next closest to ours. Some guru masters have experienced these and report back on their nature, giving suggestions how to reach a mind state wherein they may be found.

But you don't see them *here*. And if you don't go looking, with a vivid imagination and pre-drawn notions as to their existence, you won't see them **there** either, wherever "there" might indicate.

My perspectives don't approach any of those, because so oriented, **the mind seeks and finds** solid evidence of any such explanation.

No doubt unlimited realms of perceivable experience lie beyond the real one encountered daily and the dream state engaged nightly. Going looking, you may well find them. You likewise find exactly that god you seek or evidence of "Natural" laws firmly entrenched in your mind. But did they exist with validity before you went looking? Or did you create them in the pointed search, orienting consciousness by setting mental intentions – then fulfilling them.

Given the proper, defining mindset – and a firm conviction of the superiority of that yogi master who explains such esoteric matters to you – you may experience chakras and orient them toward health and improvement in life. And it may appear to work.

You may otherwise, with alternate experts to trust in, find apparent benefit from vitamins, attribute power to crystals or pyramids, perhaps find causality in the orientation of the stars and planets. So inclined, you may encounter forest nymphs romping through meadows or deceased Indian spirit guides to point out the true path.

But these conceptualized sources do not empower Reality; they draw energy, indeed their veritable existence, from **you** through imagination fixing itself on recycled conceptualizations.

My message is remarkably simple, relying on no defined accounts, no paradigm of esoteric being, no conceptualized entities to believe in or bow to. I use no fancy, foreign terms to impress naivety, nor do I dress up in robes with incense burning or rituals to conjure up special effects.

I speak of **mind** – that evaluating, experiencing, thought-generating aspect of your consciousness. You know of mind, because it is an innate part of you. You experience thought directly.

And I speak of **reality** – the flow of events and relationships that constitutes personal life. You know of reality, because you encounter it daily. You know of the joy you feel at accomplishment and acceptance, the disappointment at failure and rejection. You know of events, for they happen all the time, day in, day out, some good, some bad. You know of relationships, for you have them with all others you encounter – to be measured in quality, not angstrom units or arcane Hindu terms.

So I tell you only one thing: the two, *mind* and *reality*, are **One** – interrelated, indivisible, one holding values, the other embodying them in unfolding episodes. What you hold in mind, the whole realm of value and belief, expectation and self-image, becomes real. You might not immediately recognize that – the interrelationship of the perceiver and perceived – but you will when you quit subscribing to all the other notions you were taught.

So you may delve into kundalini, some god or other, "natural" laws and definitions, or astral planes. By all means expand your point of view by exploring new avenues of consciousness. Those explorations will at least (and likely at most) serve to break you away from mundane, archaic conceptualizations otherwise rampant in cultural lore.

But when you do break away, don't just absorb new ideas – fancier, more spiritual-sounding notions – as though they were facts. You just have to outgrow all those new explanations and esoteric conceptualizations, ultimately, anyway so that eventually your Self becomes apparent with clarity.

For the destination on this particular life journey is back home, out of direct engagement with this realm, back to the intangible, integrated non-corporeal Self. But growth comes *in the journey*, during life, not by virtue of having arrived at the destination. And the Singular Oneness of your being is only to be clearly seen in this moment, encountered now – not ever in conceptualizations, esoteric or fanciful, eastern or western, scientifically sound or religiously attested.

So I only ever look at consciousness here, embedded in its integral values during the life experience.

Being an Unteacher

Nullifying Non-Functional Knowledge

Many coincidences occur in life, none of them based on chance. My given name at birth has some unique connections, mildly amusing and apropos if not earth-shattering in strains of enlightenment.

Since I make no claim to haughty titles, the hidden meaning my name carries is at least worthy of note.

Thomas was the name of the father of my mother's mother. Living in Bangor, Northern Ireland, near Belfast, about 1870 he made the less than strategic move to marry an employee of the Kinkead family's business and was disowned by them for marrying beneath his status. On a level of inner meaning, that gesture embodied struggle in life, a quality I did, indeed, inherit via absorption across the generations.

Daniel was a name commonly given to males of the Nehrer line. My middle name recalls that of my uncle, my grandfather and my Great Grandfather along the male side of the family tree.

Daniel Mathias Nehrer left Dobsina – a town now in Slovakia called Dobschau then in the Austro-Hungarian Empire – around 1870. Actually, research showed his name to be Mathias Daniel. With a father and two generations before that named Mathias, though, he seems to have willingly switched monikers.

Prior to all those Mathiases, though, was my great-great-great-great-great grandfather Daniel, born in 1735. *His* father, born in September of 1711 to Joseph and Zuzanna Nehrer, was named...

Take a guess...

Yes, good guess: Daniel.

So I was named ostensibly after my great grandfathers. But those given names carry meaning beyond family usage in a Christian culture. Indeed, many names assigned at birth in European tradition were drawn from Biblical roots. It is there that my names elicit some curious connections.

Thomas was one of Jesus' disciples – the one who, according to tradition, didn't believe that Jesus had returned from the dead until he'd seen him and touched wounds in his hands made by spikes driven through them during crucifixion. So Thomas was known as *the great doubter.*

Or so tradition has it. Oddly enough, having reviewed the Synoptic Gospels (Matthew, Mark and Luke of the New Testament), I find not a single mention of Jesus being nailed to the cross, nor any reference to Thomas during the period after the crucifixion. Various accounts of Jesus' reappearance after death are highly inconsistent among Mark, Matthew and Luke.

But none, reporting various sightings of the reconstituted Jesus, mention Thomas *at all*.

Only John – the latest gospel, composed 80 years after Jesus' death – makes fleeting mention of Thomas touching the wounds of Jesus when he was supposed to have appeared to disciples days after the crucifixion.

The Gospel according to John is generally regarded by scholars as the least reliable gospel in biographical terms. John presents a Jesus considerably different from the Synoptic Gospels, as well as accounts that contradict various details of those earlier writings. Only the writer of John (whoever he was – certainly not the disciple of that name, who would have been a centenarian by the time this account was written, having morphed into being a sophisticated Greek writer rather than the peasant Aramaic speaker of Jesus' time) has Thomas declare he needed to see and touch the nail marks in Jesus' hand and the hole in his side (where he'd been stabbed to be sure he was dead) before he would believe.

John 20:26 continues a week later when Thomas joined other disciples and Jesus came into the house – even though the doors were locked. Jesus, as reported there, then had Thomas put his finger on Jesus' hand and touch his side – at which time Thomas then believed in Jesus' return from the dead. (How he recovered substance again, having passed through a wooden door to get into the room, isn't reported.)

So the doubting part fits me well. Indeed, I doubt much of the unrealistic lore of the gospels altogether.

I don't, however, doubt Jesus lived. Nor do I doubt he had an awareness rather attuned to the inner-outer Oneness – a feature he termed the "Kingdom of Heaven *within*" (although that referential phrase eludes John).

And I don't doubt Jesus was crucified: if you haven't cleared out your own inner conflict and go off verbally questioning the commonly accepted religious definitions of a primitive folk, you are very likely to annoy their long implanted, politically powerful priesthood. Your own negative inner propensities invariably entice negative consequences.

But I doubt pretty much everything else haphazardly reported in the gospels about the Jesus' resurrection scenario. Much of it appears highly concocted, meant specifically to convince an impressionable reader of Jesus' super-human status.

So count me in as a doubter well in excess of Thomas, but certainly in that vein.

Daniel, on the other hand (this one intact), was the "great believer" in Old Testament lore, i.e., the scriptures of Hebrew tradition. Living about 600 BCE, Daniel was a trusted and beloved character during the period when the Hebrews had been removed to Babylon. Embedded in politics resulting from his reading the meaning of dreams – having done so for key figures in the empire's hierarchy – Daniel was thrown by his enemies into the lions' den to eliminate him from the scene, doubtless with the added advantages of not having to clean up the mess or dispose of the body.

Normally that would have been a pretty effective means to curtail his career as court favorite, but...

But Daniel's trust in his god kept the lions at bay, as the story goes (without mention as to why Yahweh let him be put there in the first place – was he powerless to stop it, playing games or just not paying attention?).

Daniel was thus *the great believer*. So my given name contains an odd pairing of opposites, the great doubter and believer rolled into one.

Oddly enough, that status, while appearing as **opposite** to Thomas' doubting nature, is rather complementary in my case. No, I don't believe in any sort of god. But I do unwaveringly trust the function of reality to support my existence in a fashion consistent with my nature. Since my first experience of healing outer issues by eliminating their inner roots, I've seen no other consequence to inner change than outer improvement.

So, having worked through layer after layer of conflict and struggle as elements of my Self, I trust the unfolding reality I encounter daily to fulfill my desires, not oppose, threaten or ignore me – because reality is qualitatively connected to me, always reflecting my inner nature. I trust my body to work very well without artificial interference – vitamins, medicine, folk cures or esoteric healing techniques. And I trust the unfolding of reality now to fulfill my will, not oppose or neutralize it.

But don't look for me to be chucked into mortal danger by my rivals so that miraculous and unexpected events might save me. Real inner peace precludes such a threat occurring in the first place rather than unlikely mitigation of the danger later.

Thus "Thomas" and "Daniel", so linked as my given names, actually have significant symbolic meaning with some accuracy.

And my family name applies as well, in a curious, symbolic fashion. The German word for teacher is "Lehrer", utilized rather commonly as a name there.

Understand, use of family names in European tradition began in about the 14th century as a means to discern people from each other. One Johan in town, a smith who shaped metal, needed to be distinguished from another Johan whose father's name was Andrew, and from a third who came from the north. Slowly, led on by the style of nobility which already had distinctive names, common folk began to refer to Johan Smith, Johan Anderson and Johan North. Each of our western family names originally carried meaning – occupation, place of origin or father's name – when first adopted by an ancestor way back when.

I don't know what the original meaning of "Nehrer" was. Neher, without the first "r" stems from sewing, *nähen*, where the "a" with an umlaut sounds similar to a short "e". But that "r" changes it in form to something like Lehrer, where it is a person who does something associated with the noun: Lehren means to teach. Kehren means "to sweep", so the original Kehrer would have been a cleaner.

But Nehrer isn't so obvious. Josef, my oldest traceable grandfather (7 greats, born circa 1685) could have come from a Nehrung, a narrow strip of land created by wave motion near a sea coast, such as the one along the eastern Baltic near Kaliningrad – then Königsberg, East Prussia. I don't know.

But in both German and English the typical sound beginning expressions of negation is "n", as in not, never, no, and their equivalents nicht, niemals, nein. Thus, Nehrer can be looked upon without stretching credibility too much (do I ever?) as the *negation* of Lehrer, that is, meaning **un-teacher**.

And that applies as well as being doubter/ believer rolled into one. All my accounts are meant, not to define or teach how Reality works, but rather to expose the artificiality and ultimate fallacy of what you've learned elsewhere – so, having shed that, you can begin to see reality clearly, doubt and accept as needed, without rational accumulation to clog your perception.

On Open-Minded and Closed-Minded

People

With six billion people in the world, spanning a vast variety of sizes, shapes and colors and an even greater variety in other discernable differences, finding characteristics by which to divide and categorize mankind is easy.

Gender is one. Draw a line, males on one side, females on the other, with a few staggering the line, perhaps.

Skin color is another boundary often applied – though all six billion+ humans could probably be lined up (perhaps with some offshoots for various hues) with albinos on one end and the

darkest-skinned on the other – with
no discernable difference between
any two people standing together
along the line.

But in my wide travels – ever
wider since publishing my perspectives – I've encountered two separate,
though thoroughly intermingled
groups into which mankind readily
divides itself: those who are open-
minded (OM for short, but not to be confused with the eastern
chant) and those who just aren't (CM, with "C" standing for
closed).

Of course, there are many shades to even **this** designator, but
generally the open-minded crew is always quite receptive to my
perspectives, although not all of them may immediately grasp
my message. OMs often have either consciously considered the
weaknesses of explanations offered by traditional sources for
accurately picturing how life works or at least have doubted it
somehow in the backs of their minds.

The rest of mankind, the CM batch, appearing to constitute
the great majority at the present moment, doesn't question the
ideas given them from early childhood. They have all the
answers they need firmly cemented in acknowledged authorities
and previously accepted explanations; they not only don't
entertain any doubt that their set of beliefs, underlying definitions and subtle assumptions might be flawed, but may well
react with considerable emotional outrage if their favorite
pseudo-truths are questioned.

Some years back, when Reality's interactive function was
already quite clear to me but I had not yet cleared away inner
conflict adequately, I used to encounter CM people at talks I
gave. (Actually, holding that inner mechanism, I was *attracting*
them.) They would either leave early (my preference) when I

came to treading not so lightly on their favorite beliefs or stick around until the question phase, their minds likely awash in counter-arguments to my illustrations. At that point they would launch off into a defense of their darling paradigm or ask a question that wasn't a question.

The latter, that non-question question, was always amusing to me. I rather miss them, since I don't attract CMs anymore. The gist of most people's questions, in that they hadn't grasped a point I'd made during the talk, was that they wanted a deeper look at that specific subject focus. Or they had missed something. Or they wanted to explore further, perhaps how what I'd said applied to some aspect of their own lives. But the non-question questioners would phrase a statement in question form with the clear implication that what I'd illustrated wasn't possible because of some reason or other that happened to stem from their own personal belief structure.

One of the most common of them was some variation on the "hypothetical deformed baby" query. It went something like this: "So my reality depends on my own mind content, eh? What about the child who grew up in Africa without a chance for a good diet or education?" Or, "what about the baby born deformed?"

Of course, this type of question might even come from someone relatively open to my message. But more frequently, it emanated from a person who couldn't fit my large perspective into their limited world-view.

And my response? No one can look into that hypothetical child's psyche to see the roots of their physical problems. To perceive the inner-outer connection, one can only look into one's own mind to relate inner roots to outer problems.

That query rides the subtle assumption that one would only incarnate to be a handsome, successful man or beautiful, glamorous woman in the western idealistic fantasy, rather than a real person with many flaws to work on throughout an incarnation, however long or short, however plagued with problems – which is what we're doing. A short, painful lifetime can be packed with valuable lessons to be learned – perhaps more than a long prosperous one.

Pondering hypothetical people provides no mindset to explore for discerning inner meaning. Even regarding real cases in life only the outer, the result, **the effect,** can be considered – for the mind of a person manifesting deformity or early demise is unavailable for exploration.

Another type of incredulity expressed mildly but proudly was fractional acceptance, often uttered by a partially OM listener: "I agree with much of what you say, but what about..." This sort of questioner would proceed to picture a consequence out of his/her favored understanding for causality – meant not to elicit better clarification for how life actually works, but to cast doubt on what I'd just spent an hour and a half explaining. In the process, such questioners would feel rather proud to have cleared things up according to their own trusted precepts and personally more comfortable at having reconfirmed their belief structure in the process.

The problem to that non-question is that I propose nothing to agree with or disagree with. Each of us perceives and makes sense of a world by interpreting its meaning through a significant array of held beliefs and definitions. **All conclusions** arise out of that complex, adhered-to understanding. My viewpoint stems from having eliminated the common world-view precepts and underlying assumptions that listeners still harbor, mostly with little or no awareness of the mental constructs involved in their ideas. So what I'm reporting is *how the world looks without a belief system* in place to distort perceptions into false views. **Of course** that differs from conclusions held by listeners based on their beliefs – but my point is for them to consider eliminating synthetic beliefs, not simply rely on their rational model to question my account.

So my answer in this case is usually that the questioner missed the point entirely.

A similar question is the percentage-type conjecture: "I can believe that 95% (or 90% or 99%) of life is caused by one's own inner problems, but there is always that chance to get run over by a bus (or get cancer / be in an earthquake)."

My response is the simple observation that any reality featuring even 1% random events is effectively *all random*. If, in any way, "something might happen" outside the scope of predictable occurrence, then it can happen at any time and all of life would be subject to that random event – thus rendered meaningless. Even a 1% random element would cause a glitch, a disaster or problem, at least once every couple hours throughout life – or a disastrous day once every three months or so.

My point is that absolutely and invariably one's life reflects one's mindset, that neither external agents, luck nor chance drive events. Indeed, there **can be no** agents, divine or fiendish, super-natural or random, outside the totality of what you are. That percentage question comes from a cloaked CM person who looks at life as though it were an objective reality with set rules consistent with ones he/she happens to believe in, when life is entirely subjective, emerging in response to the psyche of the experiencer.

So, in regard to OMs and CMs, my approach has long since settled into a peaceful, comfortable relationship. I discuss anything with the former, give talks, chat freely, open my heart and my sincere concern to nurture their curiosity and promote their journey toward better understanding. With the latter, I chat about the concrete world: sports, politics, music, culture, automobiles, the weather, indeed, anything – except the nature of life and what's going on here. Nothing is gained addressing the fantasy interpretation of the world a CM encounters, wrapped in a cocoon of notions seeming more protective to the holder than the conceptual prison it really functions as.

But, very much at peace now, I don't seem to run into CMs much anymore.

From your angle, coming to see yourself as fully causal, gaining through the journey freedom and peace of mind, you will likely feel motivated to share insights. But most others aren't on that same journey – not yet recognizing life *as* a journey; thus, they don't share open-minded curiosity, that openly seeking attitude that got you so far along. As much as you feel drawn to communicate the wonders of Clear Awareness with friends and family, you may find them the least receptive to your unusual views.

That thought brings up several points...

First, as alluded, the degree to which you encounter people not open to greater understanding is the degree to which you still harbor inner conflict. Keep moving along the path; you aren't as far along as you need to be. When truly at peace and fully at ease, you find the correct means to express it and encounter OMs who want to hear you rather than CMs who don't.

In that regard, second, many seekers mistake minor advancement beyond standard thinking to be arrival at the ultimate enlightened destination. Among the ever-growing numbers of spiritual teachers are copious sincere speakers, workshop organizers and writers who have come some distance down the trail. Based on change they've experienced, they think that the improved state of mind as predicted by and achieved through their discipline is *it*, Nirvana, Moksha, The Kingdom of Heaven and the Tao all rolled into one. They often launch off to commercialize their newfound enlightenment extracting money from followers to their cause or selling many books based on their recycled wisdom.

I suggest avoiding that diversion as you proceed; that detour along leads to a cul-de-sac. Having not only attained a clear view of your connection to reality, but also cleared away inner restrictions and negation, you won't need to extract money from people in exchange for your perspectives.

Third, you know when you've arrived at that advanced point, as life works very well without rational manipulation. Health is achieved without medicine, vitamin supplements, preventative intrusion or any other action to outsmart natural body function. Fulfilling relationships are attracted and pathways opened up consistent with your talents to express your views openly – without fear of reprisal from CMs whose beliefs you expose as phony. And your gesture of expression succeeds – along with other fulfilling ventures – without restriction and push-back.

So, of six billion humans in this time, the vast majority are closed-minded. But more and more are coming along who are OMs, looking for answers that you will be able to provide. As one OM to another, I suggest that you put yourself in a position to help them along the path as I've helped you. Do that by proceeding until you not only perceive the Oneness, but have thoroughly purged self-limiting inner elements. Only then will you be positioned to assist other open-minded seekers along their paths.

The Illusion of an Objective Reality

Drawing Lines Where They Really Aren't

I have often mentioned illusions commonly taken as real, based on perceptual distortion of the observer due to preconceived understanding. The most common of all is the notion of an objective reality – a universe of solid objects that functions in a physically predictable manner.

Thinking of a stream, a small river or creek, you immediately picture the flow of water through a natural setting – passing over rocks and boulders, wending through its valley trough on the way, ultimately, to the ocean. You understand the word and "know" what it means.

But what is a stream? What does the noun connote, in reality, beyond general mind-images and culturally shared conceptualization? Where is the boundary that sets a stream apart from that around it which is *not* stream?

Water from rain and daily condensation seeps through the soil constantly. It travels from a greater saturation to a lesser, heading downhill until its molecules join with many others on their trek. That journey might lead to the ocean, or shortcut out via evaporation; it might end abruptly as a deer sips some of the stream or the water is again absorbed into the surrounding soil. From there it might head underground into an aquifer or continue into an alternate drainage pattern through underlying rock. There it might stay lodged in a small crevice of a rock for ages.

So, again, the question: what is a stream? At what instant does the seeping molecule suddenly become stream? Is it a part of the stream as it begins its downhill drift, having just fallen as rain? Or is only "groundwater" then, and becomes stream stuff just as it passes over the last grain of dirt and catches the flow of all the other molecules? Likewise when does it cease to be stream material? If a fish drinks it, does it instantly become fish material and no longer stream component – or is the fish, along with suspended sand and minerals, bugs and debris, part of the stream, or just something *in* the stream?

Well, all of that, observed closely, is answered only by your – or somebody's – definition. In reality, **no boundary** exists. The flow is continuous, and what you call a stream is just a portion of the interrelated Oneness that consists of water passing through many apparent forms and different media.

So the stream is an illusion.

Now that doesn't mean that a stream doesn't exist, that we can't discuss it or wade in it. It just means that clear awareness of the stream allows recognition that a stream is not a thing unto itself, but a defined portion of *all that exists*. Its essence is appreciated only in context of all else.

Another way of saying that is to note that rain runoff doesn't flow into the stream, the stream into a river, the river into the ocean, where its water evaporates – but rather that all these apparently separate things are simply parts of the same complex, interactive Oneness. They just have different names given to them through the act of defining – of setting boundaries.

I live near Pittsburgh, where three rivers are said to conjoin. But the Allegheny and Monongahela cease to exist when they mystically become the Ohio only because early pioneers or Indians named them differently. I've been at the Point (the downtown "triangle" where the rivers meet) many times, and my perception discerns one contiguous batch of water heading westward, some from one angle, some from another, the Mon a bit muddier than the Allegheny until they mix. But I see one trough of water, however many names have been affixed. And that stream, indeed, is only a subset extracted from the whole picture.

A wave, like the stream, is easy to picture. Imagine one crashing on the beach and running up the sand to cover your feet. But what is that wave in terms of being? Does it end at the deepest point of the trough between it and the next wave? Or does the wave end at some median, sea-leve point halfway down its sloping side toward 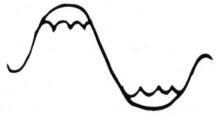 the neighboring trough? When the wave crashes on the beach, does it cease to exist? Or is the flow of its former mass back down the beach to undercut the next wave – is that still wave material, or just water running down the beach?

Of course, it is whatever you accept **as the definition**. And that is because a wave does not exist out of context, without the surrounding medium to set it apart – and certainly doesn't exist at all without the observing mind to define and interpret.

If you've followed my thinking this far, you might be pondering a more solid object – like a rock. Might that be a clear example of just that concept, an object that truly exists?

Not really. You might find a rock that has survived with little change for a few hundred million years, but any one exposed to surface weather is constantly flaking off, affected by wind and sun, and any one embedded underground is being metamorphosed by pressures from the inexorable movement of earth's crust or infiltrated by water seeping into the ground from the stream we considered earlier.

An asteroid, perhaps? How long will it drift before it encounters another body? Regardless of its isolation, an occasional particle will collide with it, slowly changing its nature over eons. One day it will impact another body, a necessity by virtue of the interrelated, changing nature of all that exists in this Reality.

What about life forms? Are horses objects in a universe of isolated entities? Or is a horse, like the stream, just a snapshot of a constant flow of material into it – food, atmosphere, water – and out – sweat, feces, urine, hair, skin, etc. Take a horse out of its environment for a few minutes – like beam it onto that asteroid – and it ceases in very short order to be a horse, at least functionally.

Indeed, a horse is not an object, but the confluence of many elements that comprise its momentary nature. It exists only within its context and relies on that environment to maintain that nature.

My point: nothing, *nothing* commonly regarded as an essence unto itself, an object, actually exists. What does exist is a continuum, a flow of parts, an interrelated interaction of all things whose individual, apparent, "objective" existence is based only on definitions accepted by the observer.

And While We're At It

What About You?

Constant change as an indelible feature of Reality is easy for most to recognize (even CMs!) and acknowledge. One can imagine that water molecule as it falls within a raindrop, makes it way to a stream, passes through a fish's gill, is sipped by a deer, absorbed through digestion into the bloodstream, is sucked out by a horsefly, consumed by a frog and passed back into a pond, only to evaporate, become updrafted into a cloud, rain on your garden, be absorbed by the roots of your lettuce plant and consumed by you. Such interactive flow is going on *all the time.* In conventional terms, those same water particles passing through your body were consumed by dinosaurs in their time and trilobites long before them – and will continue to support the biosphere long after you are finished with them.

As you consumed that water molecule, so you consume and absorb nutrients daily, whereupon they disperse to each cell as needed, all the while sweeping out waste material to be passed back into the ecosystem. That your physical aspect, your body, changes constantly, is easily imagined with each breath.

But the real flow in life is much more subtle, for that standardized view attributes a default solidity to matter, a separate realness that it doesn't really have.

You hold in mind intent and desire: with many avenues in life where you wish to accomplish things. You would like health for you and your family and some degree of prosperity to attain needed and wanted things, travel and pursue personal interests. Security from threat and crime would be high on your list, but acceptance by others in various relationships may be higher.

In recurring patterns, your life responds to all of those and other intentions – a cohesive, collective, interactive response wherein situations including other people involved in them fulfill your inner requirements. But unfolding events and relationships don't necessarily *fulfill your desire*, for aspirations are only part of your mindset. The inner-outer flow, manifesting the total psychic content, also incorporates into the mix fear, worry, inner conflict, self-deprecation and whatever other negatives you hold.

So, forget the water molecule as a featured player in the program of your life. It and all real things fit into those patterns you attract. The real stars of the show (your life, the main feature) are your inner propensities: structures of mind dominating your mindset emerge from that intangible realm into events and relationships that fulfill your self-image and world view. Feeling powerless, you attract relationships that dominate you. Fearing bacteria and conditions, you experience real health issues. Hosting inner struggle, you lead yourself into difficult situations.

The real flow is from within outward, from latent inner characteristics into outer manifestations – where they are experienced, perceived, evaluated and absorbed as meaning back into the psyche.

Thus, the real **you** is seen, not in the physical body you ride through an incarnation (**that** only exhibits part of you), but in the extensive range of distinctive elements held within your psyche. And it is seen clearly in patterns repeatedly manifested in life: people come and go, but the types you attract are consistent. Health issues flare up and heal, but the intensity of them, the impact they have on living and the cost to your finances – those aspects unfold in discernable patterns.

So *what you are* is even less an object than that illusory stream, wave or rock, not even a physical essence, processing nutrients as a biological entity. At your core, you consist of complex meaning and value, held in the psyche as latent complexities, manifested in reality as health status, events and relationships reflective of, indeed embodying, that meaning.

How long have you existed? Because you change all the time, responding to experience and growing in the process, arguably, this current version of you is as fresh and new as spring growth. But the Self doing the experiencing exists outside of time: there was never a time when you didn't exist and there will never come one when you don't.

Paradigms and the Psyche

Regarding Life, not Conceptualizations

After giving a talk, I often encounter questions concerning my message with the questioner having trouble finding an appropriate word to describe what indeed my message *is*. Sometimes people comment on my "theory" or refer to my "philosophy". Actually, neither word applies.

A *theory* is a scientific proposal attempting to describe some portion of reality with the intent to subsequently investigate the

viability of the proposition. Results from this strictly controlled test – obtained either in a carefully formulated laboratory experiment or controlled observation in a natural setting – should either support or disprove the principal proposal of the theory. Results that support the theory, if subsequently reproduced by other researchers and able to withstand criticism of technique, precepts, etc., are seen to validate it.

In science, technically, a theory is never to be calcified into the status of "fact", with no further consideration. But theories that withstand repeated empirical testing tend to be deemed established facts – in practice.

My perspectives illustrating the psyche's innate tie to the Reality it encounters are not theoretical. Science, by virtue of core definition, looks for real-world causes to any results. I see inner, driving values that always elicit outer effects – *always* – whether positive or negative in the resulting consequence to the meaningful regard of the observer.

Notation of that inner-outer causal relationship is not personal theory open to proof or rebuttal. It is an awareness – a direct perception of Reality's core attribute – that results from having eliminated from my own psyche a complex of synthetic definitions, rules, tenets and laws as well as the subtle assumptions underlying them in common scientific understanding. From my standpoint, the Oneness of Self with the flow of events and relationships, of the psyche with the Reality it generates, *is obvious*, as apparent and clearly discernable as this book is to you.

But consideration of metaphysical causes to reality lies **outside the paradigm** of science. As such, attempted scientific confirmation of inner-outer ties would most likely fail any purely scientific test – not because of its inherent invalidity, but because the scientific testing procedure simply does not feature inner causality.

This is not to render science itself as anything less than a useful tool for exploring complex effects in the real world. There is much to be gained by intense, detailed, controlled exploration and examination of the physical realm. Science has obviously served to promote development of a broad array of technological developments.

But science, as a mental endeavor, as a blind promoter of quantitative exploration, has accomplished absolutely nothing in overall effect of improving man's quality of life. Through modern communication – one oft-cited accomplishment of technology – literally hundreds of television stations and thousands of programs vie for viewers. Yet the literary, intellectual quality of 99% of these media statements is lowbrow and trashy, serving to keep most of modern man addicted to archaic ideas and turn the non-critical thinker into a mindless consumer.

Modern science has helped farm technology produce enormous output of food – yet its "advanced" techniques and chemicals lay waste to the land by severely damaging widespread ecosystems with artificial fertilizers and destructive, short-term practices. And it provides for unnatural, environmentally damaging industrialization of farm animals, supplying humanity with meat from horribly mistreated cows, pigs and chickens. Science, in regarding reality as a hollow shell of interactive particles and meaningless objects, has encouraged a mindset that not only mistreats environmental systems, but provides easy justification for mistreatment of other people.

This is not a diatribe against science. But by ignoring the innate inner-outer connection, science sacrifices consequential meaning to its discoveries to the discovery itself. That the application of scientific research has led to the destruction of widespread, major eco-elements of our whole planet is not a problem within the science itself – principally because science, as an entire mode of thinking, *doesn't care about meaning*. It only focuses on the objective realm, answering functional questions, while holding no consideration of impact and outcome. So its developments can be applied without empathy or conscience by CMs looking solely for profit.

My deep insights into the interactive function of

Consciousness/Reality are decidedly not *theory*. They constitute an explanation of the flow going on in reality for each of us at all times as perceived clearly by an individual who sees the innate shortcoming of science for discerning what is going on here.

Is my message a philosophical statement? Angle Four delves into philosophical explanations of man's greatest thinkers, individuals whose explorative, deep and penetrating minds have led man up a gradual slope of understanding through centuries of resistance by CMs.

Still, philosophy generally builds ideas onto ideas, taking rationalized notions from previous thinkers and refining or refuting them via logic and argument. My perspectives come from a mind exhaustively cleared of standard rationalizations and the faulty assumptions on which they rest. So, in discussing aspects of life that philosophers have long explored, my perspectives appear to be philosophy.

Yet points presented here emerge from direct cognition – not by rational conviction, proffered for argument and intellectual discussion, for agreement or disagreement, to establish or refute or confirm. I illustrate life, having cleared away limiting ideas – not building on them – so that this existence could be seen clearly.

So my insights are more like indicators to open-minded seekers than brilliant ideas, rationally supported with tight intellectual argument.

The listener/reader who disagrees with me – or even agrees with me – has *missed the point*. All rational regard put to examination here is based on already-accepted notions held in the mind of that listener or reader. And my point is singularly that so long as any such conceptualizations are held and nurtured, they will interfere with perceiving the Oneness of life's flow and role of the psyche at its initiation.

Closer in a way to an accurate depiction of my message in whatever form is, curiously and not without ironic humor, theology! There is a god in this reality, **and you are it**. I'm only providing perspectives to bring recognition of your innate, inviolable status as sole creator of the patterns that constitute your life.

Shifting to Second

In painting a large picture here of the psyche and its meaningful engagement of Reality, I now turn inward – from general perspectives to an explicit illustration of *how the mind works*.

ANGLE TWO: YOUR JOURNEY

Inner Structures within Your Mindset

Consciousness and Reality are intimately conjoined. Reality cannot possibly be understood without understanding the workings of the psyche that encounters, interprets and ultimately manifests it.

Many predecessors in the intimate regard of life tried to discern life without understanding its inner source. And many illusions have resulted from each of those time-honored ventures. For quite some time philosophy and psychology were closely knit in studied consideration, i.e., within academic approaches. But the two became separated late in the 19th century as each underwent reasoned development, with both of them heavily influenced by science's bent for exploring the outer while ignoring its psychic interior.

I fuse the two into a proper amalgam: the innate Oneness with which life functions requires *both* philosophy's regard for Reality and psychology's focus on the mind to meet in common recognition of the process – but without the distortion both disciplines introduce.

For now, the psyche is illuminated from a different angle; rather than simply exploring *reality* and ideas entertained about it, we explore characteristics of the mind that *does the regarding:* specifically, *yours*. You use your conscious abilities daily, considering reality in its many aspects and then responding – interacting in ways that, to some degree, you've learned, but to a greater extent are core to your attributes, to your conscious capabilities.

There is very much more in play as you interface with reality than simply referencing the many lessons you were taught for tilting that interaction in your favor. The mind works in specific ways, some learned and otherwise absorbed, mostly practiced since your youngest days, while others are innate to your conscious functionality, whether or not you recognize just what that is.

The former, those learned aspects of mind function, are variable – some useful, enhancing to your life track, others highly detrimental to your welfare. The latter, inherent to being, are simply attributes you should be aware of, qualities beneficial to recognize so life can be engaged with greater fulfillment.

Turn to the Right

And Proceed Forward – As Long As You Have To

My mystic experience presented a momentary but crystalline view of the Oneness with which life emerges. Many eastern mystical traditions attempt to glimpse that flow through practiced discipline – mostly via meditation with an effort to quell the thought stream that interferes with awareness.

Basically the mind constantly churning a steady flow of thoughts diverts focus from the present *Now* moment, deterring focused engagement *in the present*. I certainly concur with eastern tradition that the flow of thought – the "crazy monkey" as they term it – absolutely clogs immediate perception. But the long tradition of regarding *thought* as the **core of the problem itself** is fallacious and must be corrected.

(For those who have had exposure to eastern thinking: it is *absolutely vital* to recognize that the seemingly spiritual approaches of Hinduism, Buddhism and many lines of yogic meditation practices have inherent limitations just as significant as western philosophies. My purpose is to expose all limitations to awareness introduced from whatever background.)

Thought, *per se*, is not causal.

While playing a creative role in revising the mindset,

thoughts do not directly drive the flow of encountered reality. So trying to change – particularly to curtail – them doesn't appreciably revise the quality of manifested experience. That gesture only fulfills inner conflict. The crazy monkey flow of intrusive thought, unnecessary to the moment, is, more accurately, a significant *symptom* of the real problem, a functional effect of a problematic situation lying deeper within the psyche.

But before I elaborate on that, let me expand on a critical concept I've emphasized already: the tendency of the conscious mind to fall for its pre-accepted tenets and definitions...

An Idea in Place of Reality

If, for example, you believe (as people did in Jesus' time and region) that evil spirits could get into your head and cause physical and/or emotional illness, **so it would seem**. Suffering from headaches or depression, you might easily attribute the problem to these invading spirits. Indeed, programmed with this notion since childhood, you might hear strange voices, might even feel self-control being usurped by some alien entity. Those demons would seem very real, threatening, very much to be feared, as they could gain control over you.

Such was the common mindset 2000 years ago – awash with religious notions passed along to each new generation of children, that powerful sources out there could dictate your life.

But in ages since then, that primitive notion has been discarded. Illness now has come to be attributed to bacteria or viruses – life forms found in infected areas like sinuses.

According to the scientific paradigm, which attributes causality to real-world agents, microbes are thus deemed to be the *cause* of the sickness. Similarly depression is seen as induced by conditions or hormonal imbalance, again with some obvious feature of the real world seeming to cause the problem.

Such is the common mindset now – dominated by empirical science taught to each succeeding generation as fact – that sources of power **out there** hold sway over your life.

The difference between the two models is significant, but might not be what you think...

Ancient cultures attributed causality to metaphysical sources consistent with archaic religious understanding then. Seeing the intangible spirit world as interactive and threatening, fearing its determinative supremacy, people felt weak and powerless against evil discarnate entities. Modern cultures attribute causality to real-world forces – consistent with scientific under-standing now. Seeing bacteria and viruses as interactive and threatening, fearing their determinative supremacy over body processes, people feel weak, with an immune system powerless to fend off infection.

So what's the difference between the two paradigms? That one is outmoded and superstitious, the other modern and accurate?

No, that's not it at all. Both paradigms are **functionally identical**, simply holding alternate illusory culprits to blame for negative situations.

The real difference – *in effect* – is that most individuals today don't believe in the first model, so they don't find demon possession threatening. But that majority very likely does attribute sickness to external causes – minuscule biological units, ambient conditions or spontaneous body malfunction. This default notion is so widespread in modern western cultural lore as to be virtually unquestioned. So the average person of modern times (and *every* generation considers itself "modern" in comparison to its predecessors) would answer that, ha-**ha**, the difference is that spirit possession is ancient myth, superstition – whereas infectious or environmental cause for illness is proven medical science.

Let's look a bit deeper...

In ancient times, indoctrinated with demon possession during upbringing, people facing these invading evil spirits would need help: a healer or divine agent, like a recognized priest or shaman, to drive out the demons. These holy men and women could neutralize the power of nasty spirits, sending them packing – a countermeasure falling nicely within the belief structure of the sufferer. And so it would work – or at least appear to. (It certainly worked well for the priests and shamans, who lived easy lives off contributions of ignorant suckers who bought into the illusion.)

In modern times, indoctrinated with medical science, people facing bodily malfunction or attack by infectious agents need help: a medical doctor or recognized practitioner to counteract the illness-inducing agent. These experts will neutralize the power of the bacteria with harsh chemicals or other treatment – counter measures falling nicely within the belief structure of the sufferer. So it generally works – or seems to. (Likewise, modern doctors live very well off the ignorance of patients unaware of the body-mind connection.)

Many alternatives are available, of course, for sufferers looking to manipulate their bodies back into proper functionality.

In traditional Chinese medicine, health is thought to result from a balance of yin and yang – perceived opposites into which all things are said to break down. Ill health is imagined to result from an imbalance of those metaphysical essences. When that disparity crops up, a sensitive operative using time-honored rituals – e.g., acupuncture, applied along specified meridians to redirect qi, the vital energy deemed to power life – will wrangle yin and yang back into balance.

This reputedly works pretty well – particularly if you believe in it or accept that such mysteries exist beyond understanding. And allowing yourself to be punctured repeatedly with long needles – particularly at your own expense – is unlikely if you don't believe it a possible healing gesture.

Faced with illness, you may opt for other alternatives, like vibrational medicine – believing that energy fields need to be reset with vibrations of a certain frequency. You might try faith healing, figuring that prayer to the god who must have first initiated the problem might elicit him to reverse the plan if properly beseeched.

Each of these – and many other healing techniques – require buy-in to the general notion of what causes the illness and what has the power to eliminate it.

Also, each such scenario for healing physical ailments works within the context of the near-default world view that personal consciousness resides in a body separate from the surrounding reality and somehow subject to external forces and sources – of whatever description – that need to be fought against, manipulated or otherwise overpowered.

And *that* manipulation or conflict, in turn, originates within rational processes of the mind, ones learned early on in life: evaluate the illness, figure out the "cause" based on learned functionality, devise a plan to deal with it, then execute that plan. The body is perceived as a stupid slab of flesh, weak and incapable of overseeing its own health. All the while qi and god are imagined as having their own agenda – or no intelligent plan at all. Indeed, reality itself is generally seen as rife with external forces ready to inflict physical harm.

Any of those options may be employed by classical gestures trying to heal physical symptoms, because those symptoms, with diverse sources and forces deemed to be manifesting them, are perceived as *the problems themselves*.

But they aren't.

What, on the Other Hand, Is

The mind – the regarding focus of the conscious Self – and the body are intimately connected. Outer ailments, whether minor like infections, allergies or propensities toward injury, more severe conditions like arthritis or psoriasis or major life-threatening diseases like cancer and AIDS, always have inner components – *ALWAYS*. Pomegranate pits could no more be found naturally occurring inside oranges than cancer occurring in bodies whose resident minds don't contain such elements as fear and conflict.

The inner and the outer are *always connected*, with inner values and specific mechanisms of the psyche being directly at the root of outer physical issues.

Providing perspectives whereby you can come to perceive that Oneness is the gist of my communication here.

But so long as you maintain beliefs and culturally shared notions attributing causality to some, to *any* outer source or force, you will neither see yourself as the ultimate determiner of life's flow nor be able to sway that flow towards fulfillment of your own desires. Some of those possible outer agents have been indicated above: one or many gods, qi, conditions, bacteria, spontaneous body malfunction. Some illusory causes are even simpler: external sources like wool, nuts, milk, spices, gluten, chocolate, specific drugs, etc., might trigger an allergic reaction. But others far more subtle will be exposed shortly.

The emergence of real events and relationships in life is part of a continuous cycle. You hold a certain complex mindset at this very moment, exceptionally deep with multiple strata of interwoven meaning. However complex, though, it contains discernible elements: beliefs and definitions, fears and hopes based on a world view and self-image that are consistent with those underlying definitions and their accompanying assumptions – and a grand array of memories that embody aspects of their innate meaning and value, related emotional underpinnings and broader intent.

From that seeming menagerie of diverse, often internally conflictual, interconnected mind-elements emerges a flow of meaningful events and relationships into daily life – where you encounter and engage them as real situations embodying your inner propensities. In perceiving and interacting with this real reflection of the inner self, you learn and change in the process, thus recycling via psychological digestion the meaning that emerged from your own depths of consciousness.

With your mindset having changed a bit through experience, however slightly, explicit qualitative content of the flow will revise accordingly through ensuing days and weeks.

Standard cultural notions, including traditional religious theology and scientific tenets contained within the mindset, attribute the content of life's outcome to conceptualized sources: an independent, divine source for the former, real agents in the case of the latter. Your psyche, to the degree it has absorbed those cultural notions and incorporated them into its world view, reinforces its comfort and contentment by interpreting causality consistent with its base definitions – interpreting a reality it has itself manifested based on those featured beliefs.

So precisely how the world appears to you, personally, and how my accounts here might find their way into your mindset **both** depend a great deal on your current adherence to common cultural "truths" vs. your open-mindedness in regarding different views.

But *regardless* of how you perceive the world and my illustrations, **you create distinct patterns** in events and relationships you encounter. While specific players in life's adventures change, coming and going through time, and your occupation, health issues and leisure pursuits might evolve, patterns as measured in level of struggle and conflict vs. ease and peace continue...

That is, those patterns continue to replicate *until you change* inwardly.

Viewed through standard lenses, the world out there looks otherwise. Based on common regard, it seems to be separate from you and must therefore be controlled, manipulated appropriately, to get it to work as desired. If your mindset, drawing from those common misconceptions, features a causal, interactive god, you will try to manipulate this deity through prayer or offerings – whatever you've learned might cajole that deity to revise his/her/its agenda. If your mindset is more heavily scientific, controlling things would be the solution, taking prescribed action to accomplish goals. In either case, *luck* might come into play where you try to affect **that** by holding a charm – a rabbit's foot, an amulet or talisman of some sort. If fate is imagined to freeze your destiny into place, the response might include depression, given the resultant despair lack of power engenders.

But each such notion and many others in common attitudes – some overt, others subtle – seek to affect a reality *that is already manifested.*

Each healing technique, trying to manipulate the body via medicine, to revise the flow of qi, to heal the body through foot massage in reflexology, etc. – each of them attempts to revise a reality that, by virtue of having been manifested based on psychic content, is a *result*, **an effect**, fundamentally a finished product. In this regard, all such healing techniques and religious or scientific means to elicit positive outcomes are preset to failure: they may fail altogether (people die regularly with the utmost medical attention), or at best, if struggle and conflict are involved in the physical illness or other situation, those inner traits may shift away from health status into some other aspect of life so that the body *seems* to heal in response to the healing gesture.

Because the outer realm is one of effects, if you wish to revise the nature of patterns in health, relationships, or success/failure, you must first shape fundamental change *inwardly*, where its valid cause lies within the psyche. All traditional gestures for healing the body or attempting to substantially improve life are illusory in their apparent efficacy.

So, specifically, how does one do that, change the inner to affect the outer?

That question brings us back to comments concerning *thought* that I presented at the outset of this Angle.

Thinking Again About Thought

Numerous great visionaries, much of eastern traditional discipline and New-Age schools in general regard thought as being causal – propounding in various ways that thought per se is the inner lever behind the quality of life entailed in the outer.

In one view, specific thoughts can be shaped and honed by the disciplined mind, with emerging reality being positively affected as the consequence. This notion is contained in popular books spanning the early 1950s, Peale's *The Power of Positive Thinking*, to the early 21st century, Byrne's *The Secret*, with many other references to basic visualization in between. The gist of this thinking is: if thoughts can be made to focus exclusively on an intended outcome, visualizing only the object of desire, that goal should manifest into reality.

As a variation on that theme, according to common eastern teaching, if the uncontrolled, undisciplined flow of thought from the cluttered mind can be quieted, Reality's Oneness can be perceived and peace attained.

This first notion labels thoughts as the bad guys, promoting personal ability to edit and reissue your thoughts as the key, ultimately, to fulfillment in attaining peace and contentment. The second pictures the very *act of thinking* as the culprit – stop the process and inner peace will ensue. Both philosophies promote surface imagination as the literal creative force. The first implies: scribble desired outcome onto the mind's chalkboard and, having been writ, it will come to pass. For the second, simply clearing out the mind should make everything peaceful and wonderful.

But meaningful events and relationships in life do not emerge from the superficial content of current imagination, the qualities of specific, individual thoughts *or* the very process of thinking. Rather, the quality of experienced life emerges from *the total picture*, as an all-inclusive quantification of the mindset.

Thoughts are like waves on the surface of an ocean in which deep underwater currents flow much more powerfully than any effect resultant from surface movement. Were a wind current directed on the water surface to change wave patterns, still deeper currents would scarcely be affected. Similarly, trying to control the flow of real events and relationships through revised thought process, specifically by visualizing a desired outcome, is no more effective in changing the currents of your life than shifting those surface ripples would be in revising deeper flow patterns.

"Random" thoughts cluttering attention, that involuntary, intrusive flow of thinking eastern mystics try to squelch – as opposed to thoughts elicited intentionally – are not *random* at all, but clear, specific indicators of your core mindset. As such, they are *results* of your mindset every bit as much as encountered events. So thoughts are **indicative** of mind content – but are not the content itself, which lies deeper and *is* indeed as much deeper within the subconscious as it is broader in scope than the simple chatter superficial thought is made out to be. Changing them would be like smoothing the surface waves in that analogy, while the deep currents continue unaffected.

Concerning those intrusive thoughts: while learning early in life how to manipulate mom (to get the cookies), you absorbed procedures for how to manipulate the world. So you now continue that process: first evaluate what's happening, form a plan to affect it, then execute the plan. Thus, most thoughts coming to mind spontaneously result from rational, learned procedures meant to manipulate things into line with your desires. Such plans reflect a myriad of ways you learned to deal with reality.

Attempting to stop those thoughts, as eastern disciplines suggest, without dispelling the underlying control mechanisms, only **intensifies** inner conflict **already there**. And that inner turmoil remains steadfastly in place within the subconscious when meditation is over.

Likewise, attempts to visualize thoughts into imagined outcomes may (or may not, depending on many other inner elements) yield a specifically desired outcome. If it does so without eliminating inner conflict and struggle, however, the psyche will only manifest them in other channels of life. Thus, while perhaps the gesture has led to realizing the vision (there is much more involved than visualization), it will have defeated the purpose and not fully accomplished the intended effect.

For example, suppose lack of money is thought to be the problem in accomplishing your wishes, resulting in ongoing struggle. Believing visualization able to solve money issues, you might repeatedly picture having a lot of money. Should you then come into greater wealth, you might conclude that outcome a direct, successful consequence of visualization. But if you hadn't fully removed struggle from within your mindset, it must become realized in other aspects of life, even though you now have plenty of money! Relatives begin looking to you for financial help, your health may deteriorate or your principal relationship crumbles. Struggle, no longer woven into financial aspects of life, would now be manifested in health or relation-ships.

However, eliminating, one by one, fallacious sources of causality underlying each controlling thought – now *that* approach would accomplish real gain in quieting the mind by eliminating the illusion of outer manipulation.

Indeed, while the typical western mindset looks to conjure up an appropriate action to affect reality (with visualization being one of these – a kind of quick-fix enlightenment), much of eastern mystical tradition rests on the illusion that thoughts in themselves engender reality or drive it. Siddhartha Gautama, the Buddha, set the pace for this principle two and a half millennia ago with his Noble Eightfold Path.

Gautama, a visionary whose life view stemmed from Hindu basics, saw life as wrought from the suffering which seemed inherently tied to all aspects of living: birth, sickness, aging and dying. He felt the source of suffering was *desire*: the craving after sensual pleasures, possessions and such. And he concluded that **desire itself** was bad – that cessation of this craving would stop suffering and end the cycle of incarnations into this innately distress-laden life format.

The Buddha's way to do that involved eight recommended actions to take to conquer desire; these included Right Thoughts, Right Speech, Right Conduct and other actionable gestures.

The inadequacy here – i.e., inability to attain real peace through this Path – lies in Gautama's mistaken impression of thought as inherently causal. Each prescribed gesture requires that the follower rationally correct thinking, speaking, conduct, etc. – that is, intercept wrong thoughts or actions before they come "out", changing them to correct ones. If negative, critical thoughts occur, stop them and substitute loving, peaceful ones; if words are about to be uttered that are blasphemous or hurtful, stop, stifle the expression and voice more positive speech.

Gautama's procedure, rather than clear away inner conflict and dispel negating mechanisms of the mindset that hinder peace and accomplishment, simply adds another layer of rational control onto the already jumbled mindset. So the

Buddha, while recognizing ages ago with true insight that the inner and outer are connected, did not discern the whole picture clearly. He incorrectly saw causality in thoughts rather than in the whole mindset.

In short, your flow of thoughts stems from composite understanding of what you are and how the world works. Words that come to mind are always consistent with your intent and world view; they hearken back to that same understanding of your nature and place in society. Actions you take are similarly consistent with procedures learned early in life for how to make things happen.

Indeed, your very behavior is an *outcome*, not the driving force – a result of your knowledge-based impression as to attribution of power and your place in the world. Each of these rests on the complex mindset held at any point during life. Much of that, in turn, was absorbed from cultural lessons and common notions you encountered through early life.

So thoughts, per se, are *not causal*. That direct connection only appears valid, *if you believe in it* – much as divine intervention, causality as a consequence of action or any other paradigm. Advanced manipulation of thought is no more causal than crystals, pyramids, hard work, lucky charms, prayer or wishing upon a star. Any of those, believed in, seem to yield real results. But the real cause lies deeper, resting subtly within your own mindset.

And herein resides a *highly significant realization* for readers who seek a Clear Awareness of life's functionality. The greatest caveat is the tendency to latch onto a greater, fancier, more esoteric-sounding paradigm for accepted "truth". That can be one offered up by a highly noted, highly vaunted visionary, by a grandiose religious movement with lots of money and big cathedrals or by a spiritual-sounding discipline of a noted yogi master, replete with white robes, incense and candles. Or a simple explanation like the Power of Positive Thinking or any sort of visualization technique: easy to grasp and apply, but ineffective and illusory. (Most people seem to prefer quick, easy procedures that don't work, rather than deep, long-term inner quests that *do*.)

The mind is invariably fooled by its accepted tenets. Abandoning old notions in favor of New Age conceptualizations is easy, thinking you've actually gained ground toward attaining greater awareness. But ultimately, to become fully aware of your own nature, you must shed old philosophical ideas completely – all of them, even ones that effectively describe the inner-outer integration (like this one) – and *come to see for yourself* the Oneness with which life flows.

The Subconscious

Making it Conscious

Consciousness and Reality are two aspects of the same Singularity: *YOU*. Values you hold within your mindset become woven into the meaning of events that unfold in daily life. In addition to disposing of notions contrary to that essence, it is vital to gain awareness of the psyche's workings, coming to see clearly subconscious mechanisms involved as your attributes are translated into real events.

And that requires delving deeply into subconscious stores of information undergirding consciousness, supporting your rational engagement of life on an even keel of daily psychological function.

As to terminology, the subconscious can be referred to as the "unconscious", but I find the former term more clearly descriptive. Meaningful material stored within is, in my experience, more accurately thought of as *below* conscious attention, thus "sub-", rather than opposite of conscious focus or a lacking it as implied by the "un-" prefix. In either case, turning your focus inward, perspectives of significance can be discerned – which again is better illustrated by regarding mind content as underlying conscious focus and thus retrievable, not out of the scope of conscious access, as implied by the *un*conscious reference.

In traditional psychology, the subconscious is commonly broken further into a state called the "preconscious", indicating a body of information to which the mind has ready access, compared to what is regarded as the unconscious, seen as housing repressed, inaccessible info. I see *no value* in this inaccurate categorization. When not curtailed by beliefs, emotional sensitivity or contrary impressions serving to limit access to a given memory or evaluation, the mind can access the full store of its own information, value relationships and derived meaning. Information access is not *innately* restricted by some hard-coded hindrance to the psyche for retrieving it, lodged out of reach due to structural characteristics of mind-function inability.

Given an appropriate technique to bypass emotion- and belief-based restraints, all pertinent info is available to the sincere, determined seeker. That includes unbounded information about every physical function at all times, how events combine to impact life and much else – but all oriented toward meaning, as opposed to structure. The subconscious is thus not delimited, a thing unto itself, either physically or in conceptual structure, but simply an extended aspect of the psyche, of the total Self.

Thus, I regard the *subconscious* here as any and all information held subtly within the psyche which is not currently in mind, i.e., in current focused attention of the experiencing Self.

Shortly I will present techniques for extracting info critical to self-exploration and improvement that may otherwise be impeded by inner restrictions.

Driving a car doesn't require knowing how they work. The internal combustion engine, complex operation of a transmission taking kinetic energy output from the engine and converting it to the drive shaft and ultimately to the wheels, brakes for stopping, the multi-dimensional function of the suspension in getting the vehicle around bends, through potholes and over bumps – all these can be well beyond understanding and yet you can still drive that car anywhere.

Likewise, you can ride your body a whole lifetime without recognizing the subconscious mind, its depth and its reliable, dependable function. For sure, you can engage the world just as you were taught, fighting for rights, working hard toward career goals, having and raising a family despite relationship problems – not one of these endeavors requires comprehending inner workings in operation continuously.

But to drive a good automobile, reliable, efficient, superior in performance and safe in handling and braking, you *should* understand the mechanics of a motorized vehicle – otherwise, you can neither properly evaluate a car for purchase, nor maintain it in top operating condition.

Similarly, if you sincerely wish to maximize enjoyment, creativity, quality of relationships, accomplishment, health, longevity and freedom in life, you should understand how the psyche operates, because its deeply stored specifics impact *all aspects of your life*.

My exposure to subconscious functionality has been deep, exploratory and multi-phased. For a time during my thirties, I gave psychic readings. For a couple years, beginning with the opportunity to work with an established psychic in a favorable setting, then later on my own, I read people twice weekly. Able to access extensive, meaningful information for people who came to me, open-minded and wishing to discern hidden aspects of their own being, I could access the intangible realm of information within their psyche. By simply clearing my own mind and opening my attentive focus to their associated information, I could tell complete strangers about themselves. Information that came through concerned their daily lives, their desires, their significant shortcomings. Seldom did I predict the future, more often gleaning information about their character and surrounding situation in the present.

Of course, the present mindset *becomes* the future if not changed.

About that same time I had begun delving into my own subconscious. Following a workshop on self-hypnosis techniques, I came across a pioneering book on the subject by Leslie LeCron. Providing added insight into technique, LeCron clarified the body-mind connection – specifying mechanisms by which the inner realm directly affects health issues.

As I applied LeCron's principles, healing various ongoing ailments that had plagued me from childhood, I discerned ever more clearly the innate body-mind connection. (More accurately, *my body healed itself* as I cleared away inner factors inhibiting health. The body really knows how to operate itself much better than the rational mind – or your doctor – once psychic baggage hindering proper function is eliminated.)

Once I'd built great confidence in the reliability of the process of healing by eliminating inner roots to real problems – having discovered significant mechanisms in addition to those pointed out by LeCron – I came to realize that the same mechanisms affecting health applied **in all aspects of life**: my nature didn't end at the boundary of my skin. Indeed, relationship issues I'd had and career problems I'd encountered throughout life – both in repeated patterns – were firmly rooted within my psyche, just as physical illnesses had been.

From my thirties onward (now 63, I'm considerably healthier, happier, more fulfilled, more successful and much freer than ever before) I have scoured my subconscious of many, many self-defeating elements. In the process, aided by earlier exposure to others' subconscious function through psychic readings I'd given, I've gained a thorough working understanding of the interactive functionality of the psyche – unique in depth and breadth.

In earlier writings, I've specified mechanisms of mind that constitute building blocks, bricks, in a fashion, that form walls within the psyche that inhibit fulfillment of the will. I review those briefly here along with techniques for effectively delving inward to be able to clearly discern those mechanisms.

Following that overview, I illustrate many specific inner structures I encountered on my long, thorough inner venture. As I addressed all aspects of my life, finding and eliminating health issues, dissatisfying elements in relationships, failures in endeavors and other disappointments, I made notes of the more complex structures – inhibiting walls made of those bricks – so that I could ultimately specify them as part of my message. Without doubt, I share some of these inner structures with others holding the western mindset, including, I have to imagine, *you*. So there should be immediate value in exposure to the specific structures I illustrate.

But even if your psyche doesn't hold exactly the same elements, you gain considerable perspective on the psyche's function by seeing just how values and impending, negating elements lie within the mindset – how subtle they can be, how camouflaged by beliefs and favored explanations *and* how damaging they are when woven into real events.

Simply reading about these deeper inner structures brings considerable insight. But you ultimately benefit enormously more by using techniques illustrated to delve into your own psyche to clear away restrictive mind-elements.

Driving a good sports car is much more enjoyable than viewing pictures of one; traveling through Europe is greatly superior to watching movies about it; drinking fine wine or tasty beer is far more fulfilling than perusing advertisements for either. Should it be surprising that exploring your own mindset for the purpose of improving it – and thus *life* – would be far superior to just reading about how to do so?

Realize this: if not approached, identified and changed, components in your mindset at the root of real problems remain intact – and troublesome patterns reflecting your total Self will, too.

Delving Inward

Playing a Home Game – For a Change

Your subconscious mind is not an entity separate and apart from you, neither some alter-ego sitting out of reach of experienced pain and frustration – nor an insulated akashic crane operator, wedged rebelliously down there, pulling levers to inflict pain and defeat on you. Your subconscious mind consists of...

Information.

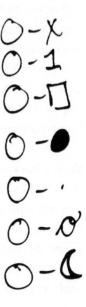

At the core of conscious being is what can best be called information, but not data as in bits and bytes, not genetic codes or isolated, learned facts alone – although an extensive store of acquired knowledge is in there, too, often camouflaging deeper elements. (Indeed, genetic function is activated by the value-image of the subconscious, wherein functionality is turned on and off – within a broad scope of potential – by virtue of specific propensity embodied in the current mindset.) Your subconscious mind holds an enormous amount of information concerning all aspects of your body function, unfolding life and all meaning pertaining to both. It holds a broad range of interrelated values associated with that information, along with corresponding emotional and evaluation references.

Much of that information – inter-cellular exchange, minute details as to life flow, hormonal regulation, hair and toenail growth particulars, how you superficially interact with two hundred strangers while walking down a busy street – you don't need to know. To enjoy a stage show, you don't have to be aware of the lighting cues, makeup provider, box-office personnel employee benefits and ten thousand other details that go into making that production happen. Likewise, you needn't know the plethora of details behind life's flow to live it.

But key information about critical aspects of your life is readily available – particularly those underlying problem areas – that would greatly benefit you to be aware of.

Realizing that life's entire flow hinges on your own nature as embodied and evidenced in the overall content of your mindset, you understand that *improvement in all areas of life depends on your making subconscious info conscious*, i.e., bringing vital inner meaning into your awareness. Once aware of inner aspects to real difficulties, then *and only then*, **can you accomplish improvement**. For only at that point and in that way can you break patterns of ill health, rejection and/or failure.

With a background cultural heritage that assumes the self to be detached from the rest of reality, most protocol you learned for dealing with the world involves maneuvering against the world you encounter. My point is that, regardless of attempts to control elements within your scope, you continue to produce and encounter patterns which reflect your own nature. So your *only real leverage* for revising the quality of actual events and relationships is to delve inward to revise mindset elements, purposely changing those contributing to self-defeat and pain.

Deeper levels of information can be clouded or totally hidden by knowledge of a more superficial nature, often inaccurate, such that you can easily fool yourself when delving inward. So the five techniques I illustrate are meant to bypass rational limitations and more directly access subconscious information.

Gaining greater rapport with deeper elements of your own psyche, having employed these techniques effectively, you may ultimately dispense with the need to use the techniques. The very limitations to accessing deep-seeded information are *problems in and of themselves*. As you proceed to remove them and other restrictive cultural notions, access to inner information becomes easier.

Techniques for Acquainting Yourself with Your *Self*

Five tools for delving inward proved to be of great and complementary effectiveness during my inner journey. I present them as I found them, utilized them, and honed their unique qualities to my own usage, so long as needed.

Details on each technique can be referenced in my previous writings or through many sources elsewhere. Without **actually applying** these techniques, you will not adequately grasp my illustrations of the psyche, nor will you fully benefit from subsequent details of inner structures. Value comes, not in perusing and accepting my descriptions, but in personal exploration of your own psychic structures for the purpose of improving personal life and coming to a Clear Awareness of your own being.

Meditation
Meditation, a relaxed, peaceful state of mind in a quiet, undis-

turbed setting, is a key beginning step to an inner journey.

Cluttered with unwanted thoughts, jumping from subject to subject, from rhyming musical tunes to pondering matters not pertinent to the moment, typical rational focus is fragmented. Vital to establishing peace and focus is an initial discipline, culling out some short period of daily life to disengage from the immediate, conflictual face-off with real events and challenges.

Meditation, as introduced into western culture from eastern disciplines, is principally meant to achieve a glimpse of the integrated Oneness with which life works, to bring to immediate awareness an uncluttered epiphany of regard. In this disciplinary gesture, you sit quietly in a relaxed posture – but not reclined so as to avoid dozing off. You let loose the thought stream that normally fills conscious background thinking.

As thoughts come to mind, release them, maintaining focus on quietude. In eastern practices, a word substitute called a mantra is provided by a spiritual guide such that, when extraneous thoughts come to mind, you release them by repeating that special – but otherwise meaningless – word. Making up a mantra is just as effective, reverting attention to it when thoughts intrude into your tranquil state.

The purpose, again, is to clear away interfering thoughts and initiate a process of contemplation. Eastern disciplines expect meditation to ultimately yield perception/experience of Oneness. But, the practice may or may not elicit that clarity because, as mentioned above, *thoughts* are not the real problem.

Whether or not it produces a mystic glimpse or two, relaxed contemplation in some form is vital in its calming effect, its disengagement from the constant stress of dealing with daily life. Beyond, that, however, meditation does not thoroughly cleanse the subconscious to quiet the mind at its core.

Self-Hypnosis

Sitting in that same quiet state, rather than clearing the mind superficially as a procedure, you can begin to clear the mind thoroughly as a *goal* – element by element.

Hypnosis is not a mystical state of trance, but a given state of human consciousness wherein full focus is held on a specific area of attention. Under the auspices of a good hypnotist, an amenable, relaxed and focused subject readily accepts a suggested reality in place of the real one observed through his/her senses. Using an induction technique for entertainment, for example, an effective hypnotist can get subjects to run around like chickens, see through clothes or whatever elicits a laugh – with the subject all the while oblivious to the absurdity of such actions. To the subject, reality is what has been suggested, not what the senses perceive.

In a more serious application, hypnosis can be used by an analyst to bypass a subject's rational resistance and explore subconscious content to shed light on inner drives and behavioral difficulties. The subject, open to such exploration and trusting of the therapist, reveals under hypnosis details of inner values not easily accessed during normal waking consciousness – including memories of events not recalled otherwise, even suppressed due to emotional trauma.

But the same induction technique applied by an experienced hypnotist can be exercised by oneself. Entering a hypnotic state is not equivalent to leaving the building – the Self is still there, only now with a concentrated focus on specific subject matter. In Self-Hypnotism, you are the both the hypnotist and the subject. Properly and sincerely applied, you can delve deeper into meaningful aspects of existence than any therapist could accomplish. And you focus on exactly that part of your life which needs illumination and revision.

This technique can be used in conjunction with another common tool of psychology to great effect to discern and revise key inner mechanisms...

Ideomotor Responses

Highly useful for avoiding interference from the more superficial rational self is a technique that translates inner, subconscious information into physical motions. Using a pendulum, consciously held in a stationary position, one can request a yes or no response from the subconscious. The subconscious will deflect the pendulum in a particular direction – away from and toward you or sideways – to indicate affirmative or negative. With some practice – and trust – all aspects of meaningful subconscious information can be explored in order to specify their nature: through pendulum movement, the psyche confirms or denies meaningful questions whose content lies within its store of understanding.

Using this technique or some variation – finger movement during self-hypnosis, grasping strength in a variation of kinesiology or other involuntary muscle response to pointed questioning – one can explore deep-seeded, meaningful information in great detail. The process produces specific yes/no answers to pointed questions, revealing to the conscious self **explicit inner mechanisms** as contained in real memories. Discerning reliable specifics allows thorough exploration of what had been subconscious information.

Mechanisms involved will be illustrated shortly. But another highly illustrative means exists to glean information from the subconscious, as displayed during the sleep state...

Dream Analysis

Dreams experienced nightly manifest directly from the psyche. They are built on that same subconscious content accessed through ideomotor responses and self-hypnotism – or read by a sensitive psychic. Dreaming is the process by which the psyche explores potentials,

evaluating life elements and interacting from the perspective of Self with deeper levels of value and meaning.

Dreams you encounter and recall can provide great insight into problems experienced in reality, revealing the inner roots you are looking for. Many times in my own journey I found my dreams to symbolize and expose exactly the overview I needed – or even contain elements of solutions to problems I was working on at the time.

Nightly incursions into the dream realm are not random displays of crazy distortions, warped by indigestion or too much cake for dessert. Each episode of interaction with characters and objects drawn from real life contains meaningful perspectives on underlying strata of your own psyche, displayed in a fashion that, while differing from waking consciousness, is very understandable – if you know how to interpret dream content.

Volumes of available publications explain common dream-symbol recognition, while others aid dream interpretation on a more personal level. Use them as needed: the path toward intimate access to deeper realms of the psyche must include close rapport with dreams to discern your own nature and ultimately spur change.

Automatic Writing

Another outlet for subconscious content is, oddly enough, doodling. Holding a pencil, you focus attention on specific problem areas, letting your hand sketch out images without rational interference – just as one does while doodling during a meeting. Images produced, coming as dreams or ideomotor responses directly from the psyche, can yield valuable info.

Both dream analysis and automatic writing can be enhanced using ideomotor responses to help interpret the dreams or figures sketched. Confidence in your ability to obtain information with all these approaches is enhanced **the more you use them**.

Core Components of the Psyche

Cohesive Whole – Not Bits and Parts

Nearly a century ago, Sigmund Freud proposed a structural model of the "psychic apparatus" as he attempted to define how portions of the psyche relate to each other. Essentially in the process of defining, he segmented off compartments that weren't there in the first place: he invented them rather than discover them. Such topographical layouts, once accepted as valid, were expanded upon by others over time. Models of this nature, commonly regarding consciousness itself as a resident capability of brain function, while illustrating various aspects of mind function, create an inaccurate paradigm from the outset – carving out conceptualized compartments from a continuous, whole – though often conflicted – inner Self.

Those models typically regard the "id" as an inaccessible region of personality containing basic drives and instincts – the only portion deemed present at birth. The "ego" part, supposedly emerging only at about two to three years of age, is seen as housing conscious awareness. The **ego** is imagined to entail the personality, make decisions and interface with the world – mediating between ongoing self-centered demands of the **id** and lofty, more idealistic focus of the "superego". This last portion, supposed to develop later still, is portrayed as idealistic, exceeding local focus in a direction toward spiritual aspects, guilt, etc.

The ego-self, so diagrammed, can only access a small portion of the whole, the conscious store. The ego is thought to be able, with effort, to dig into "preconscious" stored info, but never really access the id region. That id ostensibly sits, along with much of the superego, deep in the unconscious. Often this is pictured as an iceberg, with the conscious above water, exposed to the light of day, the preconscious just below the surface and the unconscious way deep frozen within the unfathomable *id*. The *ego* is shown as spanning the exposed area, just below water surface – while the water itself that the iceberg floats in is simply not available, not contained within the whole.

Models like the above create deceptive divisions where they don't exist. Like most paradigms, they proceed to formulate the perception of one who studies and accepts them, tinting Reality to conform to their intricate layout. This is particularly so for students who learn such diagrams as hard-coded explanations issued by vaunted experts for tests upon which they will be graded.

Remember *always* that innate tendency to validate your own belief structure. Once students learn and accept the model, they build upon it and in the process fossilize that notion into "hard" science. Such paradigms, tending to *really* harden – indeed, *petrify* – through time, never clarify the workings of the mind. They only construct images that then become pseudo-reality for believers to build ever more elaborate notions upon, layer after layer.

Allow me to melt the iceberg...

No severed ego fights with competing forces of id-survival and superego-philosophication. What exists is a single Self, a conscious identity capable of discerning all needed information from within its own conscious-subconscious store. And that Self exists fully formed as a conscious entity before birth – it doesn't emerge with newborn brain function, but rather manifests capabilities consistent with its propensities.

(But internal information may not be detail-oriented to a degree satisfactory to analysts or academics. It is, rather, meaning-based in scope: oriented to how things impact the Self to fulfill or negate personal intent – purely subjective in nature, not objective in profuse structural detail. E.g., the subconscious isn't aware that your newly purchased used car has worn McPherson Struts in its front suspension. But it does recognize conflict held within. Based on that propensity, it will integrate real elements to yield a disastrous spin-out on a dark road two years from now, wherein that car will ultimately manifest this pattern based on its handling characteristics.)

Conflict does come into play, not as an intramural ping-pong match between id and superego, refereed by the ego, but only regarding explicit meaning – on many potential levels – embodied within the content of the mindset.

From Freud and Jung onwards, through generations now of psychoanalytic and psychiatric fields of science, impressions have long since become regarded as facts – the general tendency of science in any case. It matters far less to scientific thinking that those "facts" rest on inaccurate assumptions and synthetic base knowledge than that models currently accepted seem to work.

Of course, any system appears operative *if believed in.*

So don't expect within my perspectives elaborate maps of how the id underlies the ego-self, interacting with charged feelings, supported as if on stilts by the collective unconscious. No such structures exist within the mind. They become apparent only when the definition is accepted.

Flawed from the beginning, the scientific model assumes personality and complex rational thinking must emerge from brain function sometime after birth. Thus interaction between various components of the psychic apparatus must *cause* emergence of the self early on, perhaps based on growth into increasing functionality of the young brain. With convoluted complexity and illusory interaction, that tidy image generated by the iceberg model **just doesn't exist**.

In Reality, the conscious Self engages an incarnation based on its inherent nature and always for a purpose (or multiple purposes), replete with a set of traits, tastes and propensities that manifest into the budding body and latent surrounding. Driving the process is not only intent but the very nature of the initiating Self. Innate qualities of the mindset become imprinted on the whole life scenario: your proclivities preempt a reality set for you to fit into. Parents, siblings and culture in general provide the stage for your tastes and talents, interests and capabilities to play out – or not, based on your inherent level of conflict and with whatever level of resistance is necessary, gauged on the measure of inner struggle you host.

The Reality personally encountered reflects your own nature – complex environmental elements are latent, preset ramifications of your own character. Life unfolds in detail as exactly appropriate events and relationships emerge from a field of unlimited potentialities.

The degree to which that sounds implausible is the degree to which other explanations have been accepted as facts.

I've spent the greater portion of my life delving into inner structures, sorting out from my mindset mechanisms that negated and neutralized my will, elements which at the time produced situations impossible for me to succeed in. Consequently I deleted those underlying mechanisms, along with a plethora of scientific, religious and archaic notions common to our culture that interfered with my view of life and, along with it, the ultimate fulfillment of my desires.

The only structures that exist within the psyche result from interacting values and definitions. There is no hard-wired mechanism involved. Structures I will proceed to depict result from conceptual components, not from an innate apparatus design that could be diagrammed, and certainly not from a physical infrastructure. Because of that, all such "structures" are malleable – regardless of how complex they are, you can change them. And because of that, all experiential life elements are variable. They can be healed or improved upon as need be – although they may be quite complex, requiring considerable introspection.

But also, of course, the precise structures I illustrate are (or "were", as I deleted the detrimental ones) customized to and by my own nature. Yours will differ in specifics, in content, perhaps even in hierarchical layout. But the overall interactive and malleable nature will be roughly equivalent, and indeed some aspects very similar, such that my presentation here can help you delve inward to accomplish change far more effectively – and certainly in significantly shorter order – than might be accomplished without the illustration.

Much of your life at any given time fulfills desires. The enormous complexity of your body is probably functioning 99% perfectly right now – including massive exchange of oxygen for carbon dioxide, communication via nerves and hormones between related bodily activities, circulation of water and filtering of waste materials, digestion of foods, bathing and rinsing of sinuses, coordinated growth of nails and body hair, healing of minor damage, etc. This complexity is astounding if considered at a microscopic level – and it all takes place without any reasoned effort. Just eat what tastes good, consume some liquid, eliminate waste periodically, and the 80,000,000,000,000 cells – give or take a few trillion – that make up your body keep chugging away, each doing its specialized job.

But their collective "job" is not necessarily to function flawlessly at peak capacity. Their job is to fulfill what your design dictates – and that spec emerges, not necessarily in accord with your will, even though *based on* it. Your total mindset can very easily contain many factors which compromise intent, often enough negating and neutralizing it. So that 1% by which the body might seem to malfunction isn't really flawed operation by the cells or attack by foreign bodies, but compliance with your own self-defeating mechanisms: doubts, fears, projections of power, conflict and compromised self-image.

Let me illustrate that. The Pittsburgh Symphony is a

wonderful, world-class orchestra. In technique and expressive feeling, they play exceptionally well, and do so to high acclaim around the world. But they play as the conductor requests. At one concert I attended a guest conductor had them play a Brahms piece quite blaring, with little nuance in expression. At another their music director, generally a fine musician, had them play parts of Beethoven's Ninth *much* too fast – normally expressive passages lost the fine emotional content Beethoven intended.

The orchestra played exactly as the conductor requested. But the end product, though played "well", was unsatisfactory.

Your body is like the orchestra, there for your conducting: it plays whatever it's told – *always*. Mostly, it works very well. When it malfunctions, it does so in response to your directives, manifesting inner turmoil and doubt woven into your mindset.

The following is an overview of mechanisms which comprise those self-defeating elements. Illustrations of larger structures – walls out of which these bricks are made – will follow that.

Mechanisms of Mind

Bricks in the Walls that Inhibit Fulfillment of Your Intent

For major portions of your body and life that feel good, fulfill desire and seem rewarding, nothing needs to be addressed. You *should be* healthy; relationships *should be* rewarding and fun; you *should* succeed in intended accomplishments. So, life in those positive areas doesn't need attention – indeed, intent manifests directly into reality with no distorting mechanisms twisting the outcome.

But if a foot hurts, the fact that your body is otherwise just fine doesn't reduce pain in that foot. If you have great friends, but never seem to attract a dependable, fulfilling romantic relationship, that issue needs addressed. Whether body part or significant other inflicts discomfort, there are inner, root components to those outer problems.

Becoming aware of the functional inner-outer flow, you will recognize what used to be considered *problems* as really only **symptoms**. The real problems lie within.

Of vital importance is the ability to step back and take a thorough look at your own nature.

Using the above techniques, you can find specific inner elements behind real problems, but recognize that those elements are **integral parts of your own nature** – elements of a complex set of psychological attributes. You maintain them, with some change and growth, throughout life – indeed, such growth is a central motive for living in the first place.

Typically, though, growth is slow and casual; it seems to take many episodes encountering the same issues in recurring – but slightly varied – patterns to learn much from them. But once you realize that real events and relationships indelibly reflect your own inner nature, change becomes the chief gesture, in order to gain improvement, focusing inward to correct troubled outer elements at their origin.

The alternative is bleak: trying, again and again, to manipulate the outer world, you only repeatedly reproduce those old patterns, regardless of effort.

In this regard, your whole life is interconnected. Suppose, for example, you face conflict and rejection in the workplace. Your job requires long hours with much expected, but your contribution is seldom recognized. So, after some effort and extensive looking you find a better position – improved pay and more accepting supervisor. If you haven't eliminated inner conflict and struggle, despite that career improvement, those inner issues will find their way out in other channels: your kids become raving teenagers or mother-in-law moves in.

As a whole, the collection of elements within your mindset may be quite complex in regard to any particular difficulties in life. They are revealed in problems faced *right now* in your career, love life, health and outside interests. But, because you repeat patterns throughout life, those same issues are also quite visible back through other times of life as recorded in memories.

Some healing techniques, recognizing the inner-outer connection, address issues as currently encountered. But it is much more effective to trace, through concentration and utilization of the above techniques, problem areas back to their earliest point in life. For me, searching back into early childhood, issues often reflected back to factors related to my mother. Regarded in that perspective, with emotional ties and experienced pain less severe in long ago issues, negative patterns weren't as difficult to deal with as in current life – where painful situations were too intimidating.

To the timeless subconscious, it doesn't matter! Patterns are simply specs being realized in this ongoing now moment. Inner change occurs when roots are identified and revised, regardless of the time frame.

So for me, I've always found it beneficial to approach the recognition phase in ways easiest to work with. Whatever timeframe is dealt with, once problematic mechanisms have been clarified and jettisoned whether dealing with past *or* current episodes, the negation dissipates **now**, too – because *you only really exist in this now moment.* (This does not imply that traumatic episodes disappear from memory upon disen- gagement of underlying, negating mechanisms. But rather, the *meaning* of that experience – the pain and negativity – will have changed once associated elements are dispelled. The episode takes on new meaning while previous pain, dealt with thoroughly, abates through healing. And the pattern, now broken, ceases recurrence.)

Techniques exist as well that relate current issues back to past lives, using hypnosis to regress a subject to previous lives and connect problems to situations then. That might work, because it is *the current state of the Self* and its integral content that needs revision. If this is accomplished referencing "past lives", great – whether or not that past existence is valid as perceived and was ever real. But I find this approach much less exacting than dealing with recalled situations from *this* life. Once uncovered, those real memories – containing hidden, sometimes repressed, elements that undergird annoying and painful experiences – yield a clarity of recognition that helps greatly to convey meaning and veracity in the connection.

So my approach, one I know works exceptionally well when engaged with intent and intensity, is delving inward using the tools listed above. Establishing early peace of mind through meditation, begin to focus on specific, problematic aspects of life with self-hypnosis – enhanced for clarity and specificity using ideomotor responses and dream analysis:

1. Choose a specific single problematic aspect of life you want to address. Generally start with easier issues, like minor physical concerns – allergies, muscle twitches, recurring illness. Then work on through more critical health and life issues as confidence and experience are gained.

2. Using dream analysis and ideomotor responses, discern key information about all underlying, root elements to the outer problem:
   - When was the first episode of this pattern? How old were you?
   - Which mechanisms (of those listed below) are involved as roots to the problem?
   - For each of these, discern details: who was involved,

what did they say or do, etc? What happened and what impact did it have then?

3. Once all inner aspects of a problem are detailed, use auto-suggestion to dispel the associated mechanisms. Review the elements one by one, consciously releasing them: "I clearly see the conflict (suggestion, punishment, whatever) involved with this allergy (rejection, foot pain, repeated failure, etc.), but I don't need it anymore. It serves no more purpose. I dispel it; I leave it in the past."

4. Continue with auto-suggestion to implant positive reinforcement for desired effects in place of deleted negative ones. Repeat this subconscious re-write two or three times a day for a week or so – until it feels no longer necessary.

You will likely experience a delay until inner change integrates its way into Reality. For simple problems, healing/improvement can be quite rapid: when I traced my nervous, kicking foot to a specific childhood tension I had and released it, the nervous kick ceased immediately.

For more complex issues, though, it can take some time – and there may be other aspects to the problem not yet found and eliminated. Issues I'd had with authority –  always finding myself in underling positions in professional situations – were quite complex, such that early efforts to establish self-reliance inwardly didn't accomplish much. But I persisted, looking deeper to clarify every element I could trace. Ultimately, my pattern of dependence on and subservience to others simply faded.

Caveat: *Make note!* During the healing process, increasingly so in ever more vital aspects of life – failure of relationships, non-fulfillment of critical interests, etc. – deletion of inner roots typically releases immediate psychological turmoil. This associated emotional release can be unpleasant – you may experience temporary depression or muscle clenching, tense reaction to inner change as and after root elements are cleared away. You may notice temporary intensification of the symptom. But the real issue does abate, and that emotional release passes as the new subconscious set takes hold.

The fleeting intensification of pain serves one positive value: clearly indicating that meaningful change, by release of negating baggage, is taking effect.

Like many things in life, the more practiced, the better you get at it. With each real improvement, progressively greater familiarity with the psyche's layout and content is gained, spurring confidence in your causal status and greater awareness of your Oneness with the Reality you encounter.

The Mechanisms

Whatever the issue is, whether concerning ill health, rejection or repeated failure, it breaks down into specific inner components in some combination of the following mechanisms. The first four are rather straightforward:

1. Accepting explanations: **Suggestion**
   - You are very much open to suggestion from early in life, absorbing explanations from care-givers as fact.
   - Much understanding was absorbed from *subtle* suggestion: values and cultural notions woven into childhood stories, cartoons, movies and language itself.
2. Copying observed actions: **Emulation**
   - From a young age, you emulate parents and siblings, mimicking those around you.
   - You learn to act as they do, believe their ideas, take on

their personal mannerisms, absorbing elements into your self-image, whether or not personally appropriate.

3. Encountering a major emotional episode in life: **Impact Event**
   - A single, charged encounter, molestation or traumatic episode can leave emotional scars that should be found, clarified and eliminated.

4. Building a notion into life: **Literal Display**
   - Common expressions can be incorporated into physical symptoms: "pain in the neck" in reference to a boss or acquaintance can occur for real.

These next four mechanisms are more complicated than simple absorption into mind:

5. A negative with a positive reward: **Motivation**
   - Parents – and many subsequent other sources in life – may have rewarded you for acting and being as they required or provided extra love and attention when you were sick.
   - In general this mechanism can be powerful – and thus detrimental – in having you compromise your own nature to satisfy others or finding yourself programmed to be sick.

6. A natural impulse negated: **Punishment**
   - Early care-givers may also have punished you for just acting natural, simply following through on impulses and natural expressions.
   - This mechanism can be even worse than motivation: experienced during childhood, it leads to distrusting the Self and relying exclusively on rational thinking, such that you question spontaneous actions before proceeding, comparing everything with prescribed procedures allowed by those parental authorities.

7. Imposed situation: **Force and Subtle-Force**
   - Parents may have forced certain actions: e.g., going to church, finishing dinner when not hungry.
   - Or, more subtle, the situation may have presented no opportunity for fulfillment of certain desires.
8. Trying to be somebody else: **Identification**
   - You come to identify with your cultural, racial or religious group, taking on their traits.
   - Or you may picture yourself like movie stars, professional athletes and celebrities – trying to be like them, not your natural Self.

And these two remaining are the most overarching in their damaging effect on your life of all mechanisms.

If life were such that you were separate and apart from the reality you encounter, that you had to assuage a god, manipulate powerful agents in life and deal with abundant threats from bacteria, viruses and the government as well as bad luck and preset fate, *struggle* and *conflict* would be very desirable to have as personal characteristics – indeed, traits beneficial to foster. With a world full of threats and dangers just waiting to inflict harm, you would be well served to be relentless in conflict and indefatigable in struggle.

But that's not how Reality works. Intimately tied to Reality, you create patterns in life that reflect your own nature.

So these two gestures, held within as mechanisms, often greatly prized in western culture as strength and durability – the core of heroism and valor – become obviously insidious when clarified that *you are not separate from the world you encounter*, but integrated into it. By grasping and cherishing these cultural pillars, you end up weaving both into real life in many ways: fighting with your body, spouse, boss and neighbor or struggling with a plethora of hindrances to accomplish your desires. All the while, with pride in personal fortitude and courage, you keep repeating patterns that embody these values *only because you hold them within.*

Apparent external forces that threaten and fight you, that inhibit achievement and limit wealth **are illusions** insofar as they appear causal. Certainly they are as real as any aspect of life, and will indeed usher in pain and defeat if not engaged with whatever weapons you learned to be effective. But they are not *causal* in the framework of your unfolding experience, making things happen; external agents are only triggers, cued effects. You *attract them* into engagement based on inner struggle and conflict. So the final two inner mechanisms are:

9. Negation of intent: **Conflict**
   - Conflict not only restricts progress, but yields negative outcome. You want something good to happen, but bad things happen.
   - If you host this mechanism, efforts to accomplish goals may lead to disasters, negating your will with bad outcome; if conflict is woven into physical attributes, you experience ill health, with pain, weight problems, ailments or allergies.
   - In terms of realizing your will, conflict not only deters attaining what is desired, but requires you to fight on some level to get anything. Likened to driving your car forward, conflict is like a headwind, not only impeding progress but pushing backwards, requiring extra expenditure of effort.
   - Adding to its insidious nature, you may, consistent with cultural values, highly prize conflict, relating self-worth to personal toughness and drive.
10. Neutralization of your will: **Struggle**
   - Struggle, as an inner element, inhibits accomplishment, health, relationships. You want something good to happen, but *nothing happens*, at least not without great

effort, if indeed desired outcome manifests at all.

- This mechanism, woven into career aspects of life, necessitates hard work to get ahead, to accomplish goals; if found in physical attributes, your health may be OK, but takes considerable effort to maintain.
- Struggle may (depending on many other factors) allow realization of your will, but only with great exertion of energy. Likened to your car moving forward, struggle is like friction in its wheels: not pushing backwards, but inhibiting forward progress.

The psyche contains information arranged in strata of values, of meaningful elements meshed together in a complex state.

But you can't directly observe values. Searching your mindset, you can't see disappointment or dejection. Nowhere within that inner realm is the intangible quality of joy to be independently discerned, nor free-floating hope, intent or fear. These are vital qualities of your Self, but not freestanding properties to be isolated and worked with.

But those qualities *are* evidenced in abundance, woven into vibrant memories of life as anticipation of and reaction to events and relationships you encountered. You see joy and/or disappointment right now, featured in current undertakings, health and the status of your love life. Similarly, looking back through life, you detect them built into qualities of situations and relationships encountered at earlier stages – right back to earliest childhood.

So in regarding health issues *right now*, career situations or relationship problems as they unfold in patterns *at this moment*, you see those same issues, situations and problems in earlier forms, tucked deep within the subconscious, woven into values embodied in memories of this entire lifetime. Earlier phases of life feature different people, involve perhaps diverse ailments and other situations, but values embedded in conditions of earlier times, patterned similarly, will be equivalent in their effect on your experience, on your emotional response.

The above techniques allow detailed rendering of undesirable situations into components that you can conceptually grasp and work with. The pain of rejection now can be related to equivalent rejection during childhood, seen within its "original" context, discerned with details of all mechanisms involved – and released.

The subconscious mind is much like a slate with a vast array of detailed information written on it. Duly registered, it functions as it currently sits, intangible but latent and real, as the spec from which all aspects of life are manifested. Wishing to revise the quality of life, you must rewrite the spec: change the inner roots in order to alter their outer manifestation.

Conscious-Subconscious Divide

Eventually There Isn't One

Used to dealing with the real world as taught – praying to a god or manipulating people – you likely never regarded your own subconscious at all. Delving inward, though, you realize the conscious Self rides an enormous, rich repository of information built into values and meaningful elements.

You also come to see – looking deeper – that that storehouse is every bit as much *you* as the commonly regarded rational self. That calculating, self-conscious, often fearful, limited self-image worn around daily begins to disappear as you discover the rest of your Self, the standard equipment you came delivered with but never recognized. The more often you delve inward to solve problems by dispelling inner roots, the more confident you become with both the process and your own nature. Indeed as your integrated nature clarifies with each step, the apparent divide between conscious focus and that innate store of information at hand fades.

Along the way, you encounter elements that create separation – common notions of limitation, mental façades that have you relying only on learned knowledge to engage a seemingly disconnected world "out there". As they are eliminated, the need for self-hypnosis and ideomotor query of subconscious details reduces as well. Directly tied to your whole inner scene, you needn't meditate, because your mind isn't cluttered anymore with intrusive, disconnected thoughts. Dreams become ever more understandable, requiring less analytical effort as problematic areas already addressed and eliminated fade.

Often, spiritual disciplines emphasize "getting in touch" with the inner self or connecting with spiritual aspects of self. Actually, you *are in touch* – fully connected at all times. The effective gesture is not "connecting", but ridding yourself of all the superficial cultural notions that inhibit *recognizing* that connection! Becoming "at one with" Reality isn't necessary – *seeing* mechanisms by which you generate an opposing reality *is*.

But getting to that point requires a significant, long journey. Because of the way the psyche functions, each problematic element must be dealt with individually. Eliminating fear tied to anticipated retribution of a non-existent god doesn't eradicate fear of falling or fear of failing. That functionality – how the psyche operates – is most fascinating. Illustrating it serves as a key prerequisite for looking at greater formations – larger, interconnected structures held within the mindset that I encountered and you certainly carry.

Inner Storage of Information

Not Like a Database

Just as the conscious mind doesn't consist of an ego, fending off id demands for fulfilling needs mixed with the superego's idealistic whims – as pictured by traditional diagrams – so the store of meaning and memory in the subconscious doesn't house data like a computer database. Often enough, the mind is likened to a big computer, where neuron synapses somehow equate to bit and byte storage. But, however intellectually pleasing such an analogy might sound, just as the mind does not work like a computer, *neither does it* store info like a database.

In a typical software system programmed to store and retrieve information, a relational structure is designed to house all types of associated data. Behind the scenes of a bank's storage of account information, for example, or any on-line merchandise purchasing system, is a database that records information entered into it in specific tables built to maximize usefulness and speed of retrieval.

A "table" is an itemized grid listing pieces of information, with single cells for each piece of data. For instance, storage of names and addresses of customers have dedicated cells for each piece of information: first name, family name, marital status, address, etc. Multiple items covering this logistical information collectively in rows are considered *tables.*

A relational database consists of such tables holding closely related data, linked to other such tabular listings that store information which is also associated, but not so directly.

Properly constructed, a computer database can house very complex structures of interdependent info, keeping batches of data separate for rapid lookup when a user queries it for whatever purpose. Its design also allows rapid updating through the entry of new data.

Software built to handle that database behind the scenes is quite complex as well. Developers design screen layouts that are understandable and easy to navigate for users. As users enter and access data, the software writes to and reads from the database.

Once created and in use, the database system controls computer storage space, too. It contains elaborate rules for indexing stored data to fulfill the demands of users – rarely corrupting information.

So each aspect of database operation is very complex: development of computers themselves and their operating systems, programming of the database, creation of software systems users employ to enter and retrieve data, training users, maintaining networks on which the software and database run, backups to protect data, security systems to disallow hacking, etc. But at the core of a database are the initial, well-reasoned design and the medium on which it runs: computers and networks.

The mind has neither an equivalent design nor a corresponding infrastructure on which to reside.

I've already debunked the notion of the brain as a computer-like structure that results, through its interactive complexity, in a conscious recognition of itself and its environment. The conscious Self, an integral entity *per se*, permeates the field of existence; its self-aware totality *incorporates* the property of having a mind. This Self rides no hardware superstructure. Rather the whole essence of conscious being manifests from inner propensity into matter; it generates Reality, based on its total nature.

Thus, the psyche doesn't straddle an infrastructure like a computer program runs in RAM located on a motherboard, while storing data on some disc media. The psyche *IS* the structure, intangible yet real, in terms of meaning and contained value. That conscious Self becomes real in the ongoing process of inner-outer fulfillment – spawning a reality of malleable matter into flowing configurations of event and relationship that reflect its innate, though current and ever-changing, content.

So the psyche, innate to itself, exists *inherently*, as opposed to being a formulaic function residing on some other media. Its memory, along with use and access of that memory and all rational and intuitive function-  ality, rests only on structures of **meaning** – intangible, multifold, multi-layered, thoroughly interconnected information and value. The psyche is self-contained and self-instigating. Its resultant Self-perspective has grown to its current qualitative level via a long trek of engaged incarnations and – particularly for those who read and comprehend these words – an exceedingly long, complex series of experiences, spanning many lifetimes.

Where computer operability rests on machines people developed and built and databases that run on them were conceived and programmed by people as well, the Self, with its complex mind is *self-generating*. The psyche engages a reality built on its own essence, absorbing and recreating ever more complex meaning to layer upon its current, extant nature. Computers are mechanisms built and operated by humans. They are only tools, not unlike the first stone implements created three million years ago – meant to facilitate intent. Humans are *vastly* more complex entities, each on a path of its own, engaged in a timeless trek toward greater awareness of Self.

To emphasize that difference let's jettison another computer-related fallacy. That mechanism stores and juggles information. It converts all input data into bits and bytes, then simply manipulates them, crunching the binary numbers mathematically based on rules programmed by humans. It has less awareness of its actions than an amoeba. Indeed, related to the meaning behind the information it processes, it has *no awareness whatsoever!*

Computer geeks tend to project human traits onto their beloved machines, ignoring all the human engineering that undergirds computer functionality. For example, programs have been developed to play the game of chess. A good chess program simply projects a set number of moves forward from the current layout, evaluating the status of the situation for all outcomes possible within all combinations of moves. It makes the best move for its side based on that extensive calculation. The number of potential subsequent moves grows exponentially for each added next move, making it virtually impossible at some point for a human player to anticipate every possible eventuality. But a computer only needs to crunch more numbers to project those possibilities many moves out.

Given adequate computing capacity to process huge numbers of possibilities, a computer *has to "win"*, as it foresees the conclusion of any strategy conceived by the human and selects a move to avoid it. In doing so, however, it is only blindly executing operations it was programmed to do *by a human programmer.* The machine is not even really playing chess; it's just sitting there, executing a human-created program.

Thus, saying a computer beat a grand master at chess is fallacious. A computer can't beat anybody at anything, any more than a shovel can dig a hole by itself. In reality, that competition featured a grand master vs. a *computer programmer* – or team – applying logic in programmed game strategy, making use of enormous digital ability to calculate eventualities. It wasn't a contest between man and machine at all. Given an automobile, I will beat the best sprinter in a race every time. That's the equivalent.

A computer stores and responds to information in pre-programmed ways. But without the human to create and program the machine, it only sits there, incapable of any action. And when functioning, it is only storing and operating on bits and bytes of info, having absolutely no perceptive recognition of its actions.

The basis of the psyche, then, within the framework of its existence and particularly in this current earth-based venture, is, at its core, *meaning*. While a computer database stacks data based on categorization, mindlessly indexing and storing items as designed – because a computer, as a machine, *doesn't know anything* and thus can't deal with meaning – your mind absorbs encountered events and relationships according to the meaning they hold. So the psyche regards and remembers its encountered reality based on intrinsic, often complex, meaning it entails. While the mind *recognizes* and regards categories as meaningful pieces of information, it doesn't store info by category but according to the meaning it contains.

Understanding the mind's predilection toward meaning rather than categories is extremely important.

When scouring the mind for roots to real problems, categorical searches are ineffective. The subconscious is enormously adept at retrieving information associated with a pointed effect. Referencing information through ideomotor responses, one can draw on an enormous store of information – recalling repeated episodes of a specific recurring pattern throughout life – all associated by common meaning. But it can't deal effectively **at all** with categories.

For example, if one has a fear of falling, focus on this inner dread can bring up various instances in life when, faced with walking along a mountain ridge or high bridge scaffolding, fear gripped one's attention. Further, the subconscious can itemize all of the mechanisms that underlie the fear, and all significant associations of that fear with people and objects.

But an inner search for fear itself as a subject, i.e., *a category*, doesn't achieve much more than an acknowledgment of having it – because each apprehension only exists in connotation of its meaningful object.

So, only within a framework of intrinsic value and meaning is information stored in the conscious-subconscious realm. The conscious aspect of mind can be regarded as information easily accessed, including that which was learned, i.e., absorbed as knowledge – though knowledge may be inaccurate or conflicting, distorted due to its own fallacious beliefs and notions. By contrast, the subconscious holds an enormous body of information that lies out of easy reach – across a synthetic but functional boundary created, again, *only* by limitations innate to held meaning: its effective, current understanding of what the Self is and how the psyche works.

Ideally, then, in practical terms, you have easy access to various types of information. Spontaneously, you can recall memories of events, learned "facts and figures", relationship issues, logistical, technical and historical information, etc. Ease of recall is aided by relative significance – unique or particularly meaningful things are easier to bring up than less important items.

But ready access to even learned information can be diminished by other mind-based elements – e.g., belief that your memory isn't so good, the notion that aging means diminished short-term memory, the accepted impression that memories can be forgotten, etc. These are all, ultimately pieces of information – in this case, inaccurate beliefs that contribute negatively to the fulfillment of your intent to recall information.

Looking deeper, but still in practical terms, you have access to much more information than simple learned knowledge, facts and figures, cultural values and such.

At some level of your subconscious, *you are fully aware* of all that is going on in your body at any moment. Likewise, within the psyche is a full, precise gauge of attractiveness to others, capacities for succeeding in undertakings and all other elements that determine your relationship to the world and other people. Some of this, in terms of details, was absorbed as knowledge and can be thus referenced. But much of it was brought into this lifetime as critical aspects of your nature. Those core qualities become impressed on the world in general as you imprint your own nature on emerging situations, and are thus reflected in qualitative terms – to be evaluated as needed – in recalled events.

The prime point is: within your subconscious resides all information necessary to evaluate and improve all aspects of health. You don't need outside data; however, you likely *do* need some useful technique to access deeper info cut off by various inhibiting notions.

The Gist, Not the Data

Along with recognizing that information is stored in the subconscious based on meaning comes the keystone recognition that meaning is the *only element of importance*. The subconscious holds many numbers as critical information; it holds expressible facts within its store. But all that information is retrievable and its engagement reliable based on the personal impact it contains.

For example, your subconscious knows exactly what you weigh; it doesn't care so much about pounds or kilograms, but rather about meaningful effect: what extra weight does to looks and capability – basically, exactly *why you maintain* extra poundage.

Underlying elements of meaning related to weight may stem from motherly prodding early on to eat your food, along with the planted suggestion to grow up "big and strong". That excess weight may rest on objective notions, stuck like barnacles to scientific thinking, implying that **bigger** is necessarily *better*. It may echo childhood experiences when it was suggested you weren't "big" enough to accomplish desired goals or be allowed to go along on certain outings, planting subtle desires to be bigger – a subconscious element that didn't go away in adulthood.

So, while the subconscious holds a large array of factual type data, that info only really supports the meaning. It is most appropriately accessed in regard to meaning, and is most useful when dealt with subjectively.

The Timeless Regard of the Subconscious

Similarly, inner stores of information hold date-related information. Within the subconscious is stored the exact age when you first got punished for a given offense or rewarded for doing as told, when you first tasted ice cream, first had sex, first caught cold – and everything else. The subconscious is privy to measured time as an element of meaning. In that all events and relationships are recorded, the relative positional occurrence is included in that info – again, based on meaning and stored in terms of significance, not categorically *or* sequentially.

But the subconscious doesn't exist in a time-based framework. Functionally, to the subconscious, time is meaningless beyond attributed notation tied to events of importance; time is a tidbit of meaningful information, not an aspect of being or its functionality. In the depth of your psyche, you exist in this ongoing, *NOW* moment: **the complex of meaning-based, qualitative mind-elements in effect now continues until changed, *their resultant patterns repeated until that change takes effect.***

So, in terms of "time", particular moments, especially meaningful ones, can be tagged with time stamps as part of peripheral meaning – but the gist to each in effect **now**, remains in effect until changed.

Clouding the View

Typical cultural notions within our western heritage strongly inhibit access to deeper subconscious information, cutting you off, effectively – quite effectively – right at a resultant conscious-subconscious boundary. Indeed, elements of our conceptual western heritage, by virtue of their inherent fallacy, *create that boundary in the first place!!*

One key factor inhibiting access to vital subconscious information is the cornerstone belief of both science and religion that you came into existence at the outset of this incarnation and did so with a totally blank slate for mind content. (Indeed, you have no stored information as per memory, save a few pre-birth impressions and, in some instances, traces of retained memory from previous incarnations, but you entail a complex of latent traits and propensities that immediately engage in reality building.)

Another is the superstition-based thought that hidden in deeper recesses of mind lurk primordial evils, animalistic drives, primitive urges and mysterious, potentially damaging pseudo-forces – a wariness certainly promoted by religious voices and scary children stories for ages. This one creates fear, effectively blocking inner focus, however unfounded in basis.

Yet another restraint to full access of your own subconscious stockpile of pertinent info is the rational notion that all you can **possibly** know is *what came in through the senses*. This impression, default to scientific thinking, features no metaphysical aspect to reality at all, proclaiming that only the real universe, apparent to senses, exists. It ignores all attributes of mind outside space-time as inconsequential.

(Indeed, in this regard, debate over what *one can possibly know* is a traditional key point within philosophy – see Angle Four.)

Were that paradigm true, that you only become conscious as the brain reaches a certain level of development and that you, a synthetic, brain-based consciousness are isolated from all other matter, then certainly you could only know what you have learned! Of course, objective isolation *is not* the case in this mode of existence; as a timeless conscious entity, you are connected to Reality, intimately so, and unendingly so. But that scientific notion, long settled into western thinking – and thus yours – by this point, is very effective at keeping your nose out of your own business, i.e., restricting access to subconscious information.

Other, more subtle limitations to subconscious access will be seen below. But these alone should illustrate why unusual means are necessary to bypass rational limitations to access subconscious information.

Use of the pendulum or other ideomotor techniques to query subconscious information is *a means to bypass restrictions* imposed by invalid understanding. These conceptual limitations are vital to not only bypass, but ultimately **eliminate** along with other negating aspects of learned fallacy. If you currently had clear, uninhibited access to all subconscious information, you wouldn't need techniques to tap subconscious information – nor this book to gain greater insight into the psyche.

Doing Your Homework

Making use of detailed elements about to be presented here, incorporating a unique look at the complexities of the psyche, it is imperative to have a thorough understanding of the basic mechanisms listed above. Direct experience via personal use of self-hypnosis and ideomotor responses for delving beyond the conscious-subconscious boundary *is equally vital*. Without direct, personal and intimate exposure to the depths of your subconscious, complex elements itemized and illustrated below appear as jumbled, confused effects.

Residing within your own psyche is a vast store of information. To fully comprehend the psyche, you need to *use* such techniques to explore your inner realm, not just read about them. Psychic aspects illustrated here, resident within my own inner strata of interwoven meaning – at least until I eliminated them – were complex, often convoluted and always wrapped with emotional connotation. But with each step of engagement, clarification and release of negating elements, my real life improved. Such is the Oneness of mind with Reality, the inner-outer connection. And such is the value of your **experiencing** these inner structures *yourself*, not just reading about them.

Important Points

Making Use of These Perspectives

During a speaking tour down the west coast during the fall of 2008, I made a point of stopping at Mt. St. Helens in southwest Washington. That volcano, long a picturesque, snow-capped cone, covered with acres of pine and fir trees, blew its top off in a 1980 eruption. At the time, under great interior pressure, its north face slumped towards the valley and, with the release of tons of rock, ice and soil, the top erupted with huge billows of dust.

We had been living in San Diego at that time and some dust even made its way down there, over a thousand miles away. So I'd always wanted to see that volcano.

While there I did a 9-mile hike along the opposing ridge to

the north, from the ranger station eastwards, along a precipitous cliff and on down into the valley. Even 28 years after the eruption, the devastation was stunning and the hike awesome. I could describe the isolation, the quiet, the grand desolation of looking up from the valley floor to the gaping crater left by the eruption – with Spirit Lake to the east, half filled in with grey dust from its previous pristine alpine state, dead trees still floating eerily, back and forth with the winds.

But no description I could possibly generate could supplant the experience of being there for you, the reader. Glowing superlatives, vivid depictions, analogies, colorful phraseology – nothing uttered can replicate that unique scene of nature.

Yet, now I proffer for your absorption complex views of an inner terrain, easily as impressive and diverse, as colorful with emotion and dynamic with ideas as any spread of earth's crust could display with physical features. I cover expansive inner topography, exploring strata of conceptual deposits, clouds concealing perception, running streams of hope and dammed lakes of disappointment.

For some 30 years, beginning with awakening to the inner-outer connection that had been intimated earlier by that fleeting mystic experience, I ventured into an intangible, yet tangled and illusory mindscape of fear and ignorance, of intent and foiled desire, of rejection in place of love and proto-failure in attempts to just be who I am and survive, if not flourish.

With each new inner venture, I approached added aspects of life not working well. First, recognizing that physical ailments all had inner roots – as clarified by LeCron's insights into self-hypnotism – I began to clear away layers of debris that impinged on my health. Later, I continued on to rectify relationship difficulties and career issues – all ventures laced with my own personal compromise.

The journey inward was well worth it: a lifetime spent – actually never much more than a few minutes per day, and *invested* is a better term – improving the quality of my own existence.

As I convey significant perspectives, I can only reiterate the importance of your own inner venture in applying my perspectives. First, as with Mt. St. Helens, I can't possibly illustrate the scene as dramatic and remarkable as the inner ideascape you experience by delving inward. And second, you can only appreciate your ultimate causality by directly experiencing real change elicited when you have revised the content of your mindset.

Your Angle, Your Take: Not About Me

While the following aerial flyover of my psyche illustrates detailed layers of value and meaning within my mindset – how it **used to** stack up prior to revision – the view and review are meant to enhance your understanding of *your own mind function*.

The following revelation, then, is not about me; *it is about you!* By reviewing the interwoven values I held that underlie what the Buddha would have called karma, I illustrate, roughly, the inner terrain you discover within your own causal psyche – if and when you go looking. (Of course, many layers of similar meaning and value reside within your mindset right now, being churned, updated and manifested into reality whether or not you ever go looking!)

Because my mother was a major player in events manifested from my mindset, I offer some background on her and her parents. This only augments your view of the process of connecting values across parent-child relationships. It was *never* important, never in any way practical or functionally helpful to psychoanalyze my mother to derive a better view of **her** personal mindset. Only one's own mindset need be explored by discerning inner mechanisms at the root of real problems.

So all values as they impacted my real life were differentiated by breaking down real effects into whatever basic mechanisms were involved in each case.

As you venture inward, coming to clarify similar connections, you may also recognize the inner status of parents who influenced you. Indeed, they may well become rather obvious. But such external effects (parents' internal issues) do not directly pertain to you.

And that is fundamentally because you are *your own being*. You bring your nature into an incarnation; only then does your mindset attract and manifest events and relationships reflective of your qualitative essence. Maternal or other relationships, as they impact you, may be convincingly involved with your issues so as to appear directly causal; but in reality, they are only peripheral in nature, *attracted* by your propensities, instilling effects reflective of your nature. Only *you* are causal.

So as I point out, for example, how Mom instilled conflict through certain treatment, referencing her roots of conflict and struggle as embodied in the native land of her parents – Belfast, Northern Ireland, long steeped in such Celtic turmoil – it is only an image meant to more fully show connections. Only by recognizing that I was the cause behind those effects could I eliminate them.

The Gesture of and the Order of Clearing

For purposes of illustration, the following inner structures are categorized under basic topics. My process of removing them from active duty within my psyche (and thus eliminating their effects from my real life) was anything *but* ordered by category – indeed, as mentioned, the psyche is not ordered by category at all, but by meaning.

Overall, any one particular category of interrelated points exemplified below had an impact on many facets of my life. If life could be looked at as divided into three ranges, those being health, relationships and success (actually those three are deeply, significantly interwoven), one given section below would have had some functional impact on all areas – though perhaps on one more than another.

But the only effective way to delve into each range of meaning was by first looking at one element of effect, i.e., one problematic issue in life. When isolated and recognized as a problem, it could then be approached by finding its root mechanisms and other connections. Once its elements were fully clarified, it could be dispelled by auto-suggestion, with *one single element at a time in focus.*

Over years, I shaved away at major categories of content, dealing with one portion at a time as each of them might impact some aspect of life: my health, my ability to engage in quality relationships (whether informal, personal, intimate, or career), my propensity to succeed (in undertakings ranging from minor projects to business and career, to sports or investment, to the very expression of my message via my website, talks and book publication).

But the step-by-step process was long and convoluted. I focused on specific features of life as they came to mind. Having cleared away one deterring element, the next became obvious. In a fashion, my subconscious seemed to lead the way, but in reality I, like you, am an integrated Self, *a whole* – my intent to scrub away all detrimental, inner restrictions to fulfillment of my will was the navigating pointer. Hindrances came up in the order best approached.

The moral to that story is: I sincerely doubt the following text can be used as a guidebook to approach other people's personal psychic content, leveraging my journey to facilitate theirs. The better approach is to simply begin exploring small issues in life and, having found and eliminated inner roots such that those issues fade, move on to larger ones. Remember, the psyche isn't structured by category, but by meaning – and that is *meaning pertinent to real life.*

But it would be tedious reading indeed if I illustrated each step along the way – if I could even reconstruct that journey. Lewis and Clark, when first crossing North America from 1804 to 1806, didn't document each step of the thousands they took, but what they encountered along the journey, illustrating meaningful encounters in various botanical, anthropological and other categories. That's what I'm doing for meaningful inner aspects encountered on my journey.

So the prime value of the following accumulation of inner perspectives is not to present a trail for you or anybody to follow, but to help clarify some of the inner details you will doubtless encounter when you *undertake your own journey* and blaze your own trail.

Order of Significance

The subconscious functions without passion. Within the range of information, its order and interactivity, the subconscious store holds no innate preferential disposition. That is, the subconscious *has no selective preference to anything!* It does not judge; it simply holds information. Thus there is no inherent order of significance for any of the following elements of the psyche; they are all overlaid on each other, interwoven in theme and content.

There may, of course, be an order of significance to *you*, for the conscious Self (e.g., you) is quite passionate – particularly when pain is realized where joy might well have been. So while you may logically want to approach some aspect of life next, subtle components within the subconscious may impact that specific aspect in relation to other parts of life – elements it is necessary to deal with *first* before your greatest aggravation is to be addressed in all its complexity.

The rational self is not nearly as smart as it makes itself out to be: your best approach to inner clarification involves integrating the subconscious into the total Self you recognize, not pushing it along a logical trail you deem, rationally, to be best. The more you push, the less progress you make, because you are only pushing *your own Self.* Psychological push only realizes more inner conflict so that greater resistance is encountered.

So, significance to you *in itself* is not a criterion as to how the subconscious holds and integrates meaning. Likewise, the following sections approaching aspects of mind function are not ordered in any fashion. All were aspects of mind I had to encounter, clarify and de-structure to allow my health, relationships and success to fully reflect my intent. For me, some were highly significant and obvious, others more subtle, tucked into the background, contributing difficulty in their cumulative scope – but all were factored into the outcome, as the subconscious is **an integrated whole**: its *total content* becomes realized at all times.

That, too, is very important to remember: effects in real life can have multiple, layered levels, interwoven with each other, but all contributing to problems – like a stool sitting equally on all three legs. So, as you deal with some aspect of, say, your failure to attract meaningful relationships, and you find one or two very meaningful root issues and eliminate them, don't be surprised if you still have problems. More, even considerably more, may remain in there to deal with, particularly when regarding major aspects of life. So keep looking...

Please Note: Not All Bad

While I focus on structures of the psyche that distort perception and contribute to negation of your will, your mindset holds much more than conflict-inducing and struggle-manifesting content. *MUCH* more.

Many details, facts and figures are quite accurate within the scope of their meaning – and most useful in the conduct of life. Mathematical and scientific formulae, recognized governmental and organizational structures, family oriented stories, historical perspectives, environmental understanding, music and its broad range of expression, poetry, cultural lore, architectural accomplishments and building technology – I could go on and on – fall in that useful and functionally accurate category. A great deal of learned, detailed information critical to the maintenance of modern society is ultimately stored within the same mindset as all the effects exposed here.

But however useful, however critical to life and modern culture such knowledge is, to a large degree they and other accepted tenets implant beliefs about *how life works* that are not accurate. To that degree they are detrimental to your life, indeed, your ongoing existence. Given artificial validity, they usurp creative power and fallaciously assign it to synthesized sources out there somewhere. Your vital interest should be exposing such power-sapping notions and ridding yourself of them – that is, *in eliminating their detrimental aspects*.

So the primary focus here rests on psychic structures that distort understanding of your own causal nature in life. Recognizing that, in scientific notation, $F = ma$ – force equals mass times acceleration – is fine so long as you understand deeply that the gist of objects moving at all falls within the confines of your life in terms of *what happens* to that object that is moving. It's important to see love and joy as vital responses in life, so long as their core expression is attributed to yourself and real people, not to some non-existent, conceptualized deity.

So keep in mind that, as I focus on problems and root structures, very much more is held within your mindset. But in terms of meaning, if it enhances enjoyment and accomplishment, supports the vitality of health and relationships and contributes to success, you needn't adjust it. Were I to regard all interactive meaning stored within my psyche, it would require volumes to just lay out an overview.

The focus here is on life problems and their roots within the mindset because *they* need to be revised. And they provide an excellent illustration of the psyche regarding and manifesting reality.

Inner Structures

How They Impact Reality

The following sections illustrate many overlapping, interwoven layers of inner troubles I addressed journeying from an issue-ridden life to where health, relationships and success in desired undertakings are very fulfilling and pleasing. Each of them consisted of combinations of the mechanisms listed above; each had to be disengaged individually with explicit focus until it was culled from my subconscious.

Projections of Power to "Real" Things

Learning during early childhood to understand ourselves and the world around us, we pick up many explanations, names for things and what comprises their essence. Further, beyond casual suggestion, we infer from the context of common motherly talk, informal references and childhood stories the nature of many other things that never get explicitly defined. With each day of curiosity and adventure come many new notions describing the world that surrounds us.

Specified or subtly implied within these definitions are boundaries cognition builds to cordon things off, dimensional surfaces that appear to separate each object from the space – and other objects – around it perceived as *not* that object.

So, while Reality functions as an integrated, interactive realm, it **appears** to the child *taught to see it thus* to be a collection of isolated objects interacting in space. Its elements seem to respond only to forces consciously applied to them – or even by divine imposition – whatever the learned scheme dictates.

To allow Clear Awareness of the operative, functional Oneness, among the most straightforward – and most important – gestures are, first, to recognize the artificial isolation of "real" things and, second, to dispel the causality defined into those sources. Close behind, as addressed in the following section, is recognizing forces, sources and processes *that aren't really there* – then ridding your mindset of their imagined causal nature.

Illusory causality projected to **"real" things**:

1. **Natural events**: rain, ice, wind, sun, tornadoes, earthquakes, etc. Often real-world forces are seen as *causing* pain and destruction.
    *   In reality, earth's dynamism is not causal. Individuals experiencing death, injury or damage via natural events owe to their own inner state – featuring fear, conflict, powerlessness – their presence in the critical location where that disaster occurred.
    *   In any destructive episode, including natural ones, war and pestilence, some people suffer great loss, while others are scarcely affected – a situation consequent to the inner conflict of one group and the inner peace of the other.
2. **Forces**: gravity and electromagnetic "forces" are part of the interactive Oneness of Reality. They don't cause anything, but are part of the operative process. Reliable, predictable, pretty much a given, they constitute background functionality of this life format. If you fall off a cliff, don't blame

gravity.

3. **Status quo** – the current situation seen as inevitable carry-over into succeeding events.

- *How things are now* can be rational justification for an undesirable situation – as causal for things to come.
  - ✓ But current conditions, in terms of personal experience, directly result not from previous conditions, but from the prior *inner state*. That the status quo remains unchanged is a consequence of *not accomplishing inner change*.
  - ✓ Persistent annoying issues result not from current aggravating conditions, but from not bringing about inner revision.
- The *status quo* is **never causal**, only indicative. Seeing it as inhibitive of improvement only furthers personal powerlessness.

4. Looking on **reality** *as a whole* as though it were causal.

- Similarly, reality as a whole is only the outer, experienced manifestation of the inner mindset of the experiencer. It has no existence innate to itself.
- Reality, then, existing as pure *effect*, does not cause anything.

5. **Conditions**: ambient circumstances – weather, dryness, etc. – are also illusory as forces. The cold doesn't make one cold; inner propensities – metabolism, lifestyle, geographical location, etc. – do that. Similarly dryness doesn't make your mouth dry, drafts don't engender sickness and the economy doesn't cause personal financial strife. Your own causality lurks behind all such apparent sources.

6. **Objects** are likewise innocent of blame:

- Beds doesn't cause back pain; glasses don't make vision better; a fancy car doesn't make you more attractive; net worth and accumulated money neither limit nor drive accomplishments or acquisitions.

- These commonly attributed causes are only triggers or catalysts to end effects. Inner mechanisms combine to engender all such problems, incorporating the apparent cause as villain.

7. That **Other Person** is not determinative of a relationship: however others treat you – accepting, ignoring or rejecting – it is you who unconsciously attracts them into proximity. Whatever traits they exhibit fulfill your propensities.

   - Thus, while responding to situations however is necessary to further your interests, blaming others for problems you manifested is unwise.

   - Not blaming them, planning or perpetrating harm on others is unproductive and ineffective – and fruitless, only recycling the illusion of their causality.

   - Even in longstanding, intimate relationships, you ultimately, subconsciously, drive events: example, your wife's cooking, nagging, tendencies, habits, cheating, etc. (your husband's sloppiness, laziness, financial deficiencies, snoring, etc.) are not causal, but rather result from your own inner conflict.

     ✓ Blaming others for problems, you will never eliminate those issues; you may rid yourself of the seemingly guilty party but will reproduce the pattern in subsequent relationships.

     ✓ Even root connections attributed to motherly input should not elicit blame on her or older generations: you attract all situations. The real problems lie in inner conflict, perhaps involving punishment and struggle as personally held elements of mind – never in that *other person*.

   - In confrontational encounters, that threatening party is not the issue either. Growing up, I harbored many fears, the worst personified in a neighborhood bully who lived several blocks away – so I compromised my endeavors to avoid him. That pattern reiterated through life until that subtle fear had me limiting my message, afraid some jihadist or knuckle-brained fundamentalist Christian would take issue with my outspoken critique of their primitive religions. Dispelling the old fear eliminated any latter day worry about physical harm: it cannot manifest if the fear isn't there to attract it.

8. **Physical Attributes** provide easy excuses for failure. Being too short, too small (in height or in specific body parts), insufficiently attractive – too much or too little anything – is never the *real* cause for failure. No attributes of the material world, including features of your body, cause anything. Behind such apparent inhibitors are always inner mechanisms stacked with complex propensities as personal inhibitions.

9. Geographical distance or physical situation: these **logistical factors** are also results, direct consequences of inner manifestation in negation of will, never causes unto themselves.

10. **Taxes** and other seemingly unfair impositions – the demands of modern culture – seem to drain your wealth. But your level of abundance results from inner complexities specific to maintaining an exact lifestyle. Given greater inner orientation toward abundance, you attract more money: tax is irrelevant.

11. **Death** – fear of, concern over or worry about this absolute given is a total waste of creative juices.
    - Death is not inherently a causal factor, neither in your life nor anybody else's, but simply an element in life's format, critical to its meaning.
    - All things end, morphing into other things. Indeed, as you accomplish inner change, leading to outer improvement, the *old* you is gone anyway. Death is just

a more focused point of modification.

- You accomplish – or fail to, having at least tried and likely learned a lesson or two – just what you set out to do in this incarnation.

12. **Exercise** – like **vitamins, diet,** herbal **supplements** and such as means to foster health – is not really causal to your physical status.

- Your health, like all other elements of being, emerges from your inner complex.
- Given an orientation within the mindset towards optimum health, you trend toward exercise and healthy eating as a common lifestyle. But external, rationally concocted efforts to coerce the body into a healthy state never accomplish that beyond the inner scope manifested by your nature. They can, however, realize inner struggle by forcing great effort to, for example, lose weight.

In outgrowing old, shared notions, you need to shed all these external elements as causes. They only create illusions, dimming any perception of you steering your own vessel. And that process requires conscious, point-by-point auto-suggestion to effectively revise your mindset – just as when dispelling inner mechanisms.

But even beyond those tangible sources lie *mere ideas* that take on the appearance of being real things – and of being causal. Believing in them as valid items or processes makes them tricky to identify within your own mindset and eliminate – precisely because they seem so real and powerful...

Projections of Power to Conceptualized Things

People and objects, death and taxes can be grasped as real. They certainly *seem* to make things happen; you face them and deal with them daily. Still, coming to see your tie to reality allows recognition that you *attract those elements* into meaningful episodes in which they play roles.

Considerably trickier to both identify and eliminate are things traditionally deemed influential as creative forces or processes, but which *aren't really there at all.* Conceptualized entities or imagined processes you learned to acknowledge – probably quite early in life – are created by the *notion itself,* interpreted into cognition by holding the belief.

As I point these out, the degree to which you mentally argue or disagree with – or reject – my connotations is the degree to which you maintain belief in them. But the following are all illusory – notions attributing substance to any of them rest on pure conceptualization.

Causality projected to **Conceptualizations**:

1. **God**: numero uno on the list of causal illusions. No such creative, overriding entity exists anywhere, outside of you, yourself – within the scope of your life's perimeters.

   • Angle Four illustrates many past notions of causal gods, but not a single one of the thousands of deities man has imagined ever existed, except within believers' fervent minds.

   • Ridding yourself of the overriding notion that some lofty entity hovers out there, watching your every move and judging you is *first and foremost* of many steps toward freedom and self-determination.

2. **Fate** – derived from ancient notions of entities even more powerful than the gods, fate or **destiny** appear as independent, third person determiners of how life unfolds.

   • No such process or force exists that dictates your life events.

   • Life unfolds precisely, inviolably in response to your inner nature. The imagined process of fate is generally assigned to cohesive unfolding of patterned events in your life – attributed by people who aren't privy to the real inner-outer flow.

- Destiny, related grammatically to "destination", a concept similar to fate, is generally applied in retrospect, with life events interpreted as preset by some mystical force in order to yield a specific, foreordained outcome. Indeed, life's flow is fixed, but not by external occult forces, rather by pattern-making inherent to the Self manifesting Reality.

- **Kismet**, from Turkish Islamic roots, refers to the casting of lots, meant to determine beforehand the intent of a determinative god. Add this exotic synonym for *fate* to the list of non-existent forces.

3. **Sexual Response**, termed libido, or lack of it as frigidity in females, impotence in males – or the now commercially popular phrase "erectile dysfunction" – provides a classic example of taking an effect and imagining it to be a cause.

    - None of these exists as a featured thing unto itself, but only as a composite resultant of other inner elements:
        - ✓ Involvement in a relationship where one doesn't excite the other (realizing inner struggle and/or conflict).
        - ✓ Self-image complexities.
        - ✓ Fear and attribution of body control to conceptualized other sources.

    - Solving them by artificial application of exotic substances – anything from Viagra to pulverized rhinoceros horns – totally avoids inner issues, relegating sufferers to addiction to artificial means for carrying out what should be a normal, natural act.

4. **Chance, odds, probabilities** and such: these traditional features grow out of scientific notions that statistical forces are impelling things to happen.

    - Within the framework of your life, out of a vast array of

potentialities one set of eventualities will ensue; that combination of events and relationships will be consistent with your own mindset.

• Consider poker, a gambling venture considered a game of chance. In any given game setting, each player has a personal proclivity toward winning and losing – complex, perhaps, and spread out over time. But during any hand, the flow of cards corresponds to those inner needs. Whatever the odds calculated against a needed card appearing, the winner-type gets it. Winners lose sometimes and losers win on occasion. But overall, inner predispositions play out in specific patterns.

5. **Hope** – a deceptively *negative* mind-stance. This optimistic attribute is generally seen as desirable, romantically setting intent on the right course with yearning and idealistic fervor.

   • But hope is insidious in casting creative power towards specific or general external forces.

   • Wistfully wishing for a positive outcome to anything is blatantly conceding that you yourself are not the deter-miner of events! Hoping for better things recycles the standardized helplessness common to a cultural heritage of religion steeped in science.

   • Seeing clearly that life emerges in *direct consequence* of your own inner state – having cleared away inner conflict and struggle – you need not hope for good things to happen. By then, you simply know they will, as no force exists to oppose positive outcome and none to diminish it.

6. **Attempts and Efforts**: a prime path toward failure. The mental stance of **trying** to accomplish something intensifies conviction of inability. Confidence in oneself toward ultimate attainment of goals precludes *attempting* things.

You just accomplish them.

7. **Blessings and Blessedness**. These gushy references aren't negative so much as meaningless. They imply an external determiner, attributing positive outcome to that imagined source. All good outcomes result from intent coupled with inner peace and ease – not at the blessing of some capricious god.

8. **Luck**: a widespread illusion nurtured by millions. Unaware of intrinsic ties between himself and encountered reality, man has long pictured a force in play that imparts specific results, good or bad, on life's eventualities. It takes many forms in practice, all illusory:

- References to *birth* or *current circumstance* as causal: neither engenders anything, but both are tied to the situation the psyche has attracted/manifested – as results, not causes.

- Conducting *rituals* to affect luck: this ancient practice originated with assuaging gods for positive outcomes. Whether the rituals work or not, the process continues. If successful, the rite, assumed effective, is repeated. If not, the ritual is reused later with *more intensity* – the practicing mind stuck in its own illusion.

- Holding **charms** – pyramids, talismans, crystals, etc. – as alternate gestures to ritual: attempts to sway luck favorably. These items and gestures are beyond silly; they serve only to continue personal impotence in life – projecting initiative and effectiveness to imagined processes, like luck.

- Seeking *omens* as symbolic indicators of upcoming luck is also a long, long practice. Man has always sought to divine the future by various means – all the while attributing causality to other sources. The future for any individual will be what *that person makes it* – but not through action or fortune, rather through being.

- **Numbers,** like so many other things, are often regarded as lucky or unlucky – another prime illusion.
  - ✓ First, numbers are purely imaginary: nature features no numbers *at all!* No two apples, blades of grass, stars, amoebae or anything else are identical, so counting numbers of them is fundamentally fallacious to begin with.
  - ✓ Then, numbers, signifying only conceptualized entities, can hardly be attributed creative force or even indicative authority.
  - ✓ However, as all things fit together in patterns, often enough associated numbers in some fashion reflect overall tendencies. So some dim correlation might well be detected between reality and numbers – but the relationship is hardly reliable and never causal in regard to the number.
- The **luck of the Irish,** basically *bad* luck – as in Murphy's Law – has everything to do with long Celtic/Gaelic traditions featuring conflict as a high ideal.
- From Sanskrit "Lakshmi", luck references a goddess, Mahalakshmi – not unlike Fortuna, probably hearkening back to ancient Indo-European deities – who supposedly bestows good events on chosen recipients. Becoming her devotee would win favor and cue beneficial outcome in life. Good luck with that gesture! Unfortunately, such ill-fated attempts are hopeless and destined – most likely – to fail, *thank God...*
9. And specifically **Bad Luck** is traditionally tied to a host of indicators – all illusory:
   - Black cats crossing your path forebode ill events only when you happen to notice them, make the conclusion, then apply it to some part of life that negates your will – which it would have anyway, based on your mindset,

with or without the feline indicator.

- The imagined devious *number 13* comes between artificial indicator 12 and 14. Little more of any significance can be said about it.
- *Speaking ill of the dead* is appropriate when they deserved it. Doing so won't bring misfortune – unless you also believe in your own powerlessness.
- **Step on a crack, you break your mother's back.** I had to include this old childhood rhyme we used to chant on the way to elementary school. It never happened, but it did rhyme – which helped its folklore popularity. All such catchy, often old, old sayings, passing like waves through the generations, are equally fallacious.

10. **Parts of Speech**: oddly enough, we nonchalantly push creative power out to such intimidating beasts as nouns, pronouns, verbs and objects of prepositions!
    - Language inherently breaks the interconnected Reality we encounter down into bits and parts that then seem to be real entities.
    - Among them are, of course, **named items** – including other people – as causal by inference. Each of these thoughts, responding to real situations, reflects a mindset that assigns causality to external entities making things happen to me:
        - ✓ **The car hit me** – as though a machine was responsible for my being in that place at that time.
        - ✓ **The wind blew the tree onto my house** – indicating a mental concession that some things happen randomly. In actuality, were I at peace, I would not have had a tree in that spot.
        - ✓ **That person was rude to me** – neglecting to regard my own self-esteem as attracting such treatment.
        - ✓ **I lost my job because of the owner's son** – ignoring personal fear and lack of authority that had me in

that position in the first place.

- But standing for those names are spurious **pronouns**:
  - ✓ **It hurts me when…** – assigns causality to something unspecified. That "it" is part of *you*.
  - ✓ **They cheated me/raised taxes/screwed up/messed up my account/etc.** In Reality, no "they" out there does anything you don't elicit in qualitative effect. This and like notions create phantoms – evil agents that don't really exist – doing you wrong. More such phantoms will be itemized below.

- Imagining oneself as being the **named** physical entity draws boundaries that solidify helplessness: I am not "Tom Nehrer", but rather a *timeless, ongoing conscious entity* currently engaged in an incarnation of meaning – one in which I was assigned that name. I am thus not just "Tom". I am the total statement of accomplishment, taste, expression, impact on other people, factor in the advancement of mankind, love and joy, father, contributor to world culture and much more. None of the real essence of Self that I embody is contained in that moniker, which reduces Self to a physical bodied, diminutive self – and entirely misses the point of life.

- **Verbs** conjure up their own illusions as well!
  - ✓ Verbs of **being** imply that isolated objects exist out of context – breaking down the Singularity into a vast collection of items.
  - ✓ **Action** verbs strongly imply that things out there move around totally independent of their impact on you.
  - ✓ Both buttress the illusion that you are disconnected from the world you encounter.

- Even more subtle in constraining realization of one's desires is **passive case** usage of parental authority: e.g., *you're not allowed to do that.*

✓ This simple statement indicating parental restriction in specific instances – issued repeatedly during early childhood – formulates in the subconscious a **very** constricting status of non-permission, implying punishment should that act continue.

✓ To the timeless subconscious, this suggestive command, once absorbed, assigns throughout life a stamp of *forbidden* on many desires. Even though parents fade from authority, the **suggestion remains in effect**, creating an undetectable authority-image still disallowing whatever actions were first prohibited.

- **Authoritative recommendations** function with similar negativity:

  ✓ The repeated suggestion *"You shouldn't do that,"* sets up a negating subconscious notion as though some decreed sets of permitted actions governed you – and fulfilling your specific desires isn't among them.

  ✓ *"You can't do that,"* meant to disallow a childhood gesture, actually suggests to the psyche an innate inability that can subtly limit accomplishment by inhibiting self-confidence.

  ✓ *"You don't (really) want to do that,"* again meant to discourage unapproved action, sets conflictual doubt into the childhood mind which really *did* want to do it – remains there to fester as inner conflict until removed.

So, there: a collection of illusory mind games posing as valid forces in your life. For me, those last few, strongly intensified by my desire to please my mother, were very detrimental to accomplishing my goals. Strongly suggested based on her values, it made my own interests seem wrong.

Such structures must have been registered in your mindset by parental correction. If so, they remain in effect so long as you host them as real functions of reality. Indeed, if you find yourself saying, "fortunately" or "luckily" or "thank goodness", those notions lie buried there in your complex mindset.

Indeed, getting rid of luck, fate, fortune and chance from your psychic store of understanding considerably improves your luck, fate, fortune and probability of health and success!

Planning-Action Projectors of Power

One complex mechanism built into logical patterns you likely picked up during childhood projects power out to sources, often unspecified, to which it attributes authority; the problem arises that these objects of planning **are not *you*.** By virtue of the mental process involved, you further your own lack of determinative influence by hosting the thought process, thereby projecting power outwards.

1. **Initiation and Plan**: to express a need and begin to try to satisfy it by rational means. Following the path laid out by tradition, likely imprinted on you by mother and culture, you try to concoct some action to attain an intended result. But remember, experienced reality unfolds in response to your composite mindset, not action taken. *Planning itself* reiterates the action-outcome illusion. Whether you ultimately succeed is a result of **your inner nature** – not action taken.

2. **Solicitation**: as part of the reasoned plan, you figure out who (or what) can satisfy your needs in carrying out that plan, then you solicit that power/source. If it works, it was not the trigger action you took in soliciting, but the propensity toward success that *caused* the result. Likewise, failure didn't result from malfunction of the plan or faulty

execution, but by inner struggle or negation.

3. **Action, maneuver**: the next step in action-taking is follow-through on the plan. Great emotional expenditure might be built into execution of the venture. Yet all phases in actuality *are merely results*, preset toward success only if your psyche and its content are oriented toward success.

4. **Reconsideration**: adjustment to plan and execution – you may rethink all phases, taking into account initial setbacks, imagining what you would do different "next time". But that next time is always different, such that any complex calculation still only reproduces the same pattern. Subsequent maneuvers only bear fruit if you have replaced inner conflict with inner peace. Struggle, if present as a mechanism, necessitates adjustment and excessive fortitude before any success.

5. **If-then** deductions, in all aspects of problem solution, involve convoluted thinking that attaches elements in an illusory causal connection. Logic is the embodiment of artificial causality – useful in practice to allow communication, but illusory in false attribution of core cause.

The whole complex procedure of planning/execution embodies conceptual separation of you from the reality you encounter. This disconnect will be encountered in many elements below. Core to our common cultural heritage, the implicit separation of self from the seemingly external world, fundamental to both religion and science, is absolutely fallacious.

Localized Focus: Authority Figures and Limits to Scope

Most mental structures regarded here concern the psyche's way of perceiving itself and the world, holding as *real* such learned ideas which attribute creative power to something else **perceived as** external.

While the Self is the *only creative force* manifesting Reality, it does so automatically, transposing latent mind-structures into real happenings, based on its comprehensive nature – its total mind-image. Should that overall picture include firmly implanted notions that *something else* out there, actual or imagined, is the creative impetus for engendering reality, then real events and relationships will manifest appearing consistent with those imagined forces and sources!

The psyche clear of such attributions perceives itself as causal – and the resulting life unfolds consistent with its intent, reinforcing of self-confidence. Embracing a mindset loaded with fear and conflict, gods and demons or any other projected sources, however, the psyche manifests a negatively charged reality and engenders fear. Consequent experience then seems to reconfirm its belief structure, rife with such threats and afflictions that need to be fought and guarded against in ways learned earlier along with the notions.

So many inner structures directly pertain to learned, externalized power sources. Until you see and release them as I did, real and conceptualized things as listed above dictate your life.

But there are more draining notions nestled closer to home. These first ones review **Authority Figures** that dominated me:

1. Clearly my **mother and father** dictated what I could and couldn't do – I had to sneak or outsmart them to get what I wanted.
   - As life progressed onward, as parents faded into non-authoritative roles or died, their authoritative position was replaced by teachers and professors, then supervisors in employment scenarios, and spouse.
   - To eliminate the subservient role, I had to dispel that initial parental authority – for I continued replicating my underling role in ever recurring patterns.
2. My older **brother** had power over me as well. His attitude –

tending to pick on me, belittle me or push me around, never expressing any sort of appreciation or brotherly affection – was the real issue. But I had to jettison **my subservient, intimidated feeling** to eliminate his type from encounter.

3. **God** was supposed to reign over all. While I quit believing in this conceptualized entity very early, I had to delete conceptual variations of the *god notion* repeatedly, as the projection of power outwards continued to get rolled into some other undefined external projection.

4. **Grandparents** and other **relatives** held sway over me to a degree. Anybody and everybody within my perimeter from birth well into elementary school had authority over me.

    *   Regardless of how free society is, a residual, intangible pecking order exists common to all life forms, from chickens up through mankind. All advanced fauna posture and vie for dominance, facing off in overt male displays of prowess or female fussing, all meant to establish domination: who is boss and what order status stacks up under that.

    *   To be prime authority in my own life, I had to work through complex issues relating to external authority – issues involving suggestion, emulation, punishment, force, and certainly conflict. You will not become an authority until you personally see yourself as such.

5. And I had to go by "**the rules**". In place from my first day at home (though I had yet to be informed) was a set of miraculously ordained laws that my parents duly enforced. Often, their justification for applying punishment to me for some natural but forbidden act was simply referring to *the rules* I had broken.

    *   The implication was that Mom and Dad weren't at fault for punishment they meted out but were just enforcing **the rules**.

    *   It didn't even seem like *they* had created these arbitrary

imperatives; apparently they'd been chiseled into granite as fine print to the Ten Commandments. Thus, these dictates were completely out of my reach. Indeed, my parents *hadn't* created them; this same set of authoritative attitudes had certainly been encountered by them as children. They blindly reapplied these control gestures from earlier generations – replete with attendant inner conflict – without ever pondering their sense, usefulness or psychological impact.

- Of course, clever enough eventually to handle that, I found ways *around* their rules. I devised means to cover up disobeying rules I found unsuitable and plotted other devious means to do what I wanted. But the process incorporated:
  - ✓ Reinforcing within me distrust of my own impulses in favor of learned behavior – a disastrous twist of the psyche I later had to explicitly dispel.
  - ✓ The notion that one *needed* to break rules to succeed – another psychic malady requiring deletion.
  - ✓ And dispelling resident bitterness at *being punished at all* – having pain inflicted on me by people who claimed to love me.
- Additional pressure to my sensitive psyche came via punishment of my brother. Much more openly rebellious than I was, he often "got into trouble" (goofy phrase used to indicate rules had been broken) and found himself in the basement getting soundly spanked by Dad. His cries of pain were at least as disturbing and threatening to me as any spanking I got. But that level of intimidation bore a heavy fear factor I surely had to work through to eliminate.

6. **Police** were also referred to in childhood stories as strict authorities to be respected, if not feared. Experiencing little or no contact with law enforcement during my childhood,

this was not a major factor. But I can imagine that, for some, the police would be.

7. **Teachers**, as noted, and school **principals** ultimately assumed the authoritative position of parents, including – in those days – the mandate to punish students. But any punitive action I experienced throughout school – from deans during college or **bosses** in the work setting – was only echoing parental relationships. It passed away when authority was no longer assigned elsewhere.

Some structures loosely related to these points were established during childhood as well. Rather than pinpointing external sources, these very subtly attributed abundance to *processes*, not specific sources.

Elements of the **Blue Collar** ethic:

1. **Earning Money**, a process of trading work for payment, was strongly promoted as praiseworthy, valued – the classic quid pro quo.
   - But life doesn't really work that way. Success, financial or otherwise, originates from within. While immediate performance might trigger arranged payment, the inner propensity is what attracts the arrangement – beneficial or detrimental. Outer effects form around inner specs.
   - To understand that, first note that the English word "work" covers many different functions, some physical and demanding, some neither. But one very important differentiation should be made: doing something *enjoyable* while making money greatly differs from doing something *undesirable* for the sole purpose of eliciting payment.
     - ✓ Pushed by parental pressures (reflecting inner conflict), I was channeled into undesirable work scenarios.

✓ Working-class families share values of doing an "honest day's work" to earn money. Indeed, in complex modern society, producing real accomplishment for money for has great value. But behind the obvious, complex inner values really lead to rewarding ventures or failures, not the work ethic itself.

• Generally, work exchanged for pay, when it doesn't fulfill one's interests, desires and intent is very negative – reflecting inner struggle and conflict.

2. **Bargain hunting**, economizing, saving, scrimping are all part of blue collar thinking – and conflict with engaged reality.

3. **Can't afford** some things, too expensive, too much money: all conclusions based on limited regard of one's nature and capability. Negating desire because of current conditions is pure inner conflict.

Blue collar thinking passes along generations, limiting each Self in accomplishment and vision. But it rides the conflicted inner realm of anyone who incarnates into that worker-mentality setting.

Supplanting Fantasy for Reality

The mind is easily fooled by its notions. As a child I watched many movies about threatening monsters – *The Beast from Twenty Thousand Fathoms* comes to mind. In that 1953 movie (I was six then), a dinosaur-like monster thawed from arctic ice and made his way to cities to wreak havoc.

Scared the Hell out of me when I saw it! During childhood it was very hard to separate fiction on movie screens from reality. I faced similar distress with *Creature from the Black Lagoon, The Wolf Man* and various other horror shows.

But explanations about a god stoked worse fears: he watched over everything I did, ready to judge and ultimately send me to eternal misery if I didn't follow his revealed expectations.

So there were many layers of fantasy notions instilled then that seemed real to the naïve child I was, *but which weren't.* Those beasts and monsters, Santa Claus and the Tooth Fairy, even outgrown and laughed at, needed to be consciously dispelled from my subconscious store of definitions…

First, let's regard other **Fantasies** as they supplant real aspects of life in cognition:

1. **Radio music** rather than personal experience of real communication.
   - My father was a good pianist. He played Chopin and Beethoven when I was little, planting seeds that became a lifelong love of music. When he played, it was direct, personal communication of his emotions to me and other listeners. (Indeed, a reflection of my inner propensity woven into an aspect of this lifetime.)
   - But, instead of making music or hearing it performed by other, live musicians, experiencing direct emotional engagement, I more often encountered music on the radio.
      - ✓ The reality to such recorded music excluded intimate, personal expression of feeling. It was but a canned image, coming out of an electronic device – not special, not sincere in meaning to me. Just an illusion.
      - ✓ In reality I was generally alone, filling in empty space and isolation with artificial stimulation.
   - In life some of my greatest joy has been singing and making music, or hearing live some of the greatest

performers even: Vladimir Horowitz, Luciano Pavarotti and many others.

✓ But, as the child I was, the *effect* to my subconscious in hearing incessant popular music was to inject confusion of canned radio sound with *the real thing*.

✓ One negative consequence was favoring the entertainment of synthetic music over bland daily life, stuck in a house with little adventure.

✓ The outcome: music rhyming through my mind – nearly constantly through adult life – engendering a preference to *dwell in the imagination* rather than engage a colorless real life. This was a **major problem**, furthering manifestation of a bland reality embodied in undesirable work settings. It realized – and continuously recycled – escape as a pattern.

2. **Television**: reality was sitting on a couch, doing nothing.

• With an end effect similar to radio, during childhood, my generation was the first to grow up exposed to the onslaught of television. I watched TV nightly – enjoying some great early comedians and creative dramas. And on Saturday, I watched a long list of cartoons, sit-coms and B-class westerns – by the hundreds.

✓ One very clear negative effect was ever deeper instilling of conflict and heroism as positive values: the tough good guys standing up against evil bad ones, always winning in the end. (Unbeknownst to the naïve little boy watching this purely synthetic input: *none of those characters were real*. They were only actors. TV and movie plots only superficially reflected real human interaction. They were idealized fantasy – life wouldn't just always work out like that.)

✓ Another was deeper implanting of religious fantasy.

Seeing grand portrayals of Moses parting the sea, of healing and miracles depicted as real, helped to solidify some veracity of religion. All such fantasy had to be discarded eventually.

✓ But *the worst effect* was this: supplanting the grand adventure of a fantasy – always more exciting, more glamorous – for the mundane routine of daily life in a small town where nothing ever happened. The fantasy world was greatly preferable to reality – a gist that absolutely contributed to lowering the ongoing quality of engendered reality. (Dumping this effect was imperative, as my life has worked out great – more interesting, exciting, fulfilling and creative than any adventure ever put to cinema.)

- Displacing the actual with fantasized, imagined realities of television, *as a structure*, had to be discerned and dismantled to eliminate its customized detriment from recycling nothingness into real life.

3. **Hearing/Reading Stories** – instead of experiencing real adventure.

- Much of the *fantasy vs. real* tug-of-war in childhood begins with story-telling. At least it did back then. Now, kids are set in front of a TV or computer – and left there for long hours – before they can even identify reality.
- Stories do indeed communicate memorable events – seldom real, though, more likely fantasized or exaggerated into myth – from the past, communicating some depth of the cultural experience to new generations. But they also pass along cultural notions and values, however fallacious or damaging. Interwoven with immanent threats and heroes to face them are notions of how life works. As stories are invariably steeped in long cultural values (stories outside culturally accepted "truths" don't get told), accepted

notions, beliefs and dogma become implanted in the open minds of every new generation with subtle but unvarying effectiveness.

- While I scarcely remember stories from my childhood, I know they involved conflict and struggle – no literary work at any level can avoid those components. Yet those elements, self-defeating when held within, have had to be eliminated, one at a time, as exposed – because they were ingested psychologically along with the story built upon them.

4. Mother was happy when I wasn't *doing* **anything** – for various reasons:

    - Inhabiting my mother's mindset were all those fears common to western thinking that sees causality in a dominant god and scores of other forces. Her motherly instincts, of course, included a high priority towards keeping me safe from harm.

        ✓ Thus, she was quite content when I was watching television or going to a movie. As early stories, often Bible yarns, gave way to broader exposure to the budding media, she doubtless saw little threat in my watching TV shows. After all, I was safe in the living room, not really in the jungle fighting leopards or riding the plains shooting cattle rustlers.

        ✓ So, whether consciously or unconsciously, she encouraged this passive status, absorbing all the negatives listed above.

    - For my mother, with her deeply embedded religious, god-fearing piety, engagement in sex and various other pleasure-inducing pursuits *was a bad thing*; sinful, they would keep you out of the post-death heaven promised by Christianity. So her general intent included keeping me safe not only from danger, but from "temptation". That, of course, would otherwise involve actual fulfillment, the reward of most natural drives and normal human desires.

✓ So, again, she was happy to have me focus on movies and TV shows – so long as they didn't involve sex – as it held my real attention and supplanted that pesky urge to actually *live out real adventures.*

✓ One traditional oddity here is the abhorrence of such religious people to exposure of even a single female breast, while they have no problem with the depiction on a screen of the bloodiest of murders and torture. If absolutely pure idiocy and unbridled banality exists, *this is surely it.*

• So, among the wide range of mind structures I had to eliminate, Mother's subtle encouragement for – or lack of restriction against – focus on media presentations was this key motivation-type mechanism.

5. **Reading the News** or following it through the media.

• Growing into adulthood, being informed of political and world situations becomes a part of life. Democracy requires, according to tradition, attentiveness of its citizens to promote informed views and wise decisions for voting.

✓ But actually mass events, including government functionality, respond to the *collective mindset* of the people, not to action taken – just as individual lives unfold reflecting personal nature.

✓ So subtle effects emerge when focus is excessive on affairs outside your immediate circle of contact: you tend to reinforce personal fear while watching negative reportage of most news sources. This adversely affects your personal life by confirming powerlessness in your own mindset. And that helplessness, shared by others within the culture, leads to unresponsive government.

✓ There are **always** natural disasters happening somewhere in the world, along with many human-generated ones. If they don't directly impact you, the relevance to your life is very limited. Yet, with the focus of media news reporting, it seems the world is rife with great danger and threat – an illusion that only reinforces negative thinking on your part.

• News always puts focus on the negative *anyway!* Our society is steeped in conflict and struggle, so bad news holds focus. Ignoring that millions went home last night, loved their families, made their living, did creative things and helped their neighbors, the news features the one rape or robbery – because that's news!

• The quality of your life is caused by your own inner content, not external sources. Until you grasp that, watching the news can only thrust its negative bent into your life.

6. **Movies**: the ultimate escape.

• Hollywood movies, with glamour, adventure, hot babes and exotic locations, meaningful events and idealized settings blasted on a huge screen, were an even greater thrill than TV. As a kid, I was whisked to exotic places, facing – and always overcoming – great challenges, for well-scripted movies always draw you into the plot from the protagonist's perspective. With their glitz and ever attractive stars, they carry a powerful **Implied Rightness** to their statement, rendering the viewer necessarily inadequate in comparison...

✓ Movie negatives were even more exaggerated than TV westerns and sit-coms: conflict involved grand beasts and dazzling special effects, embellishing conflict and struggle with exaggerated glory and heroism. Emphasized as desirable components of self-esteem, conflict jammed ever more deeply into the mindset.

✓ Inflicting pain and damage on monsters, aliens or animals – or even characters – was regarded as just fine if they were defined as bad. The negative message here covers many layers, with an overriding implication that conflict is ingrained in life, and *you have to win it* in any way possible. Total illusion! Absolute conceptual garbage.

✓ Yet another negative was fear crushing into my sensitive mind. Great monsters – thawed dinosaurs, that Black Lagoon creature, huge ants and spiders, supernatural creeps, men becoming werewolves, aliens from space were all out to get mankind, including little me. These drove that conceptual wedge between me, with my intent, and a frightening reality *out there*.

• Other **confusing illusions** abounded: while handsome heroes always got the girls in movies, life turned out not so amenable. As it happens, orientation toward big-screen fantasy as **ideal** strongly contributes to diminishing real, manifested events by energetic inclusion of fantasy as preferential in one's values and overall mindset. Orientation toward fantasy inherently hinders real relationships.

• As an added annoyance, the projection of thrill and wonderment into movie fantasy also contributed to background **music running through my mind**.

✓ To help clear away that irritation, I had to release the preference toward glorified cinema pseudo-existence over real life – the thrill over mundane existence.

✓ Indeed, my life itself has featured grand adventures that outclass the grandest Hollywood episode. Yet, I still maintained the orientation to the imagined rather than real engagement – a real detriment to my accomplishment and enjoyment, until dispelled.

- **Emphasis on conflict** and dominance – protagonists overcoming various encountered forces of evil is standard fare in movies and, by inference, in life – promote as a goal and emphasize as a highly desirable attribute *being good at conflict*. This idealization of conflict yields separation between self and forces out there; it reinforces and idolizes toughness as the ultimate trait – one which then highlights and perpetuates conflict in real life.

- Compared to movies seen as a child, as life progressed into adulthood, I could **never measure up** to the looks and bravado of the grand movie stars, or their inevitable success at dealing with their problems.

  ✓ Of course, consequential to this unavoidable comparison, I judged myself inferior to the cinematic ideal. Why should a pretty girl fall for me when I wasn't as handsome as those movie stars? How could I succeed at beating bad guys without the bravado and confidence those film heroes had? (Of course, bravery is easy when the plot calls for enemies to miss when they shoot you and fall over dead when you shoot them!)

  ✓ By and large, I was failing in life in significant part because I could never match up to the glorious, heroic images I'd seen in so many films. Finding this connection, though, I could easily release it: those movie heroes were only illusions, actors walking through a script in front of cameras, not real characters succeeding at their every undertaking.

  ✓ And I came to see that, by comparison, I was by far the more significant character in my real journey, far more impressive than any Hollywood façade – as my life was shaping into a significant one for real, not as a fictional projection, fleetingly popular, but soon relegated to film rental and past glory.

In all these ways, imagined effects interfered with real life. The above six points were encountered repeatedly in seeking out roots to life's issues. Their presence impacted my health and real life negatively until I rid myself of them.

Most fantasy-based effects entailed the specific mechanisms suggestion and emulation, as the child I had been was very open to such input – the *Creature from the Black Lagoon* was as real and frightening to me as every western hero was romantic and brave. And of course, with struggle and conflict built into every single plot, the ideal – virtually the goal in life itself – became standing up against bad guys and veritable monsters of all sorts, being tough in the face of adversity.

All these intertwined inner elements combined to embody – and manifest – a great deal of conflict, not only in various relationships, but in professional situations I encountered. Idolizing those traits, I was attracting opposing figures, not cooperative ones, in professional and personal relationships in what should have been supportive connections. So my continuous intent was negated, not fulfilled.

Self-Image

Your psyche right now holds a complex, composite image of what you are in all phases of life. It consists of a detailed evaluation of your nature in terms of quantity and quality, covers a range from the physical (looks) to the very psychological (self-esteem). It dominates resultant manifestation of your ongoing situation. Your own evaluation of yourself, even including comparison to others real and imagined, impacts all phases of life: health, relationships and success.

Health issues can rest on detailed self-perception in regard to how your body works generally and within your particular environment. But in terms of interaction with others pertaining to relationships and success at endeavors, your self-image is absolutely critical.

I was a reasonably handsome young man – tall and athletic, humorous and outspoken. But, as noted above, I couldn't match up in my own evaluation against the hunks of appeal that populated TV and movies, nor did I seem to have the great sex appeal of the more down-to-earth, less intellectual guys where I grew up. So, my self-esteem featured one well-founded negative: I was somehow inferior. This detrimental element of my mindset had been previously exacerbated by my older brother, wont to ridicule me and push me around. Indeed, during my formative years, he was always bigger and stronger – inevitable, given a 4½-year head start. I could only feel inferior to him in many ways.

Indeed, our household came preset in a pecking order stacked against me, as noted before. Authority was an issue in itself, one I grappled with for much of my early adult life – at least until I cleared away negative mechanisms such as punishment and suggestion that registered me as inferior in my own evaluation.

Adding to the downside of things, I started to lose my hair – male pattern baldness – by my early twenties. Whatever bashfulness and lack of confidence, whatever state of inferiority to movie stars and local ladies' men I'd had before increased at that point.

Now, consciously, I've always been more than confident of my own ability and my own ultimate success. But in pursuit of relationships, while I approached attractive females, inwardly I didn't evaluate myself very high in terms of looks and colloquial "coolness". Thus, unconsciously, I didn't even *judge myself worthy* of any female attractive enough to interest me. That mix was doomed to frequent failure – realized by leading myself into encounters with females predisposed to not respond positively.

Of course, I later came to realize that all the overt elements commonly attributed to initiation and progress of relationships – looks, coolness, money, flair – were *irrelevant*: phony overt causes.

In essence, one attracts exactly those people who fulfill explicit inner needs. Mine at that point featured rampant struggle and conflict. So overtures to attractive women – encountered in fulfillment of those inner, negating and neutralizing mechanisms – generally led to rejection or indifference.

As to **Self-Image**, here were two other key factors:

1. Evaluated **worthiness**: my own take on what I *deserved* in life. Much of my accumulated understanding as a young man rested on scientific notions and leftover religious values implanted earlier. Even long after dumping religion as invalid – and later science – I retained many synthetic notions from both. So my Self-Image and its innate level of esteem rested on this dichotomy of values (religious and scientific), often themselves in conflict...

    •   In science's presumed objective reality, desirability in any relationship stems from elements of personal worth in competing or engaging in conflict with rivals, thus dominating the scene. Strength, courage, bravery, commitment to justice – such traits would be positive attributes. Set against inimical forces of reality, in order to be the best, one would have to display these characteristics.

    ✓   But, by nature I was never particularly aggressive or conflictual. I never felt, even well before understanding the functional Oneness of things, that inflicting damage on others was appropriate for accomplishing anything. While this inherently peaceful nature serves me well now, it was detrimental (or appeared to be) for engaging the world while holding to science's distorted understanding.

✓ The negative value was, as is always the case, in my *feeling* weak, somehow less worthy in a world that offered success to the Darwinian "fittest".

✓ In larger, more encompassing terms, holding scientific tenets as true imparts considerable damage to anybody's self-worth. Picturing a vast universe out there, billions of light-years across, populated with untold billions of galaxies holding trillions of stars, our sun and its diminutive planet Earth hold precious little significance in the scheme of things. Implications of that image as background understanding for any person, one of six billion scurrying about the face of an insignificant wet rock floating through space, renders the perceived self as worthless in the grand scheme of things.

✓ Add to that insignificance a *default meaninglessness*, embodied in the scientific notion for the essence of consciousness: a functional outcome of evolved brain function. The consequence to one's existence becomes ultimate nullification: a cessation of existence at death and eventual total dispersal of any and all accomplishments, ultimate destined demise of all offspring and their progeny, thus eventual irrelevance of any creative production. Held in the mindset, this limited view fosters underlying futility for everything in life, save perhaps for immediate sensory pleasure.

• From the standpoint of religion, specifically the Presbyterian version of Christianity my mother cherished and inflicted on me, my self-image took an equally damaging hit from defined subservience to the grand creator god.

✓ In comparison to the grandiose, all-powerful deity – or his wonderful, perfect son, the bloatedly idealized Christ – this meek, temporal being *I was* paled in significance and value.

✓ Taught to pray to that omnipotent entity – or his miraculously conceived offspring – for anything, including my own salvation, I was rendered to seeing myself as little more than zero in power and worth.

Seen in the light of those two great pillars of modern understanding, science and religion, the Self shrivels in value to a negligible quantity. But in reality, you, just as I, are the *absolute most important entity* in existence, seen from our respective angles of existence.

It took more than mere recognition of the Oneness of Consciousness and Reality, more than realizing that I was the only force causal to the quality of my being to divert my life towards a rewarding, fulfilling quality. I had to chip away at all the false suggestion, all the illusory, implanted ideas that both paradigms contained, before life actually fulfilled my intent rather than negate and neutralize it.

The second key factor directly, harmfully impacting my self-image was a twist on values implanted by my mother based on those religious notions. You recall the basic effect of motivation – a reward as positive reinforcement for a negative situation. The normal, positive side of life includes real, appropriate compensation for positive accomplishments, for success or just as a course of being. Yet I was never rewarded for anything:

2. **Lack of reward** connected to positive events, enhancing a

joyful outcome:

- For Mother, hooked on the fantasy perpetrated by Paul on Christian tradition, the real prize in life was *always in the future*, in **heaven** – that idealized post-death wonderland posited by Paul (but never referred to by Jesus, as his Kingdom of Heaven was *now*).

    ✓ As touched on earlier, for Mom, receiving rewards during life was *not good*. Quite the contrary, in fact: suffering in God's name would help secure heaven later – doing without, being humble, giving rather than receiving.

    ✓ So Mother only increased affectionate attention at times of distress when her sense of motherhood trumped religious fervor – *never when things went well*. This bizarre form of motivation was a critical, negating element for me to uncover and eliminate: I spent much of my life never reaping benefit from projects I succeeded at, reproducing the bland experience of early life.

    ✓ And Mom's ramped up affection during sickness only helped to motivate repeated sickness, trouble and failure.

- Further in that vein, heaven was attained by subverting urges and repressing desires *NOW*, while always holding out for that grand reward, the carrot at the end of the celestial stick, based on divine judgment later. In the ultimate life twist of Mother's sincere religious understanding, pleasure experienced *now* would be judged *negatively* later.

    ✓ To help secure post-death heaven, she avidly repressed anything gratifying at all, particularly in a sexual context. In reference or deed, pious Christians tend to be hung up on sex as sinful. In fact, one of the most disastrous episodes in my early life resulted from my mother's prudish bent. About age 5, a neighbor girl and I had discovered that it was rather stimulating to take off our clothes – rather clueless as to why. We code-worded our game "dee-dee". At some point an older neighbor girl, about 11, initiated such a game in her basement, adding a feature we hadn't invented: rubbie. She rubbed my genitals (*wow*, quite an enhancement, I quickly noticed) and I returned the favor. My 5-year-old playmate didn't join in the action, though. In fact, she proceeded to tattle to her mother about the whole episode. When my mother got wind of this innocent little encounter, she flew into a rage – so severely and fundamentally had it offended her values. Her response, multifold punishment and reprimand, plagued me in many ways *for decades* – right up until I specifically jettisoned her Victorian response along with the rest of her strait-laced sex-oriented inhibitions.

✓ The overwhelming oddity to that religious attitude was the absolute avoidance of aspects of life that brought pleasure and fulfillment – sex, travel, ribald humor, partying, whatever. Looking for a wonderful Heaven to reside in for eternity, she turned this life into an ongoing Hell. (I often pondered what her heaven would have been like with all real sources of pleasure disallowed – eternal card parties with tea and pious gossip about those who didn't make it?)

✓ To complete the picture, my mother was often ill – not surprising, given what must have been enormous inner conflict. The drain on family resources resulted in us *never* taking a real vacation. She unconsciously scuttled all other forms of pleasure. While I had fun friends to play with and some interesting relatives to visit, we never went anywhere of interest – Europe, out west, to the ocean, the desert, the mountains, *never*. My parents always had money for cigarettes (further scuttling health), but never for adventure or pleasure: miniature golf was a big treat in their minds.

✓ One other point of core consequence to the notion of after-death heaven. This archaic image stemmed from Zoroastrianism and likely from superstitions even well before that. But the gist itself is precisely as damaging as it is deeply embedded in the subconscious: the place of contentment and happiness is off there, **somewhere else**, sometime in the future, in some other dimension – decidedly not *here and now*. Accepting that during the absorptive, formative years of childhood builds a default mindset that, by its base definition, *precludes fulfillment now!* (In Reality, there is only **now**. Life is fulfilling, rewarding and joyful *now*, i.e., Heaven-like, or not – either boring or painful, either of which is Hell.)

Thus, unconsciously, my mother added affection when I was sick or troubled, but actual reward for what was meaningful and fulfilling for me now was out of the question – dreadfully sinful.

I worked through all those stratified effects. As for baldness, I came to see that this particular incarnation was well served with this classical intellectual, philosophical sort of look. And I came to accept that, not as deviating from the norm, not as a "condition" or negative physical circumstance, but as a masculine trait that was just fine; it no longer deterred me in any way.

As for all other factors deprecating to self-image, they, too, are long gone.

I have no use for humility; I recognize the meaningful,

expressive force of my lifetime in cutting through ages of myth and fallacy and value my Self highly. Only from that standpoint can one ever truly value *others* in the same vein – as we are all unique, rich of character, and on a long, long journey. Perceiving the timeless nature and innate meaning within each thread of life spurs absolute creative joy that life can and should entail.

Yet another key curtailment to my self-image, though, was put in place by early definitions:

3. **Self-Identity** was established very early on: similar to **naming objects** was being named *myself*. This conceptualization, covered in **parts of speech**, should be appreciated for its profound gesture of separation – and damage to self-worth.

   - No perspective was ever presented that the reality I encountered was a cohesive Oneness, a blend of interacting objects and people all of which fit into a single, meaningful flow.
   - No, those huge adults feeding and nurturing me split me apart from all things by naming and treating me as separate.

Adding to personal limitation is the tendency toward **Group Thinking** – pressure to *conform* to cultural norms. In early times, individualism was much less prized than today. Still, though, conforming remains as strong peer pressure from childhood onward: go along with the crowd, wear popular styles, do expected activities, watch trendy TV shows, get the latest techie devices, etc.

That tendency reinforces notions of separation and everpresent threat to the loner: safety and security are deemed to lie in numbers – being part of a group provides protection. And that includes conforming to accepted ideas and bowing to commonly acknowledged authority – like preachers. That sort of compliance strongly crimps the Self, substituting emulation and identification for self-expression.

Having worked through the above, my self-image **now** is no longer limited and powerless, but rich and joyous, full of humor and accomplishment, top shelf self-esteem, optimism and positive anticipation. It got here by shedding negating rudiments of both science and religion, all the downer suggestion and punishment from parents passing along cultural limitation and all the consequent inner conflict. I could only have achieved this current positive status by so doing.

World View

As well as notions conceptualizing the nature of self, the psyche holds complex ideas as to the natural world around it. These, like many impressions of self, were introduced through explanations during childhood and by inference from exposure to common, shared understanding.

Indeed, so many such core defini-  tions are held – the nature of this planet and its diverse ecological system, earth's solar system floating about the outer reaches of the Milky Way galaxy, houses and how they are built, the evolving track of primitive man, imagined creation by a grand deity, cloud formation and weather patterns, political structures, road systems and other key transportation, communications, behavior patterns of others, cities, entertainment, natural disasters, music, cuisine, sports, on and on – that the vast conceptual diversity precludes going into detail.

I must only emphasize in regards to your psyche and its perception of the real world: you were taught to see external reality in ways consistent with cultural values and understanding. Much of your understanding is so deeply accepted and so interwoven with personal security and integrity that you can scarcely see it, let alone question its validity. All details, though, affixing a functional nature to the biosphere of this planet, serve to separate you – in your own mind – from this extensive world and the vast universe it occupies.

Behind that environment, however, driving details as to how *you personally fit* into daily interaction with it on any scale, is your personal propensity for creating patterns in the customized interface of you with that world. For whatever happens elsewhere on this planet or beyond, how it impacts you qualitatively is set only by you.

So the many definitions creating mind-images regarding aspects of the real – all of them – serve only to functionally separate you, the meek, small individual, from an unbounded, vast universe surrounding you. While useful and practical to maintain many such elements, highly critical to recognition of the unlimited Self in imprinting quality of being on real events is profound recognition that the grand universe only impacts you according to your own specifications. To fully realize your own timeless nature as an integral conscious entity, definitions constituting your **world view** must be put into perspective.

Truth

One core distortion that plagues the typical psyche brimming with standard western notions is something defined as a **core truth** that *really isn't*. Of course, much of what I expose here involves fallacies parading as defined truths – gods and other fantasized sources, gravity and other conceptualized forces – which create illusions appearing real.

But the notion of truth *itself* is, to the undiscerning mind, a prime trickster: truth creates its own pseudo-validity by painting everything its own color.

The only thing that really exists is *you* as the total essence of meaning: inner propensity emerging into outer manifestation. All descriptions concerning your nature and that of the surrounding environment you encounter are patently artificial, generated conceptualizations, thus functionally false: no assembly of symbols or sounds which formulate words representing ideas which again symbolize Reality can be exact.

While I discuss this and that aspect of being, how it works, how to change it, etc., in the end I'm only trying to illustrate consciousness and its resultant so that you can come to see it for yourself, perceive it, nurture your own intimate connection personally and clearly.

Any attempt to depict Reality in detail, rendered through any language, sputters in its own grammar and limited definition. The Oneness with which Reality functions in response to Consciousness is perceivable, but not describable: words create boundaries – Reality hasn't any.

Based on perceived sources, though, I worked my way through many illusory forces functioning as: **Externalization of the Internal.**

1. **Rebelling** against perceived gods.
   - When things don't go well, one who believes in a god can try to make a deal, promising to be better – or whatever action might be deemed in the best interest of that deity – in exchange for a good outcome in that crisis.
   - Similarly, one can rebel, defiant, against that imagined god's apparently negatively inflicted event.
     - ✓ Neither reaction to real events has viability as a gesture, because there is *nothing out there* to bargain with or rebel against.
     - ✓ Engaged reality – what you see in front of you – is a

result, an outcome, a consequence of your mindset. You are only dealing with or rebelling against a reflection of yourself!

✓ Any such gesture only reiterates struggle and conflict.

2. **Railing against** something out there, unnamed, that one is frustrated with, angered against.

- Having cleared away old notions of a kibitzing god, you might, in frustration, turn your wrath against some vague thing out there, shaking your fist at undefined forces that seem to impose bad things on you.

- This subtle effect, this dangling shade of an external source, I call **discombobulated convolution**: residual elements of illusory forces already eliminated.

  ✓ Having long since ended belief in a god, I still carried subtle notions from childhood *attributed to it*.

  ✓ Part of an ongoing inability to succeed was tied, through punishment, to the god-notion picked up from Mom. Between ages 2 and 10, I sincerely believed this creator being would punish or reward me based on my actions. Ceasing to believe this fantasy, however, didn't eliminate **all subconscious values** in place attributed to it. Lack of success lay rooted in non-reward from this god-mind-image for me not believing in him!

  ✓ Having jettisoned the god, I also had to clear out meaningful attributions to it that the subconscious still held. The subconscious, not ordered by category, didn't delete all functional features of the deity when the principal notion was expelled!

"Truth" in any expressed context is a hoax. The gods, apparent forces "out there" seeming to mete out bad news, are only external projections of notions you hold within. If you catch yourself railing or wailing at your ill fate, understand first that *no causal force lurks out there at all.* Truths depicting one aren't truths.

Reality is a result, a source-less, forceless *effect* culminating from your own inner, causal nature. Defiantly confronting it is no more effective than beating a straw dog perceived to be piddling on your leg.

Compressed Effects at Birth

Patterns you create throughout life give valid, clear indications of your mindset's many elements. Problems encountered now will be found echoing back through earlier episodes of life – as far back as you can recall. Clarifying their inner components at any stage is key to identifying those specific inner elements so you can eliminate them and change the pattern.

As I was working through critical issues – problems covering the spectrum from personal through health issues – I used the basic techniques illustrated above with excellent results: I was able to trace core problems back to the **first four days** of my life.

Mostly we assume we can't remember much from those early times. Common sense, rooted in scientific and longstanding cultural notions that consciousness rests on brain function, would tend to support that. But common sense rests on shared belief and accepted definition – its impressions as flawed as the mindset it emerges from.

Distinct memories were already accumulating *even before birth.* So looking back to early stages of life is possible, provided sheer disbelief doesn't deter access. Indeed, as I found, major patterned situations are already in play from the outset of this present incarnation.

To understand the situation I uncovered, first imagine an ideal birth. With a relaxed, confident mother, the baby bloops right out into somebody's waiting, loving hands. After minimal wiping, it is laid into its mother's gentle arms and, in short order, latches onto a warm, nurturing breast. Very natural, that scenario played out in some variation – perhaps not quite so idyllic – over thousands of generations of ancestry right down to each of us. Ideally, that baby feels warm, soft skin, smelling natural odors. It first tastes colostrum, nutritious precursor to breast milk. Its first eye contact is with its mother, a loving entity strongly oriented to protect and nurture.

Generally that's how it worked before medical science took over.

In a hospital not far from where I live now, at 10:30AM on June 10th of 1947, I made an entry to this world stylistically well outside that ideal...

Upon arrival, hit with the cold, I was inverted and slapped to make me cry – it worked. Warm mother? Cuddling? Breast milk? No way – I was summarily wiped and wrapped in a sterile, stiff hospital sheet and whisked off to the nursery. And that began four days of clinical Hell.

Understand, time goes faster as one progresses through life. Now 63, I find a day shoots by amazingly quickly – three meals, various duties, a long walk or run for exercise, do email and some writing, buy some food or take care of a chore and *zappo!* – the day is gone.

It wasn't always like that, though. I remember as an 8-year-old, driving out to my grandparents' new house: that 15-minute drive took *forever*. I remember saying: *when are we ever going to get there!!* Now I drive 1200 miles and scarcely notice it. The earlier you look in life, the slower time goes.

That first day in the hospital was like months now – literally. But in place of warm tones from a loving mother and natural scents, I had hospital clanks and bangs, crying babies all around with medicinal smells and an occasional whiff of those fellow inmates' poop. When my eyes could focus, there were no homey colors to see, not the golden hues of the sun, green of plants or colors of flowers – just glaring, white hospital lights and colorless walls, metallic cribs and white-robed nurses. Hour after hour after long, long hour…

(For all my subsequent years as a child I always disliked it when my mother changed my sheets weekly. On delving into these first four days, I realized why: it brought back the hospital Hell.)

As social beings, we all want love and affection – a chick or duckling, even simpler life forms, looks immediately for its mother to bond and interact with. Yet no such connection awaited me. I had nurses – people too busy and too distant to provide affection. They picked me up briefly to feed and burp, then put me down. Or worse, *much worse* – stuff a pacifier into my mouth.

I'm a sensitive sort of person. I've spent much of my life culti-vating tastes in good food and drink, enjoying great music and exploring the world for its visual and experiential wonders. Those are timeless traits of mine, certainly at the core of the intensity needed to travel my long journey and communicate it. I drink good beer and wine, buy raw, delicious milk from a farm. My wife bakes our bread and we grow much of our food in our organic garden. During travels, I always keep an eye out for good honey and preserves or locally produced maple syrup.

But in the hospital, I got *formula* – artificial crap not remotely like mother's milk: synthesized slop. Horrible stuff, unnatural, unsatisfying – unwanted.

So I was miserable, alone, uncomfortable, frustrated, confused. Sleep was the only respite. It got worse: next came day two…

Medical Science pictures a newborn as a dim-witted lump of flesh, not aware of much, focused only on survival needs – which can be replaced by artificial substitutes. Psychology doesn't do much better, figuring that early phase is only oriented to rote fulfillment of biological processes – food, piddling and pooping.

They are wrong, though – dreadfully wrong.

For those males of you who may not recall, and for those females unacquainted with such details, a baby gets erections at an early age: standard equipment on the model.

On day two, while I was yet to see my mother for a couple more months-long days, I ran headlong into her religious bent: they circumcised me. And they did so without so much as asking.

So, added to the misery of loneliness, periodic rejection by nurses, a pacifier to shut me up, the din of other babies protesting the same torture, medical smells, incessant noise, stomach cramps from the pig slop they fed me, they saw fit to snip off the foreskin from that most sensitive of body parts. So then, for some long time afterwards, urinating burned and erections stung. And when I cried, they again shoved a pacifier into my mouth.

All senses faced an onslaught of negative input. Whether audio, visual or olfactory, taste or touch, I experienced an offense to every channel of experience. At some point, faced with rejection and pain with no means to counter it, I initiated a retreat back into myself, into a comfortable, imagined world. I built a wall, a psychological barrier against the hurt – and spent my life retreating there when failure or rejection played out yet again...

As interesting as my life has been, I've faced many issues that grew out of (or echoed back to) that original set of conditions. During my younger years, I had recurring colds with little respite, allergies to various things like wool, feathers, and cinnamon. I had assorted ongoing aches – my knees hurt during and after sports and I often enough sprained an ankle or suffered joint problems. Headaches were an issue, later ear problems and as I matured, my prostate acted up.

In terms of career, my degree in chemical engineering reflected a system – and parents – that guided me into channels I really didn't want. It did serve to keep me from being drafted during the idiotic Vietnam War and having to shoot – or be shot by – people I had no interest in or complaint with. But it led, following many years of travel and searching, to a "career" as Systems Developer of various software systems – again not what I desired, but something I could do well. But while I did earn a living in each setting, as recurring patterns, I always found myself in a position managed by clueless superiors and lacking authority over projects and my own focus.

In relationships over the years, I found myself unable to win the heart of females I most desired – either they rejected me or ignored my entreaties. Even having ultimately met and settled with a good mate, I encountered ongoing problems and issues.

So from youth until realizing my innate connection to the world, I suffered the same set of issues traditional to man – with enjoyment of life always tempered by events tainted with pain, emotional and physical. And until I began to correct negative issues from the inside out, I always ended up in retreat, relegated back into the imagined world, justifying or ignoring hurtful patterns and continuing on with hope dimmed, but never extinguished. Only having come to perceive myself as the root cause of difficulties, could I discern the specific inner issues and dispel them. Only having experienced real improvement could I begin to tear down my own inner defense shields and engage the world, finally expecting positive outcomes and enjoying them as they unfolded.

In that whole process, I could relate ongoing situations very clearly back to those first four days. The parade of females I'd approached were *just like the nurses* – never providing sincere love and affection, but a temporary glance then rejection, if not ignoring me in the first place. My various bosses in professional settings were giving me nothing more than formula – recompense inadequate for the good job I was doing – or that hated pacifier, yielding no reward at all.

Sexual encounters hearkened back to that circumcision on Day Two: yielding pain in rejection far more often than the fulfillment of acceptance.

Using the pendulum to explore pure subconscious meaning and self-hypnosis to cleanse and restructure troubled areas, I could revise that early isolation. Once ignored, unvalued, I now can be who I really am without compromise and be accepted as such, communicating sincere perspectives to many appreciative listeners. Once fed unnatural slop as formula, I now eat better, healthier, more delicious, nutritious foods than the grandest king ever did. Where I struggled for decades with finances, I now live in abundance – able to travel and enjoy many aspects of life without having to compromise myself under the authority of bosses reflecting my parents and uncaring nurses before them.

Doubtless, your own overall conditions lie rooted in life's first experiences, for all patterns experienced *now* echo back through similar, equivalent instances in life. Whether or not you can focus back so far, root issues identified in patterns *at any juncture* can be culled out of your subconscious tote bag of traits and propensities. And razing any inner defensive walls is in your ongoing best interest, too. If you don't, you continue to reproduce current miseries over and over, in ever morphing but remarkably consistent patterns.

Generated External Forces

One of the trickiest aspects of discerning projections of power out to external forces is stepping back from common thinking, typical responses and everyday engagement of life to actually observe yourself in action. You will find many phrases and gestures which repeatedly, literally extend power to some conceptualized externality. Such gestures continue patterns of powerlessness; they repeat and thereby recycle the notion that not you, but some outer force or source causes issues in your life.

Many of these you simply picked up from common expressions learned while absorbing the language (suggestion), while others you copy from "grown-ups" or older children while little (emulation). Using them may make you feel independent, rebellious and tough – venerable characteristics highly cherished when you see yourself pitted against an alien, opposing world, but less than *worthless* when you realize that you are the creative source in your own life.

Here are several logical **Opposing External Forces**, mostly unsubstantial, often anonymous:

1. Some "**You**" out there:
   - Railing at some indeterminate "you", as in: "Damn you!" Your thought blasts an epithet aimed at some unspecified, external force, or...
   - "Fuck you!" – a defiant statement leveled at that undefined force that just seemed to hit you with an undesirable event.
     - ✓ Such mental gestures further the illusion that some opposing determinative **you** out there causes problems.
     - ✓ Defiance/rebellion/toughness, exhibited outward, re-emphasizes inwardly that stoic toughness to endure whatever that externality had in store – reflecting strength of character in oneself as unbending and unbowed by pain and failure.
     - ✓ As always, this self-fulfilling signal simply recycles grit into subsequent, repeated negative events that then also need to be endured. Defiance manifests a need to defy.

2. **"They"** – a similar illusion
   - Referring to unspecified authority figures, uttering a lament blaming your problems on some third-person plural nefarious group.
   - In so stating a condition, the mind detracts from its notions of personal power and causality when projecting it to this "they".
     - ✓ As a child, I asked my father who "they" were, as he often stated, "They're raising taxes again," or "They screwed up the economy." "They" seemed to be causing a lot of problems.
     - ✓ Dad said something about other people, various groups that had power. I doubt he would have concurred, should I have been able to correct his thinking at the time, that "they" are illusions.
3. A spontaneous, unspecified, **blurted negativity** and personal frustration:
   - (God) **Damn!**
   - *Oh, shit!* – or the fanciful, fleetingly popular pseudo-wisdom: "Shit happens."
   - You may know and spontaneously use other ones – all of which are worthy of elimination.
     - ✓ Not exactly projecting creative power to imagined forces out there, expletives recycle tacit acknowledgment that bad things might spontaneously occur.
     - ✓ And indeed, bad things certainly will – but *you* manifest them, partly because you expect bad events, partly because you mindlessly regenerate negativity with habitual expletives.
4. The flagrant, mean and nasty **"it"**:
   - Damn it!, fuck it, *to Hell with it* – as in frustrated dismissal of any more attempts to struggle in the face of repeated failure.
   - "It doesn't matter…", stated when it actually does.

✓ "It" in these expressions refers to *all that is*, as a reference of futility when no action taken seems to bring fulfillment.

✓ And the frustration is accurate: action isn't causal. But *you are* causal, by virtue of your nature, not through rationally worked out plans.

✓ Changing this aspect of expression requires shedding such pronouns as forces, for they are only illusions: no "it" lurks out there, only aspects of you reflecting your own nature.

5. **Visualization** – focus on desired outcome.

• This time-honored illusory procedure suggests that if you imagine a desired situation, holding it exclusively in focus, then it will happen. Various disciplines suggest that such mind focus preempts non-compliant potential events while manifesting the one event desired.

✓ I've already pointed out that the visual screen of imagination is not the direct source manifesting your experience. The Mind-Reality interactive blend is enormously more complex than this simple gesture implies.

✓ In the real inner-outer connection, your **total mindset** gets rolled into complex events and relationships that constitute real life, not just the visual field of imagination.

✓ Visualization may *seem* to work – just as any imagined function does if one believes in it. While the desired effect may indeed come to pass, it wasn't elicited by visualization any more than by some vaunted deity, but *by the whole Self.*

• The **innate negative** to visualization: this gesture *automatically* presupposes an otherwise negative outcome, based on the obvious preemptive assumption that your desired intent won't happen without specific intervention. (Otherwise, you wouldn't be visualizing in the first place.)

- ✓ Failing to recognize the connection of self with reality, when visualizing a desired outcome, you seed expectations with doubt and negativity.
- ✓ Thus, holding the very notion that *visualization is necessary*, projects doubt and fear onto the flow of Reality and virtually guarantees an unsatisfactory outcome overall! And the actual gesture of visualization, rather than realizing desire, further negates the will.

6. **Reasoning** – trying to project an argument to an imagined externality when frustrated by life's outcomes.

- • "What do you want from me?" you might plead in frustration. But there isn't any "you" out there – remember point #1 above?
- • The default other entity you are reasoning with in such pleading is conceptual residue from many an imagined externality, phantoms to be outed shortly.

Automatic Projection of Power

Some latent elements of mind and associated gestures that result from them *inherently* result in a manifestation of their objects. That is, their very presence within the mindset manifests fulfillment of their gist, thus recycling it.

Fear is principal among these. Fearing anything projects power – within the scope of your recognition – out to that conceptualized object of your fear. Recognizing how the fear was first implanted is very helpful to eliminate it – suggestion, perhaps emulation and/or punishment? Of course, no isolated force or source out there holds sway over life's flow, but any such notion to that effect negatively impacts anticipation. Thus, it can create real fright by contributing to manifesting that feared object, real or imagined.

The best approach to ending fear is not fighting or overcoming it, avoiding its object or just living with it, but rather (as always), finding inner mechanisms involved and dispelling them. The only causal source in your life being *you*, personally held fear becomes woven into experienced reality, manifesting uncomfortable situations to suit. Worry works the same way.

Similarly, various other mind constructs or gestures, by the very process of holding them, project power outwards to pseudo-sources:

1. **Saying prayers** is the ultimate de facto projection of power.
   - First of all, praying projects creative power out to conceptualized deities who really exist only in imagination. That very gesture defines you as powerless within your self-image.
   - Then it reinforces the status quo of reality, particularly that situation specifically prayed about, as an undesirable aspect you acknowledge you are incapable of changing. That act solidifies the current state of affairs, recycling its negatives.
   - And finally, it exacerbates fear of the world, reconfirming the negative situation (in your mind) as something you need god to overpower (which he presumably instituted in the first place) to deliver good events.
   - ✓ The power to stamp your life with desirable effects

lies only within you.

✓ Praying inherently distorts personal creative power, twisting it into a form that guarantees a negative ultimate outcome.

2. **Overwrought engineering**: machinery, like your car or computer, may break down, so it's good to know how to fix it.

- Generally mechanical or technical expertise is a good thing. But connected to qualities like heroism, excess inner conflict and pride in your technical prowess may lead you to encounter – if not subconsciously create – situations that need your attention.

- This effect is something like owning a pickup truck – if you do, people likely request your help with jobs needing one.

3. **Shame** – the real shame is harboring it, along with its cohort, **Guilt**.

- Common sayings I encountered growing up featured shame in various roles: "Shame on you" issued by my mother at unapproved acts, or its alternative "You should be ashamed of yourself."

- These phrases, likely with overdone religious connotation, were spoken in response to anything involving sex – playing with the genitals, saying "dirty" words, etc.

  ✓ Sounding simple and innocent, these phrases' early negative connotation can inhibit natural response or deter performance.

  ✓ Of course, the subconscious implication to the child's naïve mind is literal, its phrasing taking on a much greater implication: you *should be* ashamed of yourself – implying that shame is actually **the proper state to be in**. That suggestion can be woven into the self-image, producing broader negative consequences.

- Guilt can carry heavier connotations, hearkening back to primitive Christian notions of Adam and Eve's fall from "grace" when ejected from Eden. Harmless sounding, phrases implying the *rightness* of shame or guilt can contribute to manifestation of unavoidable situations in which the programmed holder does indeed feel ashamed.
- **Guilt** must be understood in light of personal causality. With increasing recognition that you attract events and relationships into experience, you correspondingly cease to blame others as *causing* your problems.
  - ✓ Consequential to that, you more easily shed personal guilt feelings – specifically, because action taken does not really cause external effects.
  - ✓ First, recognizing your own inherent causality, you no longer engage in acts damaging another's interests.
  - ✓ And second, any synthetic theological guilt you absorbed is easier to dismantle.

4. **Military honor and pride** – march, stand erect, take orders, etc. to defend *us* against *them*. I grew up shortly after the Second World War, so many movies, games and toys I encountered involved weapons and war. As the US Army had gallantly saved a troubled Europe, hoopla abounded over wonderful heroes who had risked their lives for their country.

- It took me some time to realize how war is rooted in primitive idiotic conflict, lodged in the minds of foolhardy leaders representing a populace ignorant of how life really works.
- And it required specific focus to strip away the illusory gallantry and heroic attribution of western cultural heritage.

✓ First, a peaceful world can never be attained by a culture whose values entertain fighting as a core, idolized, hallowed value.

✓ And your life will not be peaceful until rid of phony external sources as well as high value placed on prowess in conflict.

5. **Eat your vegetables** was the mantra of a dedicated mother. But this commanded rational override implies that your body **and you** don't naturally know what should be consumed, so you have to ignore taste (your own indicator) and eat something that will generate health.

- The deeper implication here is suggesting that *acquired knowledge* – often forced on you by all-knowing parents – is needed to overcome innate limits to realizing health.

- Growing lots of veggies each summer, I consume as natural and organic a fare as possible and certainly promote eating vegetables. But food does *not cause* health good or bad. However, holding inner peace and ease, *which are causal*, spurs taste for healthy, natural foods.

6. **Toughness, grit, determination**, long prized qualities, are deemed necessary to overcome implied opposition – thus desirable traits to emulate, even better to have. The trouble: holding them within your mindset as highly valued contributes to *attracting that opposition*.

7. **Size and strength** matter only in the illusory world of external causality.

- Because causality doesn't stem from action taken, physical strength – while practical and generally healthy – does not result in prowess at fulfilling real desire. Of course, it might fit into the picture if the goal – e.g., weightlifting, football and other sports – requires physical strength.

- Alternately, **belief** that strength catalyzes manifestation of intent virtually guarantees failure if coupled with a self-evaluation of weakness.
- In any case, accomplishment results from intent and inner peace that allows its realization.

8. **Death**, that ultimate *bad* thing, seems daunting.

- The scientific paradigm implies that you, no more than a perceived self resulting from brain function, cease to exist at death. This flawed notion generates near-terror of dying, such that extreme measures must be taken to fight it (which actually only postpones it).
  - ✓ Fear really stems from implied cessation of being, not ending a lifetime.
  - ✓ But the associated apprehension often dictates how life is lived: setting focus on health concerns, strict diet, workouts, vitamins – whatever might prolong life.
  - ✓ The logical consequence of that: life is spent *just trying to extend* the boundary, wasting an incarnation by trying to hang on to it.
- Christianity posits judgment upon death, imagining near impossible criteria to meet for passing the test.
- The resultant effect cascades into modern efforts to keep people alive at all costs – regardless of the lack of quality of life experienced.
  - ✓ So fearing death tends to reduce accomplishment, enjoyment and positive outlook to life when extreme focus is spent, not on *living* but on extending a lifetime judged as meaningful more on length than quality.
  - ✓ Recognizing one's timeless conscious nature in the present moment renders death as moot. Health is a consequence of the mindset, not the rational efforts to engineer it. And life is measured by qualities of

growth, accomplishment, creativity, love and artistic expression – not by sheer length.

9. **Passing the test**: the need to seek others' positive opinions – or approval – for actions taken.

- Given the notion that the world exists already at the time of birth, survival suggests that one should fit in however possible. For me, pleasing that first judge, my mother, later became pleasing teachers, bosses and other authority figures (yep, God again), so they would grade me well and reward me.
  - ✓ This deferential nod to outside authorities also typifies scientific thinking: that reality features many powerful authorities to contend with and assuage.
  - ✓ This world view, in actuality, is fallacious. Those apparent authorities, insofar as you encounter them, vary in impact *according to your own mindset*, not based on their own agendas.
  - ✓ But, after growing up under authoritative parents plus 12 to 20 years of education, pressured to conform and impress – to pass the test – a feeling likely remains that the self lacks authority. It only does so long as *that impression remains*.
- So escaping from subservience requires removal of mind elements featuring external sources as authorities and judges. Life really isn't testing you. You aren't obliged to do or accomplish anything, pass any test, please any authority.

10. **Waste**: the highest priority of the troubled mind is efficiency – struggle against a sparse world. Every entreaty to clean my plate, every patch on jeans and shoes worn until soles had holes implied struggle in life. Nature is very inefficient, yet works very well. Only mankind, with worry and trepidation, pinching every penny and saving for anticipated disasters, looks on wasting precious resources as bad. The

message and resultant manifestation of such apprehension – lack of confidence in the self and in the world – furthers inner turmoil without respite.

With these many rudiments clarified, the real work becomes ridding yourself of all variations on the theme of *automatic projections of power.*

The next grouping looks at more focused projection. While this last group, automatically, passively defrocks you of power, the next set – likely woven as well into that wrinkled fabric of your mindset – drains creative energy more directly.

Active, Conscious Projection of Power

Fear of death, inclusion of shame or orientation to strength, by virtue of their simple presence in your mindset, negate and neutralize your will. Other means of doing so involve stirring up your own creative juices in confrontation of perceived external threats or authorities. You find yourself thinking up ways and means of manipulating such external forces – except that, lo and behold, *they are illusory.*

On my pathway, I cleared away a host of non-existent "phantom" elements – entities conjured up mentally that I found myself planning and plotting various ways to confront. Much of my base thinking hearkened back to early techniques I'd absorbed for how to manipulate Mom. But those were solidified and enhanced by a host of dramatic movies and TV shows.

A more active gesture I call **Phantom Otherness**, not unlike the background images illustrated above, recreate inwardly the very conflict they attempt to work against, thus recycling the illusory opponent into subsequent patterned episodes. The gesture, then, *per se* – when unobserved as emotional confrontation with what is really only a mind-image – furthers your own inner conflict unabated.

Once I'd realized how *conflict*, wedged into my mindset, served only to repeat patterns of engagement, I was puzzled how I should rid myself of such inner strife. The paradox was this: confronting elements of one's own mindset only repeated and intensified the inner clash of interests! Leaving it alone peacefully, on the other hand, allowed the conflict to remain.

The psyche, timeless in its engagement of Reality, never spontaneously sheds its values, holding them indefinitely while continuing to incorporate them into manifested Reality.

There seemed no way out of the loop!

Meditation rather passively takes the second approach – trying to establish peace within the mind through relaxation and mantra repetition, imagining that peace displaces underlying conflictual substrata. But peace never does waylay conflict. The multifaceted psyche, harboring conflict along with diverse other values – and attached to specific elements – revises its content only as *change* is introduced – consciously through pointed auto-suggestion or slowly through lessons learned in life.

So, if inner conflict isn't explicitly deleted *in each of its instances*, the mindset simply holds peace on some levels while containing conflict on others. Peace never just displaces or *replaces* inner conflict – both simply manifest into different aspects of experienced reality.

No, to eliminate conflict from events and relationships, i.e., fulfill intent, one has to revise the mindset: clearly recognize the psyche's complex makeup, discern its components and mechanisms – with whom or with what conflict emerges – and dispel each element, **just as with any inner problem**. Of those steps, the most important as well as trickiest is that *initial recognition*. These basic mind gestures you might commonly carry out against phantom externalities *right now...*

1. **Threats and warnings** pondered or issued by you. If you find yourself posturing toward perceived opponents, either physically or mentally, *you host inner conflict*.

2. **Mental push** against indeterminate opponents: a gritty crush, that grimace of determination, indicates problems within.

3. Building up a **mental opposition** of your own: thinking you can't accomplish something because of some hindrance, *any* hindrance – stronger foe, great odds, inadequate resources, lack of help or financing, personal ineptitude – allows such inner conflict (or struggle) to manifest itself.

4. Accepting that the **dead, spirits** (good or bad) or **other intangible entities** hold sway over real events can deter your success. In reality, *no other force* is involved in the unfolding of life patterns than the overall content of your mindset. If some of that content includes beliefs that supernatural forces plot against you, **so it seems**, as that superstition simply manifests into real events, where perception reconfirms it based on belief.

5. **Opposition** to government policies, corruption, pollution or other widespread cultural maladies stems from early opposition to parents' dictates.

   • And that opposition, functionally, came from their treatment and behavioral expectations incorporating long traditions of struggle and conflict.

   • Your personal opposition to *any external condition* sprouts from pure conflict, held *within you*. The opposition you encounter hosts similar conflict with different sets of values.

     ✓ The long-term solution to systemic, cultural ills is

not fighting with the people who perpetrate them – action that only realizes inner conflict. Nor is it passively accepting those major issues, which reverts the conflict inward.

   ✓ The only effective solution is to rid yourself of conflict within. Only from that standpoint can you help explain that same state of mind to others and dispense the fundamentally peaceful mindset.

   ✓ Exactly that, you might note, is what I am doing.

6. Trying to be **heroic**, to be the **savior**, the grand, long-awaited **messiah** of modern man.

   • Most people don't really want to be "saved", preferring their own little fantasy worlds. Thus encased, they don't grasp what causes difficulties and can't fathom being the source of their own problems.

     ✓ The only things people need saved *from* are distorted notions as to life's functionality.

     ✓ Until **you** see life's operational Oneness clearly, having eliminated your own inner turmoil, being the great messiah is impossible. And once you see it, you won't care to be that savior.

     ✓ Further, until your psyche holds absolute peace and ease, the only people attracted to your message will be confrontational or rote followers.

   • So settle on achieving a state wherein you can just be yourself, which holds as prerequisite being *absolutely at peace and ease*.

7. **Rejection for a reason**. This mind game was likely first experienced from parents – as in my case – who disallowed desired items or endeavors based on some stated reason.

   • We couldn't go on vacation *because* Mother was ill or we didn't have the money. I couldn't have a Winky Dink kit (a plastic screen to put on the TV set so I could draw on it with crayons during that interactive cartoon show) *because* I shouldn't sit too close to the TV.

- ✓ There was always an officially issued reason why my intent wasn't being fulfilled. The reason seemed valid in my parents' view, but it was just a subtle means *to reinforce inner conflict.*
- ✓ Indeed, the reasoning itself was confusing. It served to drain power, as the impression became implanted that many causes lay out there to defeat my desires – all outside my reach. In reality, the very act of accepting their explanations created the drain by implanting phantom causes.
- ✓ In end effect, the subconscious image imprinted was powerlessness – a component of my self-image I had to jettison.

- Each of us tends to turn this same procedure around when raising children, passing to them the same phantom causes we absorbed.

8. **Problem solving** – pride in one's cleverness actually inhibits success.

   - How's that? Being proud of intelligence and native ability to solve problems and engineer solutions is somehow negative? Motivation as a mechanism contributes to ongoing encounters of problems if some warm glow of accomplishment compensates such cleverness.

   - So cleverness isn't the problem, but rather overly lavish self-evaluation can recycle the need to solve ever more problems, thus the motivation to encounter them.

9. **Clumsiness and klutziness** – this pure negative can be enhanced within the mindset by motivation – early comforting applied to the toddler at each fall or head bump. That band-aid, lovingly applied, along with extra attention and sympathy, by a mother relishing her motherly instincts, ultimately emerges as motivation to fail in later life.

10. **Group Think**: feeling the need to conform projects power to the group as well as compromising the self-image.

- Much of traditional thought, reflecting ancient ages, emphasizes fitting into tribal thinking patterns. Unlike modern times when individualism has become vogue, ancient cultures didn't value personal expression at all. In conformity was unity and strength against threatening neighbors.

- Each of us is unique. Efforts to follow fashions and fads, dress, talk and act alike, buy and use the latest gimmick project determinative power to elements that cannot be aligned with one's own nature.

So those structures supply phantom external sources within one's focus to vie against. Yet, in reality, no causal source lurks 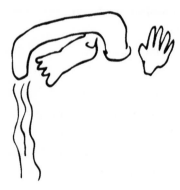 **out there** to contend with – only qualitative, resultant reflections of your own nature. Whatever manipulative processes you learned for dealing with those externalities – push, protest, outsmart, reject for some reason, solve problems – your reasoned plan can only be applied to the real world, which is actually already finished, a manifested consequence of the inner-outer flow. Your psychological reliance on learned mechanisms to deal with such phantoms only recycles the effect for subsequent encounter.

But more bad news: *phantoms* don't cease with those itemized effects. We generally learned while growing up that dealing with people required convincing them of your viewpoint or otherwise manipulating them into doing things your way.

In that case, you will find, as I did, a verbal dialog running through your mind preparatory to an encounter. In this mental discourse, you try out various lines of reason to convince the other party of your line of thinking. Then you imagine how he or she (whether that phantom represents your boss, spouse, potential hot date, child or other figure) will respond. This can go on and on as you wrack your brain (just an illusory expression, as the brain doesn't do the thinking) trying out possible lines of argument to convince the phantom of your view.

Of course, that discussion never ensues in subsequent actuality the way you imagined. But the act of carrying out that mental discourse furthered – within your own mindset – the conflict and reconfirmed your lack of authority. The few useful phrases conjured up for real discussion aren't all that practical in light of the continued hole you keep yourself in.

Here are some specific **Phantoms** created by the mind play of mulling over an intended discussion:

1. *"Plead With"* **Phantom** – really drains your self-image of authority by recycling pure acknowledgment of that other person's power as you concoct arguments to convince him/her of your case.
2. **Phantom of Justice** – appeal to common values of justice and what's culturally right to convince another. This also serves, in the very act of conceptualizing, to reinforce lack of authority in your own self-esteem.
3. *Defy* **That Phantom** – tough, rebellious stance against a perceived authority serves the same purpose, however different the approach. Whatever mental attitude is exhibited against some opponent or authority figure, the effect of **conceding power** is the same.
4. *Hold Out Against* **That Phantom** – hard line against adversary likewise recycles conflict.
5. *Command and Control* **The Phantom** – turning the tables

here, your exercise of control *over others* furthers your own conflict as well. As you plan out procedures to exercise your apparent power over other people – children, employees, students, underlings – you simply recycle the apparent need and efficacy of manipulation. (Not all interaction implies conflict. The issue is style and content of relationship: do you need to threaten punishment to force others into compliance? Is force via strength or manipulative dominance necessary? Those indicate inner conflict at the root of your Phantom-manipulation gesture.)

6. *Resist* **That Phantom** – making plans to get around annoying, negative issues also simply recycles the situation. Because that status indicates inner problems, acknowledging the status of things and exploring inner roots can lead to change; creating new plans and carrying them out won't.

7. *Calculate* **Phantom** – working out the affordability of an item concedes, and thus reinforces, your own perceived shortcomings. "Can I afford that?" as an inner dialog means to the subconscious "I lack power". Such notions, always reinforced in the now moment, solidify the status quo.

8. *Ward-Off* **Phantom** – planning preventative measures for fighting off disease, financial difficulty or relationship issues, like others just listed, simply reinforces those opposing elements as causal within your mindset.

9. *Future* **Phantom** – hoping for improvement and great things **in the future** or in that wonderful, promised Christian heaven after death. *There is no future;* there is only this now moment. The patterns you realize now persist in recurring episodes until you change your inner nature now.

10. *Phantom* **Phantom** – this most insidious mind element consists of an unnamed, unspecified non-self imagined out there to push against. Similar to the "Oh, shit" or "Damn you" uttered in response to negative events, this puts focus

on some nefarious source out there. Particularly once you quit believing in a conceptualized god, but before you have cleared away negating inner elements, this object of anger can replace any railing against a deity or fate with an anonymous externality.

So, in addition to any phantoms you might create, various common gestures, behavioral or even linguistic, project your power outwards just as effectively.

Have you yet noticed, having now encountered the above mechanisms – many of which you likely share – how complex the mind can be?

Several **Gestures** projecting power outwards:

1. **Blame** of others. Finding root elements in your mindset pointing back to, for example, your mother, it's easy to blame her (or your siblings, your boss, your culture) for bad situations in your life. But they aren't to blame – *ever!*
   - You dissipate negative orientation by releasing that blame through explicit forgiveness of those apparent sources. *They did not cause* your problems, as you attracted them into your realm. They are only symptoms of your inner issues.
   - Blame harbored within only furthers negative patterns, spurring recurrence in subsequent incidents.
2. Even blaming **yourself** reflects negativity back onto your rational self – probably carryover from being blamed for things during childhood. But action is *never causal*. Blame of self, obviously counterproductive, only furthers negativity. Consciously releasing the self-criticism breaks that negative pattern.
3. The word "**Because**" as grammatical, logical projection. Obvious when you notice it, this word affixes causality of situations to actions or conditions. Indeed, *you* are the

ultimate cause of all aspects of life; external agents are only triggers. This grammatical construct subtly projects power outward, quietly sapping your determinative power.

4. Likewise, the word "**if**" deviously projects causality to **conditions** as though they impel events. They didn't; you did.

5. "**Fortunately**", even used casually in common speech, tacitly concedes that a process, *fortune*, drives events.

   • This archaic reference stems from Fortuna, the Roman version of the Greek god Tyche, goddess of luck, good and bad. She was thought to be behind capricious, unexpected turns in life.

   • Mindlessly reiterating it or other variants – "**luckily**", "**thank goodness**", etc. – maintains this illusory external force in your subconscious store of attributed life functionality. This is more casual and unfocused than real references to fate, luck or destiny regarded above. But even such informal references are **equally rooted** in the mindset: the psyche does not discern casual meaning from solid belief!

Simple **God projections** can do the same as the above: saying grace before eating to thank god for providing food, usurps power just as any such notation. The very expression "*thank God*", functions just as does "**fortunately**" and those other phrases to allocate cause to something external.

From these overt structures, I now refocus on more personal, directly detrimental factors found underlying many aspects of my life that didn't work well. Some of the above will reappear from a different angle, but many new twists will be seen rooted in...

Direct Mother-Related Elements

Hitting Home

So, you bring your nature into this incarnation, manifesting from the outset events and relationships reflecting it. Perceiving interactive, root elements within the psyche is greatly enhanced by dissecting the many ways in which care-givers treated you early in life. Memories of meaningful childhood events reveal your effective nature.

As I personally scoured my mindset for detrimental elements, most related back to my mother, for she was my primary interface with the world.

Delving into many aspects of our relationship, however, I want to be explicitly clear on causality: my *mother was not to blame* for my problems, as she did not cause anything. Only I cause the effects in my life, as you do in yours. My basic nature attracted her and all subsequent iterations of the conflict and struggle she embodied at the outset of this lifetime.

My own inner issues, though, are clearly observed in many operative gestures she carried out.

So I had to discover and dispel them as they were found woven into my memories. Language used to explain these effects might sound like attribution of blame to Mom or other sources, but I must emphasize it was *only I* who drew all aspects of the relationship into my experience, just as I did with subsequent rejection, authority, etc. Only on taking personal responsibility for the detrimental effects manifested, ceasing to affix blame on any external source, was I – or will you be – able to fully clarify and eliminate such negativity in life.

I already explained various life problems embodied in those first four days. Those same effects continued on. Mother was my only source of affection – Dad being a great guy but not at all affectionate and my brother more a source of threat or ridicule.

But Mother's expression was compromised by her values: if I conformed with her way of thinking, thus compromising my own nature, all was well and good. But if I expressed my own ideas, contradicting her and my father's points of view or arguing when told to do something I didn't want to, I could get reprimanded or punished. The intense difficulty was – looking back, as it really wasn't clear then – if I trusted my own impulses, I could offend Mom, in which case I could be punished in various ways, thus becoming completely isolated.

So my choice was: obey and please Mom, thus compromising my own integrity, or rebel and face punishment. Either track available *realized conflict* – the first inner, the latter outer. At the root of that lay my own inner conflict, allowing no peaceful alternative. I manifested a reality with no way out of conflictual engagement.

In this way, overtly, my parents unconsciously joined to pass along traditional inner features of struggle and conflict – reflecting, again, **my own inner turmoil** – by forcing me to trust my rational thinking rather than my natural impulses. Straight from ancient Celtic/German values of valor in battle and heroism in combat, they passed on rebellion by *making me* rebel against artificial, limiting rules, enforcing them by punishment, using motivation and even love to make me behave like *something I wasn't.*

Thus, many insights into mind workings I list here should be seen as common means by which, functionally and apparently, older generations pass along restrictive inner attitudes to offspring.

But always bear in mind this **very critical point:** *we all bring our own nature into an incarnation* during which we attract situations and relationships that reflect it.

Blame is thus never to be assigned to any external agent – mother, spouse, dictator or slave master. **I was the cause of my problems** – it was my inner tumult that led to the relationship with Mom, then attracted all subsequent iterations of difficulty. *You are the cause of yours:* by virtue of your mindset, you attract relationships, painful to the degree that your psyche manifests.

Recognizing that, my task remained to trace down all avenues of interaction that could reveal my own limitations – and eliminate them.

By the time I became aware of the inner-outer connection, Mom had long since died – though of course problematic patterns persisted because they emanated from me. I hasten to mention Mother was a loving, caring, wonderful person. But her inner turmoil doubtless twisted love and inherent gentleness into a life of painful health issues and emotional hurt where the world wouldn't conform to her Christian idealism. My problem was to discern how that impacted me.

For you, though, the challenge remains of sorting through such early-life treatment. Root, initial events fester there, generating patterns you continue in the present.

Conflict Be With You

First, I again consider Mother's **allegiance to Christianity** and its broad-based impact on me.

As clarified under **Guilt** and elsewhere, Christianity, innate to its tenets, doesn't want pleasure and fulfillment *now*. You only get that later through denying your own nature and accepting the mythical Christ as savior. (Saved from what? The mythical judgment faced at death from the mythical God.)

Because my mother bought into this notion – deeply and fully, with sincere commitment – her treatment of me *had to* **reflect those values** in overall fashion, even with some illogical twists. (Forgiveness, for example, ideally would not involve punishment, inflicting pain, in any form.)

So the following items reveal her conduct of motherhood based on her mindset, as well as my engaging nature from the outset of this incarnation, eliciting conflict and struggle held then.

Consequences of Mom's religious attitude:

1. She never **rewarded** me for anything. I could get punished for not doing what was required. But rewards would come in the future – never now.
    *   Indeed, I was more likely to be put down when excelling at something like exerting my intellect.
    *   This effect spread through my life as inadequate pay for various projects, plus...
        ✓ A propensity to get involved with untrustworthy business contacts and incompetent supervisors.
        ✓ And overall financial issues for much of my life.
2. She promoted **humility** as deference to God and to others.
    *   This meant that she punished "showing off" or acting "smart" (difficult for me to avoid). Being a "wise guy" or "know-it-all" was a negative that received scorn, not praise.
    *   Acting *humble* is so far outside my normal character that it broached my integrity to feign it, trying to fit into her standards and be loved.
3. Her values promoted **putting others before self** – forcing me to share things (toys at that point) with the less fortunate.
    *   This Christian value of empathy, of course, overlooks the reality that people manifest their own lives. Trying to even the scale by generously giving to the downtrodden generally leads to a lot more downtrodden offspring to give to later.
    *   The superior gesture – totally beyond the ken of Christianity – is to present to people greater perspectives on real life. Those open to new understanding outgrow their downtrodden status and do not need

help.

- What I ended up with, having shared my toys, was even less than I started with.
- Mother always said to not get her anything for Christmas – consistent with these humble Christian standards.
  - ✓ My comment to her ultimately was: how could I be generous and giving according to Christian edicts if *she wouldn't accept a simple gift!* Of what value is generosity when people receiving are so non-material as to choose to live in bland, simple surroundings?
  - ✓ The proper, normal state of being in nature is abundance. If you aren't living with reasonably abundant resources to maintain freedom (and thus peace) in a lifestyle consistent with your intent, then you host problems within.
  - ✓ The converse is true also. If your lifestyle is overly materialistic, such that your primary concern is attainment of money and acquisition of expensive objects, you harbor significant inner issues as well.

4. **Fighting evil** has long been a favorite pastime for the ostentatiously holy, too. The problem with this is that **evil doesn't exist** in and of itself. There is no satanic source of inflicted badness.

- People who wreak pain and detriment on others have extensive inner issues themselves. They attract the powerless and are very weak and fearful themselves.
- Goodness and evil exist only in manifested human values as exhibited in man's treatment of his fellow beings, human and otherwise. Evil doesn't float in space or hover in some other dimension, waiting to jump into people's lives. It isn't inflicted by some mythical devilish character. Negative values only

manifest into the experience of fearful, powerless people who perceive themselves as controlled by external forces.

5. Mother didn't respect **my point of view**, particularly when, age ten, I explained that Christianity couldn't be true.

    *   Christians are very poor at listening to ideas outside their frozen, archaic mindsets.

    *   Mother was aghast at my rejecting religion, which I did increasingly throughout my teens. She prayed for me, no doubt, and likely felt crushed that I would be judged negatively by her god. I imagine it contributed to her inner turmoil that she had borne a tried and true heretic.

    *   During my early years, though, imagining me young and malleable such that she could force me into religious fervor by coercing me to attend church, she taught me to pray and focused on Bible stories (selected ones that left out blatant murder, lechery, incest, brutality, sex and such). Motivated – and faced with her wrath and thus isolation – I went along with things until I figured out the impossibility of the whole notion.

    *   Another factor, though, was mixed in: I really didn't want to hurt my mother's feelings. But that was part of the twist – forcing inner conflict for just being true to one's own self.

6. Given her archaic **fear of evil** setting in (especially on her innocent little boy), much of Mother's efforts were spent trying to ward off or overcome temptation.

    *   And this fixation on temptation preempted many fun aspects of life, not the least of which was sex. That was **never mentioned** in any reference in our home – rendering great confusion to me as I surged into adolescence.

    *   Unconsciously, Mother's various physical illnesses –

hypertension, kidney issues, etc. – along with her smoking habit avoided temptation automatically by removing any excess finances from the family budget. Thus, we never went anywhere that I could actually see what was happening in the world.

7. Possibly the worst of all effects coming out of Mother's devotion to fallacious notions was her accusing me of being **contrary** to her interests – even **contemptible** in my standing up for my own way of thinking! I always faced tremendous pressure – mechanisms like force, suggestion, punishment and motivation were commonplace – to buy into her religious thinking and its unnatural attributes.

This issue of rampant evil in the world, along with my mother's fear of infection, accident, and other threatening sources led to effective isolation and overemphasized mothering. In her eyes, during my whole childhood, I needed constant protection...

1. **From perceived threats** that the world was full of.
2. **From temptation,** to protect me from my own sinful drives.
3. **To hoard my affection,** because others around weren't as caring for and about her.
4. **To avoid damage** to other parties or things – such as the bisque china and other adult valuables (things out of reach, yet enticing to play with), girls' honor, etc.
5. **And as punishment!** Isolation was one way to discipline me: send me to my room as punishment for doing something that seemed to me to be right, but didn't fall within **the rules.**
   - Again, this isolation was very damaging, always forcing conflict, as I could either trust myself and be ostracized or compromise my own impulses and sense of rightness and be accepted.
   - Doubtless Mother viewed her treatment as very

important to get me "in line" with her values – to protect me from harm later on when her big God (the uppercase "G" god) would judge my eternal soul.

- Note: I wasn't often punished – it shouldn't sound like I was disciplined daily. I could get around some rules, but mostly I obeyed. But the **pressure** to conform and obey, quash my impulses and follow *the rules* was **ever present**, as the prosecutor/judge was never off duty.

So the only thing Mom accomplished in all of that hyper-motherly protection was to pass along her fear and that intense inner conflict derived from deep Northern Irish roots.

But the overall impact rendered on me by my mother's treatment involved more than just the religious slant. Not unusual for western culture, she had also bought into medical science as the means to counteract the body's "weaknesses". So not only did I learn to ask God for things, but that my body was susceptible to attack from bacteria, particularly under certain conditions. Fearing that the "Almighty" had bad things in store and that getting my feet wet, sitting in drafts, getting coughed or sneezed upon would make me sick, I was very wary of a dangerous world around me.

Also wary, for certain, was Mom: her attitude yielded as end effect that ideal situation wherein **Nothing Happens**. With **pleasure** out of the question and **pain** from illness undesirable, no other option remained but maintenance of an unthreatening, non-tempting, uneventful present state. Best possible outcome from Mother's angle: a bland, uneventful present – TV, movies or playing games.

The consequence of this overall pattern was enormous **inner conflict and struggle**. Remembering that one brings one's core nature into an incarnation, in my case inner conflict which my psyche hosted became manifested as a grating, ongoing, irresolvable turmoil. It ground daily between my nature of adventurousness, vigor and desire vs. this staid, bland state of religious piety and humility – the intense desire to realize human resolve *now* opposing negation/neutralization of all such endeavor by the key authority in my life. And it twisted my very engagement with life: following my impulses invariably led to disobeying Mother. That likely triggered punishment from Dad while hurting Mom's feelings and, by suggestion, should lead to eternal damnation – all negative outcomes from simply trusting myself.

So I did *what we all do*: I compromised my own nature. I learned to compare all my natural urges to an extensive conceptualized list of what was *allowed*, what was *recommended*, what was defined as *good*, what I could *get away with*, etc. To gain my mother's affection (and avoid punishment), I learned to play the role of the goody-goody little boy she wanted me to be.

And in that process, faced with motherly pressure, threats of punishment, a god looking over my shoulder and ready to judge – even Santa Claus watching my every move – I basically retreated into my own safe space. From those first four days through hurt feelings of childhood, a part of me withdrew back behind a defensive psychological shield, where I could just be me and nobody could hurt me.

That pattern continued, complete with defenses: being what teachers wanted me to be to get good grades, being what employers wanted me to be to get paid, trying to be what a female wanted me to be to get accepted – and otherwise either rebelling against the world or compromising my very integrity to try to please authorities "out there".

The Big Five

And that resulted in five major patterns in life that only began to dissipate as I discovered these connections – the grand complex of psychic turmoil above – and eliminated them:

1. In life, I rarely had the **money** to do all the things I wanted to do.
   - This reflected the early pattern that I never, ever was rewarded by Mother for anything as she *never* provided positive reinforcement for me just being my own self.
   - And that pattern persisted throughout life in professional connections and often personal relationships.
2. I couldn't get the **sports car** I'd always wanted.
   - The pattern with cars repeated itself so often, it was funny.
     - ✓ At about 18, an old guy down the street promised me his '55 Chevy (V-8 with a stick). But he traded it in without saying anything.
     - ✓ During my college years, I sent my dad to check out a fancy '59 Chevy convertible for me, but he ended up coming home with a plain 2-door sedan.
     - ✓ At 21, while visiting a college friend, I saw his grandfather had a '61 Pontiac convertible sitting there unused. He said I could buy it, but two days later, when I called, he had sold it to somebody else!
     - ✓ During my twenties, I bought a '69 Corvette. But it was front-heavy, handled poorly and I wrecked it.
   - These events, meaningful although I'm not heavily oriented to material goods, echoed that lack of reward, that unattainable pleasure and fulfillment in this moment that Mom had so dictated in early life.
3. For years, I'd owned land in a very scenic spot to build a **house** on – 1.4 acres on top of the highest hill in Allegheny County. But I couldn't get the finances in order to build there. The comfy, homey type house I did own – a structure well in scope of my mother's non-ostentatious persona –

seemed to hold me like the vice grip of her religious humility.

4. **Acceptance** is a major part of life. The most vital sense of **love** *itself* is acceptance – simply accepting the other **for what he/she is,** valuing the essence of that person.

- **In effect,** Mother didn't accept me, didn't love me for what I was. I had to compromise my own nature, to quell who I really was and simulate her ideal to be accepted.

- And that rejection/disinterest pattern was to plague every relationship I engaged through life until I could see and dissolve root structures – and the walls I'd created to hold out the pain of rejection.

5. And that same mother-based inner turmoil attended to my life statement as well: **accomplishment of meaningful things.**

- As a long-term accomplishment, I had pulled myself away from projects meant only to make money. In each of these, I'd encountered employers or business partners who wanted to make me be what they'd wanted – just like Mom. But they were invariably some blend of untrustworthy and incompetent.

- So, having cleared away the inner debris that kept me running to Mom for attention, having to compromise my very being in the process, I received an offer, unsolicited, from my publisher to publish *The Essence of Reality*, should I wish to convert my extensive website to book form.

- But even though that book was the best, clearest vision of the Mind-Reality connection ever expressed, and despite extensive travel to promote it and dispense key ideas within its content, it still hadn't "taken off".

- So, on a personal level, I still was facing my mother's rejection.

This all considers general, overall effects consequent to Mother's attitudes, stemming from her beliefs. But the immediate means by which she forced inner conflict and struggle (reflecting those qualities within my mindset) were many.

Of course, Christianity itself prizes both versions of inner turmoil. The Jesus character portrayed in the Gospels is laced with conflict, levied against the Jewish religious hierarchy, the sect of the Pharisees, non-believers, the elements, and *reality itself* – the act of healing somebody, as oft depicted, is in direct conflict with the state of affairs of the sick person.

Indeed, that scenario implies that Yahweh, the current god then, was highly conflicted himself – not surprising, as he'd evolved from being a war god earlier (imagining what he'd done to the Egyptians and repeated brutalities he'd encouraged against neighboring tribes). Of course, Jesus pictured a more loving, forgiving deity – but Paul and subsequent founders of Christianity obliterated that peaceful entity, substituting a more archaic judgmental, vengeful sort of supernatural being.

So it was a highly inconsistent deity Mother imagined – loving, yet strict and judgmental, imparting negatives readily, but maybe yielding when prayed to. And exactly that internally contradictory image dominated her – and much of society's – attitude.

Passing the (Inner) Torch

Added to the above are many simple, straightforward imperatives Mom, along with Dad and other family members, hit me with. (As did most parents through untold generations of western culture.)

Understanding suggestion's powerful impact – intensified by parental authority, motivation and threat of punishment, literally **forced on** the naïve listener – you should grasp how these commands and rationalizations left a longstanding negative imprint on my mindset:

1. **You can't play with the big boys** – uttered repeatedly by Mom as I wanted to play with my brother and his friends. Logically correct, it instilled an inherent deficiency in my self-esteem that didn't simply go away when I was older. It had to be pointedly jettisoned – otherwise my deep perspectives (as voiced here) would never be regarded as the major illustration of human consciousness they are – I couldn't play with the "big boys".

2. **You aren't *big* enough to do that** (not strong enough, not old enough, not smart enough). Again, a very negative suggestion that persisted in the timeless psyche for much of my life.

3. **Save money for the future** – big priority for the generation who had lived through the Great Depression. The problem: the *future never arrives!* This mental attitude held in the present secures only an ongoing self-doubt and mistrust that yields lack, not abundance, in *the present.*

4. **Preventative Measures**: take action to prevent illness or other maladies. This common cultural wisdom is invariably **counterproductive**. Fear of consequences and mistrust of bodily function prompts rational means to avoid calamity. But fear and mistrust engender problems *anyway* – no matter what action is taken – because they reside in the psyche and are always included in manifested reality! Preventative means thus **empower** illness by reinforcing notions of one's own weakness!

5. **Take** your **vitamins** – Mother implored. Sounds like good advice to avoid missing some dietary nutrient. But your body extracts what it needs from any decent diet – without rational help! Taking supplements only serves to imply the body is too stupid to extract what it needs from real food. The notion, then, replaces confidence in natural systems

with that eternal need to override natural function – of body and life in general – with reasoned manipulation. (Now I never take any supplements or medicine, never needing either!)

6. **Self-sacrifice** – for the good of others or some ideal, ranging from generosity to martyrdom. This heroic gesture imagines a dangerous world controlled by negative forces, a high ideal for my Christian mother – after all, Jesus *gave his life* to save us from our sins. (How wonderful, except it's a fantasy.) To the psyche truly at peace, such actions bespeak only conflict in a martyr's mind and ignorance of life's flow in concert with the inner nature.

7. **"Don't be selfish"**, was a chant I heard a thousand times. But not valuing yourself and seeking peace of mind, how can you – or anybody else following your philosophy – ever be content? The real issue here is placing limitations on abundance in reality. Fighting over toys leads to fighting over resources and lifestyles – and reflects vividly the inner conflict of western man. My enjoyment of meaningful material items never comes at a cost to others – because the lack others experience results *not from my action* but from their own inner struggle and its manifested consequences.

8. **"Don't be a show-off"** – yet another frequent entreaty – was part of the artificial humility Mother held, so prized from Christian heritage in trying to score brownie points with the judgmental deity. She could have said: "Compromise yourself! Hold back your vigor and inherent character! Let others run the world and dominate the scene! Spectate, don't accomplish! Be what I tell you to be, not what you are!" Lots of very negative, self-restricting ramifications in that command.

9. **We're just regular, middle-class people, an average family** – the banner of our family group, living in a comfy, but modest house in an average town in a typical American

setting. The implication, never missed by subconscious absorption, was that I was nothing special. But actually *I am special* (we all are in our particular way) and to realize that I had to dump the average guy self-image.

10. **Settle Down!** – or its many variants: **calm down, sit still, behave, be quiet,** meant to keep me in line actually only intensified my inner conflict. Kids have energy and vigor – elements that should be nurtured and encouraged. Mine was crimped and strangled within a lifestyle where nothing happened – at home during the week, church on Sunday, later school. No travel, little stimulation (we went to the museum or planetarium once in a while – wonderful places!), only entreaties to compromise my own nature.

11. **Be Careful** – such a common warning by Mom has lately become a valediction. The notion implies a world wrought with many dangers, so that you can't trust your own Self to navigate a course through it. So you need constant rational oversight to survive. In reality, carefulness displaces trust.

12. **Discipline and self-discipline** were big features on Mother's list. I had to toe the line, conform to her wishes and *the rules*. It served only to intensify inner turmoil in a psyche whose intensity aimed at accomplishment, not restraint.

Along with all those came various other comments, commands and basic treatment that, through repetition and force, left an imprint. Grouped into general categories, they imparted conflictual or otherwise detrimental effects on the psyche:

1. **Standard sayings** were often voiced at home, carrying the heavy implication of truth – which they often had precious little to do with. Clichés were repeated interminably and mindlessly as situations triggered them: *Little amuses the innocent; children should be seen but not heard*. These come

to mind as well as a plethora of Biblical quotes – the better ones of which, I noted, were ignored by Christians in daily life.

- They all just passed along standard cultural thinking, including low value to children's (and thus my) ideas and significance.
- And they all implied, reinforced by repetition, that reality was well defined by cultural tradition such that creative thinking was unnecessary.

2. **Additional maternal entreaties and commands**, repeated endlessly, registered in the subconscious for the value they contained. Each one **functioned**, as absorbed and hardened into my psyche, to limit my own self-determination and quell confidence in my own natural responses. Here are a few, followed by their *real* meaning, i.e., the value registered within my subconscious:

- *Don't do that!* You have no authority here and obviously poor judgment.
- *Be Nice!* You are flawed. Try to act according to our rules, not your own impulses.
- *Be a good boy!* Follow my every command or you are inherently bad!
- *You're a bad boy!* Innately flawed, your only hope is that I can force you to improve.
- *You can't do that!* Intended to mean I wasn't **allowed** to do something, but really planting the idea that I was **incapable** of it – a very negative suggestion.
- *You aren't allowed (to do that, go there, etc.)!* You have no authority.
- *Do as I say! Do what I tell you! Do as you're told!* All typical parental gestures trying to maintain order, but reducing self-esteem as it obliterates self-determination.
- *Eat your vegetables!* Disregard what taste tells you and eat this annoying slop because I have authority over

your life.

- *Go to bed!* Trust me, your all-knowing parent, not your own body, to know what is right for you.
- *Come here!* You have no authority to even go where you want to.
- *Don't talk back!* Whether correct or incorrect, you lack authority. You can't express your point of view because I'm in control and thus always right.
- *What's wrong with you?* There *really is* something wrong with you and you should know what it is, but you don't even know that much!!
- *You have to: go to church, go to school, take a nap, clean up your room, cut the grass.*
  - ✓ Overt meaning: you are powerless here – just a schlep, knucklehead kid who has to be told everything.
  - ✓ Meaning communicated to subconscious when absorbed as suggestion: this is something necessary for you to complete – a mandatory task. Failing to complete it triggers other definitions of guilt and punishment.
- *You should* – coupled with some directive. This is the corollary to earlier suggestions to things I *shouldn't do*. Highly damaging, it made me question my own sense for living and reinforced the reliance on rational action, particularly that suggested by Mother.

3. *Making sure* **nothing happens.** Promoting the ideal Nothing Happening, Mom even motivated it by allowing me to eat while watching TV and get popcorn at the movies. But various elements of repeated suggestion helped reinforce Nothingness as the default state of

being. Here they are, again with subconscious meaning:

- *Money doesn't grow on trees.* Attainment of money is next to impossible. So, forget fulfilling your desire.
- *Save your money!* Don't enjoy life now; prepare for a time which never comes.
- *Work hard (to get ahead).* Struggle is mandatory and honorable; life is never easy.
- *Don't waste money!* Life is unyielding and sparse.
- *Take care of your toys (possessions).* Life is so tough you might not get anything at all later so guard and preserve all you have now.
- *Wait until...* something else happens, some other event or miracle, before you can get what you want – meaning you get nothing **now**!
- _____ Absolute silence concerning **sex** – a totally neutralizing suggestion by virtue of its complete absence in the scheme of life.
- _____ Similar total non-discussion of travel to interesting places, hikes in the forest, exploration of mountains and deserts, ocean voyages, adventure – anything stimulating in place of Nothing Happening.

4. **Punishments:** doubtless my parents simply emulated punishments they'd encountered when children. These could be inflicted for various forbidden acts, listed below. None ever accomplished what was intended – to spur the desired behavior; they only imprinted the same inner turmoil my parents carried (realizing, of course, my own) by:

- Yelling at me: verbal punishment.
- Sending me to my room (isolated, alone). The more severe option was to be so banished without dinner. (Seldom applied: Mother was big on me finishing my meal.)
- Not talking to me: the "silent treatment".

- Cutting off allowance.
- Disallowing certain things – often activities I most wanted to do.
- Forbidding me to go out to play; or later, use the car.
- Spanking me.
- **Threatening** punishment (which was punishment itself.)

Imposing adult authority was likely meant to, as other clichés went, *teach me right from wrong, properly discipline me, not spoil me*, etc. But what they did was fulfill my own self-deprecating propensities by instilling reliance (financial, psychological, etc.) on them.

Enforcement of rules and ready coercion to that end ultimately built inner turmoil: natural urges and inclinations spontaneously occurring through my very nature had to be questioned and compared to a set of demanded rational actions. Thus, throughout life subsequent to such childhood conditions, I couldn't trust my own impulses toward action. I had to run any desired action past a long list of what I should do, could do, was allowed to do, was wise to do, etc. before I could proceed.

I guarantee *your* psyche functions with similar restrictions. They are foundation elements of old thinking.

Here is a short run-through of things I wasn't "allowed" to do or shouldn't do as a child – and could get punished for – along with general consequences to the timeless psyche, setting up lifelong restriction.

1. *Exuberant self-expression* – tempering my abounding energy as a 2-year-old set up failing confidence in subsequent interests, thus cramming my aggressive desire to succeed into a rationalized apathy.
2. *"Dirty", "vulgar", sexual thoughts* (or worse, actions) – this Victorian prudishness negatively impacted not only my

sexual fortitude, but my confidence in the rightness of my own natural drives in all aspects.

3. *Skipping church* – forced to waste a half day in a pompous, superficial, staid, boring environment nurtured resentment and inner turmoil, nothing more – certainly not belief in archaic notions.

4. *Not believing and accepting religion* – facing attempts to force me to think other than I thought right could only spur rebelliousness and even vindictiveness against authority.

5. *Speaking out* – whether "showing off" as kids are wont to do, or talking back to parental injustice, the force by authority to contain my natural impulses only solidified conflict and resentment.

6. *Doing what I wanted*, not what I was told – again, the lack of freedom and need to restrict my tendencies simply handed me inhibitions and inner tumult from earlier generations.

7. *Crossing the street* – of course, at an early age running out into the street wasn't advisable. But that restricted area was exactly where I wanted to explore! Later on, older and aware of the occasional car coming by, having still to ask permission to go play with friends was demeaning and overly restrictive – particularly because any disallowance of my going was based on purely arbitrary parental leanings.

Basically, Mother was just being herself as she tried to maintain order in daily life. But her own turmoil, a conflicted mindset undoubtedly rooted in religious fervor, led to her death at age 57 literally of a broken heart – her lifelong high blood pressure produced an enlarged heart and painful deterioration, all the while praying to her god for deliverance from her horrible pain.

Whatever her guilt feelings and allegiance to a non-existent god she held, her treatment of me stemmed from those values. It comprised forcing me to conform to her ideal, all the while disallowing my just *being myself*. Her gestures embodied a long, traditional heritage of inner conflict based on conceptual separation from a world "out there", decorated with illusory gods, phantom forces and conceptualized sources.

But more importantly, viewed from my perspective, while she was *never the cause* of my problems, her actions revealed my own nature as they invariably embodied my own inner issues. The real cause was a deep-seeded *unrest in the moment*, a turmoil brewed from conflict and struggle innate to engaging a reality perceived to be separate and apart from the isolated self.

For me, discerning and eliminating the punishment, suggestion, force and conflict rooted in each element of that unrest spanning all aspects of life proved to be a long, winding road to peace within and a manifested Reality that fulfilled my intent.

PUFF the Magic Curtailment

Frolics in the Things You've Missed in a Land Called Your Life

Were fulfillment of your will regarded as white and negation/neutralization of it as black, life rarely manifests purely as either, but rather emerges as many shades of gray – blending good with bad as things unfold.

Item by item, as I worked my way through all the issues, phantoms, punishment and threats, entreaties, fallacious definitions absorbed early on, hallowed religious falsehoods, control and restrictions, I came to see an overall trend in how life had manifested. Rather than pure failure or major health issues, instead of absolute rejection or abject financial plight – and certainly in place of joyous fulfillment of my intent – I had regularly manifested a qualitative Reality I termed *Partial, Unsatisfactory Fulfillment,* or **PUFF**.

PUFF recurred over and over in life's episodes: instead of the great car I desired, I ended up with a decent, yet far less exciting one – repeatedly. In place of that ideal female I'd fallen for (the latest iteration of the nurse and her pacifier), only a less congenial, more conflictual one would respond. Rather than realizing that house on the summit, designed to my specs, I could only manage a comfy, homey, but less than ideal house in a modest neighborhood.

I never completely failed, but my successes were compromised, diminished, unrewarded. My ventures in basketball, volleyball and other sports were generally successful, but never championship quality – often due to the shortcomings of others, twists of unfolding situations which rendered the team effort a bit short of winning. My projects in computer systems development were completed with creative, often brilliant results – yet any glory and reward I should have had was usurped by supervisors. Worse, my contribution often led to retribution from management in place of reward, as invariably I'd exposed the boss's shortcomings during the process.

So in one instance after the other, I'd never reaped my reward – just as with Mom. The reward always dangled out there in a promising future, one which never arrived. I only manifested the PUFF.

So, as you delve into your mindset, take care to observe subtleties. Recognize that all aspects of life blend in complex patterns fulfilling, negating and/or neutralizing your will – mostly in complex PUFFs. Beware your own *Partial, Unsatisfactory Fulfillment* – an unfolding reality that covers your needs, but doesn't satisfy your desires.

Separation

The Bottom Line – Literally and Effectively

Virtually all traditional views of life build on a core assumption of separation: you are one thing and everything encountered is separate and apart from you. Religion – i.e., Christianity, along with Islam, Judaism and pagan, superstitious precursors – science, eastern mystic traditions, various healing techniques and spiritual disciplines *all* pit an isolated you against some depicted, defined externalities.

That duality of *you* vs. *not you*, separating self from an alien universe, underlying all traditional thinking, is exactly what I saw **through** with my flash of a mystic experience. And exactly that illusory dichotomy is the fallacious core cultural assumption to be eliminated.

As culmination of all the above effects whereby my mother forced me into struggle and conflict, the very notion of Separation needed to be bailed out of the boat I was paddling through life. It made it impossible to get anywhere. The implication of division was overwhelmingly imposed through Mom's actions and statements listed earlier.

But looking more closely, Mother's *actions*, listed here, functioned as *suggestion*, every bit as suggestive as imperatives, severing me from the reality I encountered by implication. She...

1. *disallowed* me doing virtually anything that came natural.
2. regularly *ignored my will*, imposing her intent on my life.
3. *taught me* about God, angels, bacteria, bad guys and all other real or imaginary forces itemized earlier.
4. *inflicted fear* on me by threatening or carrying out punishment when I attempted to follow my natural impulse.

5. *inflicted medicine* on me as a rational solution, further separating me from my own bodily function.
6. *inflicted ongoing discomfort* on me by smoking incessantly and raising me in a drafty house, dry in winter, muggy in summer, always smoky.
7. supplied my needs, but *rarely my desires* – and then only in compromised form.
8. always *opposed my natural impulses*.
9. formed a strong *boundary* between herself and me through the initial word, "mama", and…
10. continued with all the other words and standard implications they entailed.
11. *gave in to my manipulation* as I wrangled to get my way, or…
12. *rejected my manipulation*. (Having forced me to have to influence her, she reinforced separation.)
13. taught me to stand up for my point of view, *to fight for what is right* – fully embodying rampant conflict. (Then punished me when I stood up against her.)
14. emphasized to *never give up* in the face of adversity – the quintessence of struggle.

All these gestures, while serving as other mechanisms already illustrated, worked here as pure and powerful **suggestion**. They carried the unequivocal message that I faced a world apart from my own essence, one that was hostile, uncaring and needed to be handled with calculated action to imprint my will on it.

And they were wrong.

My life reflects my own nature down to each *exhaustive detail*. Yours does the same, reflecting the explicit mindset your psyche holds ingrained in its subconscious store. Until you rid yourself of all the rampant, imprinted suggestion of separation, the reality you face manifests with opposing forces included.

Vulnerability

Across That Line

Implied in separation, an extremely subtle but damaging effect lingered just beyond my inner view while I scoured all the elements above from my psyche. It didn't comprise real conflict, actualized in life events where they could be seen, specified and released as all the others, but only threatened, hanging as a feeling of *vulnerability*, exposed to potential danger that might strike at any time.

I felt vulnerable the first time Mom spanked me. Here was my protector/provider inflicting pain instead of loving support, an act clearly indicating that I couldn't trust her; thus I could trust nobody. I recall that episode vividly; though not even two years old, I'd infuriated my mother somehow – however that happened doesn't matter. I was just being myself. She grabbed me angrily and spanked me with a ping-pong paddle. It didn't hurt much physically, but in addition to reinforcing separation, it yielded a personal vulnerability: a feeling that, if I was in this most secure place, at home with Mom, and was exposed to spontaneous physical harm, then some lurking danger must threaten *at any time in any place.*

This mind-element, affixed to the self-image, impedes fulfillment of intent in all regards. Feeling vulnerable, realized in this moment, you either won't attract abundance or *can never accrue enough money* to feel secure. This inner feature precludes reliable business relationships and entices flawed personal ones. It may spawn health issues that aren't debilitating or particularly painful, but always threaten potentially greater difficulties.

Exceptionally subtle, tricky to detect with no distinct events in memory, this insidious structure never brings disaster, but holds the psyche in a constant state of wariness, of concern and tension, anticipating a pending, lurking disaster that never comes.

Behold, The Psyche!

A Vast Scratchpad

All psychological elements itemized here had to be discerned and scoured from my psyche, one by one, as I evaluated unfulfilled life aspects. The psyche, not unlike a vast scratchpad, must be rewritten, item by item, mechanism by mechanism. As noted at the outset of this Angle, meaningful detail held within the mindset can only be discerned through experiential reference – by delving into memories that hold emotional content corresponding to disappointment and pain. They can only be released as discerned individually, not categorically, not by groups, but only one item, clarified and released, then the next.

Many spiritual disciplines look to grand, simple gestures to solve all life's problems – accept Jesus as Savior and all will be well, master focused thinking and you can create anything, visualize your goal and it will manifest, clear your thoughts away and you will attain enlightenment, etc.

In reality, these solutions, wrapped often in esoteric terms, eastern jargon or new-age icons, are all illusory.

The psyche, core of *your* being as my focal angle is of mine, stores information. Your base nature consists of interwoven meaning and assigned/innate value compounded from that information. *That's what you are!* The inner meaning manifest into outer events and relationships – life is that simple in process, however complex in actuality.

If you want to change the outer, recurring patterns which result from your mindset, you *have to* revise the inner.

And I could not possibly over-emphasize this point: adding new items of definition, including greater philosophical perspectives, higher spiritual knowledge is not enough. *You must consciously delete older, distorted beliefs and definitions* – otherwise, they remain intact within the complex psyche and continue not only to be woven into the reality you encounter, but also to confuse your ongoing awareness.

Final Points

A couple useful, important points not quite clarified above:

1. **Reliance vs. Trust:** two different aspects of personal regard.
   - I was taught to **trust** God, my parents, doctors, teachers and various experts in specific fields. From parental treatment as well as overt teaching, though, it was pounded home *not ever to trust myself* – that is, never expect my natural impulses to lead me in the correct direction, and only sparingly have confidence in my rational, calculating, planning mind.
     - ✓ In reality, that whole process of doubt, imprinted during my formative years, inevitably yielded its own negative outcome – making it appear that trust was unjustified. By *never trusting*, even calculated actions – preempting the intuitive – always led down paths of failure and pain. So mistrust of Self always, always, always fulfills its own negation.
     - ✓ This twist, by the way, results in many intrusive thoughts springing to mind – that crazy monkey meditation would wrest.
   - In quite another vein, though, I was motivated to *rely on* my mother.
     - ✓ Untrusting of Self from the earliest times – again reinforced by Mother's constant correction and pressure to impress on me her value system – I had to rely on others, Mother at the beginning, but ultimately on many others throughout life.
     - ✓ So, in addition to establishing trust in myself, I had to delve into other areas to establish *self-reliance* to

go along with self-trust.

2. **Duality/Singularity**: Not Two or even One.

- As emphasized from the outset, no two things, disconnected and intrinsically separate, exist in this integrated Reality.

  ✓ You are tied to all things you encounter. That connection is experienced in the oft-illustrated patterns regenerated throughout life and clearly perceived upon eliminating contrary beliefs.

  ✓ Neither are you separate from any other "thing", nor are any two aspects of Reality unrelated: not yin and yang, good and evil, up and down, in and out nor balls and strikes. All such defined items are only part of the interconnected whole of manifested Reality.

- But, as much as I discuss, reveal, illustrate and emphasize the "Oneness" of all things, there really isn't a *"One"*-ness to life at all! The notion of "one", the number, the unit itself, subtly implies a boundary to existence – of which there isn't any. You are connected to all things, not really in a Oneness, but in an unbounded, all-inclusive essence. "Oneness" is just a handy word to use to shave away at the multi-object universe typical to the western perspective.

3. Thus, as you complete your inner journey, you must also remove even those other definitive impressions encountered here: **subconscious, psyche, mind** and any other word needs to be jettisoned as though you were painting your way out the door of a room. *You* are the essence: "subconscious" and "soul" or "psyche" are just words. Using them is necessary for communication, but absorbing them as defined elements can only distort perception of the all-encompassing Self. You need to arrive at the place where those ideas aren't conceptualized, but perceived directly. Otherwise, however concise and descriptive, those words

only conjure up illusions as did notions about gods, fate and other causal sources.

4. And regarding *"conscience"*:

- Folklore and basic religious leanings have yielded a notion about an ingrained judgmental system innate to human consciousness that discerns right from wrong, particularly regarding moral consequences to action you might take.

- Indeed, you do know intrinsically what is "right". But your value system can be so distorted by common illusory precepts – layer after layer of definition and self-image absorbed throughout childhood – that you may not have any access to it. As you come to trust your own intuitive facility, reliance on that traditional "small, still voice within" becomes unnecessary. Your intent and gestures will only be positive and creative, not detrimental beyond fair consideration.

A2 Wrap

A Personal Note

As I assembled the above from notes jotted down along my multi-decade journey, I felt considerable sadness for my parents. Dad was a brilliant inventor and wonderful pianist (through his principal piano teacher, a student of Alexander Siloti, Dad's musical training stemmed directly from Liszt, Nikolai Rubinstein and Tchaikovsky, thus back to Beethoven via Czerny, Liszt's only teacher) in addition to being a great, caring person. But the baggage of conflict he received from earlier generations, carried throughout his life, severely mitigated the success he could ever realize in various business ventures.

Mother was an intensely loving, sensitive person, whose

great feeling and concern, so twisted by inner turmoil, could only internalize pain. With that ever-present, religious-based conflict channeled into physical symptoms, her decline and death were miserable and painful.

I do trust, though, that the clarity with which I could discern *my own* inner issues via memories of their treatment of me will serve as a lever for you and many others to engender great improvement in your and their lives. Given that, the various difficulties they suffered as well as the equally painful lessons I had to work my way through *will have been worth it.*

The Gist

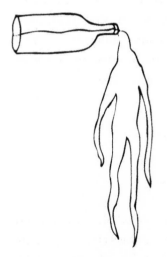

Your nature comprises, as its core, *information* – held in an extensive mindset comprised of interrelated values and meaningful elements. The overall content held within the psyche manifests continuously into real events and relationships whose meaningful gist reflects it absolutely.

Misinformation, held as true, not only distorts perception of the Self as the cause of things, but becomes woven into meaningful outcome. Thinking itself separate from Reality, the psyche manifests real situations in which the self is ignored or rejected. Believing gods or other external forces drive Reality manifests a flow that opposes one's intent.

Seeing that inner-outer flow and its inviolable, unremitting progression in recurring, patterned situations requires elimination of many distorting notions that attribute causality to illusory external forces.

Actually changing the qualitative content of the flow requires initial and initiating change within.

Exceptionally simple as a process, the Self/Reality Oneness is highly complex for advanced human consciousness due to the mind's great complexity and inherent multi-dimensionality of the life experience. And it can appear much more complicated due to fallacious notions that attribute grand appearances to illusory sources.

Any sincere seeker can see the pattern-forming tendencies in operation within his/her life. Changing inner roots in order to restructure negative patterns, that sincere explorer not only improves life with each step but becomes ever more aware of the innate connection between Self and Reality.

So the journey illustrated here is one away from perceiving life as an engagement of external forces through conflict and struggle, facing pain, body malfunction, potential attack, rejection or indifference, toward a life status where the body maintains health without resort to rational intervention and success unfolds with confidence and acceptance. That journey is one of inner scouring to clear away the debris of archaic myth and modern fallacy.

Along the way lie other hazards, cluttering the path with conceptual rubble. Let's regard a few as we change Angles...

ANGLE THREE: YOUR PATH

Down That Other Road

Only by recognizing you are on a journey with some inkling of the destination can you selectively choose a pathway to get there. The journey towards clearly seeing how life works, though, is particularly tricky: many common paths purported to lead there don't go all that far before they dead-end at a façade not much different than the starting point.

Life, of course, *is* a journey, one of change and general growth through experience. It can be movement in circles, with steadfast, illusory ideas keeping you fixed within contained notions, recycling the same patterns, thus engaging similar problems manifested repeatedly. Little is gained through this plodding, slow movement when focus remains on material goods, career advancement or simple survival – conventional gestures learned as necessary.

But when you realize consciousness spans lifetimes, building new ventures based on its status and ingrained values, the picture changes. Seeing that the real world is tied directly to your nature, the journey turns inward. It becomes a process of inner cleansing to scrub away the debris of separation that turns life against you.

At some point even the scouring phase of the journey ends, yielding a creative, fulfilling period of successfully accomplishing your intent.

Having fully illustrated so many elements of the psyche to clarify the journey, I present three more specific hindrances likely blocking the path to accomplishment...

The Lord's Prayer

Projecting Power and Glory For Ever and Ever

Perhaps the worst roadblock hindering progress consists of early exposure to repetitive chants of religious phraseology. Because the subconscious, as accumulator of definitions, is quite sensitive to input – both in regarding its meaning and weaving its content-value into experienced reality, then ultimately into your life – frequently repeating invalid, inaccurate expressions can be exceptionally damaging.

This disaster occurs rampantly in Islam. There are 6-year-olds who can repeat the entire Koran from memory, indeed quite proudly. In reality, because that archaic text is full of conflictual, primitive and very often self-demeaning quotes, such a practice inflicts that child's subconscious to an onslaught of fallacious definition. The practice only drives intrinsic Islamic conflict ever deeper into his psyche. (I refer to a 6-year-old **boy**, because girls, of course, are held as lower-level beings in the primeval Islamic mindset, thus less likely to be praised as crowning examples of religious dedication. But for females who memorize all the suras, demeaning effects are even worse.)

And conflict, integrated within the mindset – you must recognize by now – manifests into real events and relationships.

That same effect is to be seen in cultures that bear a heavy Christian influence. I grew up learning to "say my prayers" before bed at night – as though that were a prerequisite for living. (Indeed, in my mother's world view, *it was!*) The text went like this...

Now I lay me down to sleep;

I pray the Lord my soul to keep;

If I should die before I wake,

I pray the Lord my soul to take.

Reciting that drivel frequently could only damage my self-image by reducing power and esteem. By repeating that simple phrase nightly with naïve sincerity, I shrank in my own estimation – prone, this minor, powerless mortal, while some powerful, dominating Lord hovered over me, deigning to consider my meek entreaties.

And this repetition took place just before sleep, when the relaxation of near slumber promotes the subconscious writing slate to inscribe most vividly the content of prayer-type thought.

So that was bad enough, particularly because I was quite young during rote mimicking of this schlock. Add to that, though, saying "Grace" before meals.

In this repetitive entreaty, I thanked the *Lord* for providing food for me to eat.

The word "Lord" itself is an ancient deferential term commonly applied to imagined deities. All ancient cultures, until early Greek states, then Rome, established embryonic representative systems, invariably featured all-powerful rulers running the show. From his level on down, various ranks of nobility controlled the population "under" them with authoritative class designations and domineering rules.

As notions of gods emerged, naturally deities' attitudes and authority were imagined roughly equivalent to governmental hierarchy, particularly when that allowed priesthoods to embed themselves in upper echelons of power as well.

All of this had evolved from early differentiation in small, nomadic tribal groups, where a chief leader dominated decisions while shamans secured healing and superstition within their domain. As agriculture took root, populations grew; these roles expanded exponentially into royalty and priesthoods, both forcefully maintaining their dominance and advantaged lifestyles.

Anyway, the word "Lord" began as a reference to the Christian god at some point early on when the Bible was being translated into Old English. In effect, though, many ancient god names basically carried the same elevated meaning, exalting conceptualized deities into an elevated status.

By about 50 BCE, Rome had reverted to the old monarchical game plan as Julius Caesar emerged into a level of ultimate control, such that he was proclaimed "dictator perpetuo". Though his career was shortened by a Senate subcommittee, he reestablished the practice so effectively that his name became synonymous with emperor. Doubtless he and his successors were addressed with an equivalent term to "Lord". To this day in various regions "nobles" prefer to be so addressed when deigned to be spoken to by commoners. Official titles like **Lord** have always been important to such privileged classes – apparently it helps keep the peasants inferior within their own mindsets. Pretty funny – unless you are caught in that system...

As to **Grace**, short prayers uttered prior to eating, I was taught to say:

God is great; God is good.
And we thank Him for this food.

Or...

Be present at our table, Lord;
Be here and everywhere adored;
These mercies bless and grant that we
may feast in paradise with Thee.
Amen

So be it! Had to say "Amen", of course – a postscript that goes way back to Hebrew utterances. Why? Because no deity understands anything without that expression? Because some enlightened prophet realized how impressive that word was to a divine being?

No, actually I said **Amen** because I was taught it was right – just as my parents had been taught and theirs before them, on and on, back and back through generations as far back as my ancestors – and yours, since back then our ancestors were all the same ones – started to attribute causality to gods.

Long ago I rid myself of the fallacy and self-deprecation knotted into saying prayers and grace. But the more glorified version of nightly prayers, far more harmful than those, encased much greater diversity in its insidious counter-value.

Here is **The Lord's Prayer** in all its opulence, replete with archaic phraseology – retained, presumably, to make it sound most reverent. One would think that a god powerful enough to have created this huge universe would keep up on modern English grammar. Of course, one would also conclude that such an enormously powerful and undoubtedly complex intellect as this god must have – were he to actually exist – would have long since tired from hearing the same old phrases perpetually repeated. But here they are:

Our Father, who art in heaven,
Hallowed be Thy name.
Thy Kingdom come,
Thy will be done,
On earth as it is in heaven.
Give us this day our daily bread.
And forgive us our trespasses,
As we forgive those who trespass against us.
Lead us not into temptation,
But deliver us from evil.
For Thine is the kingdom, the power and the glory, for ever and ever.
Amen

As this verse is repeated frequently, a composite value becomes embedded into the subconscious of anyone doing the praying. Here is the gist of each line, along with the resultant meaning the subconscious absorbs...

- First two lines: some parental-authoritarian source, existing in a superior alternate reality somewhere, you are wonderful.
  - The word "Father" implies, consistent with Christian theology, this entity created me. By rights of fatherhood, particularly in that primitive mentality, he should domineer over me.
  - Indeed, "hallowed" extends that implication: this grandiose being is *far* more sacred and thus *much, much better* than I in any regard.
  - ✓ The literal value to this phrase, duly registered in the subconscious – since neither the "Father" nor his heavenly abode exists – carries the meaning that I, stuck here in mundane reality, overwhelmingly lack value and importance.
- Next three lines: this conceptualized source should come and gain control over not only me but over *all of reality* so that **his will** would control everything here as well as in that alternate, imagined reality.
  - The ancients could only imagine operative systems in which kings controlled the realm – this authority protected them from neighboring tribes, an ongoing threat, particularly in the Middle East of ancient times (actually even now).
  - So they willingly entreated their conceptualized entity (somehow this deity wasn't, on his own, ever so inclined) to come and take over earthly rule, imposing his will on everybody.
  - ✓ Of course, the meaning to the Self is straight-

forward: some other entity's will should be done here ideally, not *my will*.

✓ And, while it looks to blissful, heavenly status, well-fed and free of threat, the entreaty actually translates into stark **personal powerlessness**. Depending on the imagined nature of that god, the implication carries an impact that *could be much worse*: manifesting a reality that **specifically opposes** my will. Clearly, my earthly desires *could not possibly* feature the same agenda held by this magnificent, all-powerful god.

✓ And that notion, in turn, pounded repeatedly into the subconscious, not only guarantees power-lessness, but even consents to that meek status – yielding invariably a life negating or ignoring one's own will.

• Next line: Please provide us with food.

o From most ancient of times, fertility of the soil and favorability of the weather, thus production of farming efforts, were attributed to divine whim. This archaic entreaty furthers that primordial notion.

✓ Subconscious notion implanted: I am so incapable and reality so alien that I need a god to sustain me.

✓ Powerlessness is reinforced yet again.

• Trespass lines: Look, I'm being nice and generous with others, how about taking it easy on me?

o Since ancient peoples believed some god or other impelled all events, this entreaty was common: any acts perceived as negative by this god (who appar-ently has nothing better to do than watch your every move) should be forgiven.

o Jesus, emphasizing the value of forgiveness, suggested a sort of trade-off: forgive others and be forgiven. But...

- ○ "Trespass", in this sense, means to sin against somebody, to offend or wrong them. (Other versions talk about "debt", but no Christian I know goes around forgiving debts.) So this entreaty almost assumes that I regularly wrong others. So the rote request functions as an *admission of general wrong-doing* – or innate flawed nature.
- ○ Added to the concession of generally offensive behavior comes inevitable projection of **judgmental authority** to this conceptualized deity, imagined to have power to punish me.
- ✓ First, of course, no god exists, sitting there monitoring six billion people every second to judge them against his list of permitted actions and occasionally allowable transgressions. That truly ancient notion is utterly nonsensical.
- ✓ Generally, forgiving perceived slights by others is a very good thing to do, because *you* attracted the conflict in the first place. But you never reach this realization following this rote entreaty, particularly when doing so only to gain parole from your own admitted bad deeds.
- ✓ Still, following the version in Matthew 6:9–13, Jesus explains that when you forgive, the Heavenly Father forgives you, too. This vague hint at reality's functionality indicates Jesus' budding awareness of the inner-outer connection. But it isn't accurate: forgiveness *of* others does not equate to eliciting just treatment subsequently *by* others. Manifested events are much more complex than that. But the thought improves on more archaic notions prevalent two millennia ago – common in primitive areas today – that perceived slights against my family or tribal unit must be avenged.

- Temptation and evil: keep me out of trouble; forgive me when in it.
  - Again, this request assumes the deity concocts all events to punish or reward his pet humans. The very statement, a double-barreled shotgun blast into your subconscious, projects all causality to the conceptualized god...
  - This, of course, renders the one praying as impotent in life.
  - ✓ *Temptation* here lumps things like sex, one of life's greater joys and imperative needs for procreation, in with doing harm to others, which is always a bad thing. The *very least* effect of this portion is rational confusion.
  - ✓ Requesting temptation be left off the menu thus becomes, if examined closely, a multi-dimensional twist of meaning: the deity is asked to *not* present events enticing commitment of acts outside the scope of behavior allowed in the first place. But why would that all-knowing entity have created you initially with body parts, needs and drives that would invariably lead to sin, then present tempting situations and expect you not to? Then change his mind when asked to?
  - ✓ And further, as requested, deliver you from any bad things – which must otherwise assuredly be coming.
  - ✓ The overall effect of these two lines is very negative to the naïve young mind urged to repeat them. They present nonsensical god-notions in how to deal with him, even in their own terms within the religious paradigm. Such pleas only accomplish another irrational projection of creative power to an imagined source.
- Last line: You're the greatest!

- ○ The classic Lord's Prayer until this point is consistent with Matthew's version of Jesus' recommendation. This line first appears in the Didache, an early Christian treatise that didn't make the New Testament cut. Roman Catholics omit this doxology, content to be delivered from evil – if the prayer worked – then cross themselves in yet another self-effacing gesture.
- ○ It says, in effect, that, **WOW**, *you're* the head honcho here and everywhere (not I, as implied, this poor, helpless blackguard, this sniveling miscreant that I am), *yours* is the power (not mine, for I'm only this weak-kneed schlep) and *yours* is the glory (not for me, humble wretch bowing to your magnificence) for *all of time* – not only now, but even when I'm dead!
- ✓ What an overwhelmingly disastrous message to feed the subconscious! It's no wonder people grow up with little self-esteem and confidence, when they've had to repeat this bunk for years.
- ✓ Neither my mother nor any of untold generations of drivel-mimicking clergy inflict such damage on me anymore, for I jettisoned negative implants derived from The Lord's Prayer from my subconscious long ago.
- ✓ And you should, too, if you want to determine your own direction and be your own person in life.

I wonder why this prayer is written in the plural. In both of its versions attributed to Jesus (gospels Matthew and Luke) as a suggested entreaty to his Heavenly Father, the text expresses thoughts as though the one praying is fixed in a group. If I'm doing the groundwork here, beckoning a great and powerful god, shouldn't I be speaking for myself and not include all those others out there sinning and blaspheming on their own?

Oh, I forgot – according to much more ancient roots (Hebrew Scriptures, Old Testament), I'm my brother's keeper.

Well, I can go along with that one. In looking out for my brothers out there (and sisters, too, as I've never shared the longstanding church bias against females as somehow inferior), I reiterate to those kin that repeating such prayers as this can only instill very damaging notions into your subconscious mind. With no god out there listening (were he there, he must be bored to Hell by now with a billion such entreaties daily) the only effect of such projected supremacy is to render you ineffective within your own self-image.

So one glorious step forward on Your Path is to review such prayers repeated as a child, parse them for harmful elements and explicitly dispel them, piece by piece.

And for those who memorized the Koran... Well, never mind – you wouldn't have read this far anyway.

Insurance

Intentionally Creating Hazards in Your Path

One faulty notion built into modern thinking, eminently worth eliminating from your repertory, is this simple and common expression, "Something might happen to you..."

Of course, the phrase implies something *bad* might occur, because something is always happening and most welcome good occurrences. Whatever life's flow is attributed to – god, luck, etc. – it is generally presupposed that a chance event might spur disaster. So traditionally, we purchase life insurance to cover the possibility of death at any time, health insurance to cover the possibility of sickness, car insurance to cover the possibility of an accident, etc.

But *chance* is not a feature of a Reality based on meaning. It only characterizes the illusion formed by the mind mired in limited awareness – a level picturing the self and reality as two separate things.

Truly accepting Christians, for example, shouldn't need insurance. If their deity were really causal, presuming them to be trusting of It, what event could occur outside Its grace? My guess is most true believers have many types of insurance – based more on quasi-acceptance of science along with religion for understanding life more than lack of faith. But at the same time, it clearly indicates solid doubt as to the veracity and efficacy of that god-image.

I don't have life insurance. For sure, I will die. But that won't happen until I've completed my various tasks here. And a list of my undertakings (as opposed to being an undertaking of an undertaker) slated for completion includes, among other accomplishments, finishing this book. (Apparently I accomplished that one.)

So, yes I will die one day. However enjoyable it's been, I have no desire to live indefinitely as this personage. But upon seeing the enormity of the subconscious, the broad and deep field of mind content, richness, creativity, humor, etc., you recognize the timeless nature of the self – an awareness that eliminates fear of even premature departure.

But I also don't have any health insurance. Bad things that "might happen to me", *don't ever*, as I've eliminated any inner negation. Never needing medical science to patch the hull, why carry insurance to pay for it? Of course, nothing needing medical attention ever does "happen to me", despite my being quite active, adventurous, etc. My body handles its own function.

I do have minimal automobile insurance – a legal requirement in Pennsylvania. And house insurance. My wife is more comfortable with both, and I can live with those expenses, tolerating a society that imagines that, at any given moment, *something might happen.*

Things do happen all the time – but they are *never* bad.

What about you?

The reliance on insurance carries default mental concessions of life's randomness or danger – that your fate is determined by some mechanism putting you at risk or open to chance events, some of which might be harmful. That notion is common to our culture, rampant, actually, as people's fears of ill health and potential disaster are fed routinely by commercial television and advertisements that are virtually unavoidable.

But insurance and the nagging need to have it are outgrown when you shed notions that life is determined by external forces – or encountered as chance events that might be bad.

Relaxation Technique

Why the Need

I recall, early in my journey, learning various relaxation techniques as a means to self improvement. Indeed, both meditation and self-hypnosis involve relaxation as an integral element.

The former *is* relaxation, both mental and physical, in its very practice – attempting to shed the psychic stress and muscle tension that seem part of human experience. Meditation in bypassing that stressful default status provides welcome relief from its ongoing un-natural state. But, as indicated in Angle Two, it won't permanently eliminate stress and tension, because it doesn't address root causes for them.

Similarly, self-hypnotism requires, particularly at first, an induction technique which integrates relaxation of muscles along with clear focus of attention.

But the question *"why?"* comes to mind – why is it necessary for such techniques to be used? Why are the mind and its vehicle in physicality, its body, in such a stressful state to begin with? Why isn't relaxation the standard mode of consciousness and veritable existence?

The answer is simple, though the corrective process may be as complex as was illustrating the psyche: you live in a state of ongoing, perceived danger, threatened by god's will, random catastrophes, the potential of accident, economic collapse, thieves and irate drivers, spontaneous body malfunction, even lightning hitting you.

Pure relaxation occurs, not following some trance-induction process, but along the path of ridding yourself of external threats common notions pose against you. So the best relaxation procedure is coming to a standard state of personal peace, free of the inner turmoil that accompanies seeing the world out there as separate and apart from the Self.

Major Blockage – The Landslide Covering Your Path

The greatest – if not exclusive – blockage along your path towards clear perception consists of a wide array of misconceptions that plague our western thinking. (Eastern thinking has its own versions, too.)

I covered inner aspects of those fallacies in Angle Two. Let's raise the periscope from the depths of mind to take an equally focused look at long traditions of speculation by western man's most brilliant thinkers. As I identify and explain conceptual boulders blocking the way, you would do well to wrest them from your subconscious rather than, having regarded them, set them neatly back into place.

ANGLE FOUR: PREVIOUS TEACHINGS

Ideas, New and Old

As I present perspectives on the engagement of life by each human, illustrating innate ties between the apparent two, Self and Reality, it exceeds mere academic interest to regard in some detail those many messages voiced about life before me. Rather, a critique of others' accounts for how reality functions is **absolutely vital** for me to adequately illustrate the real flow.

Some messages through the ages have been quite insightful, with originators privy in varying degrees to the Oneness with which life flows; these are eminently worthy of review for their intrinsic value. From my standpoint of personally perceiving the inner-outer connection, I recognize any faint hint of that awareness in others' messages, even when cloaked in translated accounts from other cultural groups in greatly divergent settings, modern or ancient.

Conversely, from the standpoint of a clearer awareness of life's innate flow, a viewpoint beyond the referenced teacher's, I easily detect flaws in that person's message. Given the superficial basis of many religious and philosophical expressions, their reliance on synthetic definitions and artificial conceptualizations – often based on invalid assumptions – exposes short- 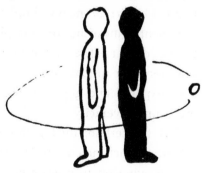 comings in their theologies, theories and stated paradigms. I have no qualms about exposing such errant thinking.

Given that – value in discerning relative insight into life's flow and corresponding value in recognizing specific fallacy – and in light of the purpose of enhancing the reader's view, the need to explore past teachings rests on several critically important factors:

1. Ideas expressed in the past can take on a luster of truth-fulness due to their antiquity – with an implied time-honored validity – well beyond any intrinsic value, a worth compromised by their inaccuracy.
2. A large following to any religion or exotic teaching, like widespread acceptance of any philosophy, e.g., throughout academia, seems also to imply validity. (How could so many people be wrong?)
3. Many concepts posed by various sources throughout civilized traditions found their way into common western thinking – thus into *your* mindset. Some are noteworthy due to their influence, sometimes quite positive, on the advancement of civilization. But for the rest, unabashedly refuting fallacious ideas is the only way to expose them as false and help others dispel them – and thus eliminate their negating effect in real life.

Point #1 carries heavy implications, however simple the statement. Hinduism, for example, has been around for several thousand years. The implication is that, if this great depth of tradition over untold generations isn't accurate, it would have been exposed and gone out of use long ago. Its long survival thus implies veracity.

But for certain, during those millennia many individuals, initially indoctrinated into Hindu cultural norms, did leave the fold, moving on to greater personal insight (or at least other ideas). All the while, though, most of the population simply maintained notions learned while growing up, such that cultural/philosophical heirs – typically their physical offspring – continue today to hang on to those old practices taught them from birth.

Continuity of old religions *should be no surprise*, given the propensity of each believer's mind to validate held beliefs – plus the guarantee that people indoctrinate new generations with their old beliefs. The same effect governs the generational stability of Jainism, Christianity, Islam or any localized version of shamanism. (Indeed, the only guarantee to avert this effect is for a religion to die out, like the Shakers, who strictly disavowed sex and reproduction and thus ushered themselves into oblivion. Zoroastrianism took a slightly more common route to near extinction: being pushed out the door by another religion, in this case Islam.)

Being rooted in ancient thinking confirms, then, *absolutely nothing* about validity. Nor – as in point #2 – do large numbers of adherents.

Years ago, during my twenties, while hitchhiking around Europe, I sat with a group of fellow travelers from various countries, chatting – likely over a beer. Somebody asked what was the correct way to speak English, noting the difference among Aussies, Americans, Brits from various regions, Scots, Irish, etc. A Yank in the group noted that, since Americans were greatest in population of these countries, US English must be correct. My comment was, on that guideline, we all should be speaking Chinese. My point, other than illustrating the silliness of that initial consideration, was that sheer numbers signify nothing.

Ditto for believers. Muslims number a billion currently, Christians even more. With differing theologies, at least one group *must* be dead wrong, as would be all the other four billion humans who don't adhere to either. Having large numbers of adherents, then, confirms only that closed-mindedness commonly characterizes Homo Sapiens.

So neither a long history nor large contingent indicates validity to a belief set.

Indeed, to me, no stated expression for life's functionality can substitute for a clear, direct awareness of it. In that regard, point #3 is vital practically as well as philosophically.

Because of the psyche's intimate tie to reality, wherein inner elements manifest real events and relationships, holding fallacious notions as facts creates two major hindrances in moving to greater awareness and improving one's life. First, the projection of creative power to illusory forces and sources builds entirely false impressions of powerlessness in one's own status and capability. Second, that debilitated self-image, as all other inner elements, gets built into experienced reality, seeming to confirm the restricted nature of self resident in the subconscious.

So, by vigorously pointing out fallacious ideas commonly shared across our culture – thus very likely occupying niches in your subconscious – I can spur recognition of their synthetic quality. Only through initial acknowledgment can you begin to rid yourself of them. That is, provided you are capable of discerning the exposé as valid – rather than subtly defending current beliefs, thus spurning my rendering as anything from incorrect to blasphemous.

With that notion in mind, I strongly emphasize that my observations never mean to be critical of people or movements, historical or present. If I point out a paradigm's invalidity, that does not imply a degradation of any person or group holding that expression as valid or even hallowed.

I honor and cherish each human as a unique and valued entity, each culture as a grand variation on the theme of man and each notion, however fallacious it might be in depicting reality, as a respectable idea in the long line of human thinking.

But each of us – *and this is very important, so please make note* – formulates our understanding of ourselves and the world we encounter based on beliefs and definitions we currently hold. Many of those are fallacious; many were absorbed during early childhood when, naïve and fresh on the scene, we were open to and absorbent of all we encountered. So, to our impressionable minds, they took on an appearance of core understanding of what is, seeming to be facts rather than mere ideas, notions and conceptualizations – constraints on understanding, not enhancement.

So I respect all people and all groups. But if ideas they hold are invalid, the only way for me to deal with them is to *expose them as such*. This gesture is vital for illustrating life's real function. But, to repeat with added emphasis: critique of an idea is *never criticism of people who hold that idea*.

Growing through childhood, I picked up most of the same notions you did. I was taught to pray to the conceptualized Christian god and did so nightly. I learned to take medicine to heal sickness, solve problems logically, work hard, bow to authority figures, respect the clergy with particular reverence, gain knowledge to improve myself, make money to succeed – and compromise myself, if necessary, to earn that money – manipulate people to realize my desires and all the other base understandings you learned.

But one by one, throughout my inner journey, I eliminated most common cultural notions and deactivated the rest because they are founded, if pared down to core meaning, on the invalid notion that the Self is separate from Reality. I speak entirely from that simple, intimate recognition of Oneness with life's many attributes.

Indeed, this highly critical point differentiates me from all the great visionaries and thinkers to be regarded in this Angle: recognizing the unbounded gullibility of the mind to confirm its pre-accepted tenets. Seeing that, I have spent my life not building up grandly constructed logical arguments, not adding to an airtight paradigm to propound nor logically refuting others', but rather deleting any and all preconceived characterizations about reality. I explain here, as well as I can illustrate it in words, *how reality looks when seen clearly*, without any beliefs, definitions and subtle assumptions to distort the view.

As I explore mankind's great teachings, emanating from visionaries, time-honored religious movements, brilliant philosophers and diverse mystics, though, I proceed with personal, sincere recognition for their earnest expression of what they all, undoubtedly, believed to be accurate, truthful accounts. Pointing out where they erred, I never mean to criticize – much less attack – their personal esteem or perceptiveness but only to illustrate ideas inaccurate as presented and thus damaging when held as true.

In that vein, it isn't that I have all the answers, such that Jesus, Plato, Augustine, Nietzsche, Mohammed, Hume, Galileo, Gautama, Locke, Eckhart, Böhme, Dante, Paul, Kant, Hobbes, Hegel, Newton, Thomas Aquinas, Aristotle, Einstein, Bacon, Lao Tzu, Descartes, Schopenhauer, Spinoza and others to be regarded below are wrong. It's more like this: all stated answers are inherently wrong – some much more so than others – and I recognize that caveat more than they did.

Life flows in a Singular, meaningful fashion. I perceive that clearly, unhindered by rational explanations.

My goal is to communicate diverse illustrations as necessary to help you and others come to see that flow as well. Awareness of it is not to be found in my explanations any more than in insights of other teachers. But a clear perception **can be** gained by sincere seekers (with or without my help, though likely easier *with*) delving inward to see inner roots to outer experience and dispelling invalid notions learned earlier as truths. Many of those notions will be encountered along the way as their originator or cultural basis is reviewed and debunked.

But while I regard earlier teachings to expose inaccuracy, I do so always with great honor due their source. I understand as well as any the journey each of them must have traveled – and the caveats of expressing perspectives beyond commonly held ideas.

Man's Long Quest for Understanding

The Oldest Endeavor?

I spoke at a convention years ago, where my slot followed a demonstration on pottery-making in early American Indian cultures. During that earlier session I shaped clay into a small vessel which then simply dried in the open air.

Chatting with the presenter as we reset chairs for my talk, I joked about the coincidence of having the world's second and third oldest occupations lined up in order. But, with prostitution traditionally regarded as the oldest – at least in terms of a *paid* profession – it wasn't clear which came in second: creating objects out of wet clay or ideas about reality out of fervent imagination.

At first glance, speculating on the nature of being seems exceptionally ancient, in play well before the discovery that dried clay, previously shaped, could be quite useful. We might romantically picture ancients, lying under the clear night sky, pondering the nature of existence. But realistically, **open-minded** regard of reality is not such a common pastime in *any* era, even in recent times – and was increasingly less so in ever more remote times. Shamans and healers doubtless held elevated niches in ancient nomadic tribes; they, along with standard cultural pressure, certainly made sure tribal members toed the line so as not to incur the wrath of their imagined deities. Thus, most people then – even more so than now – simply absorbed notions they are taught, accepting them as baseline truths. Man's preponderant majority never looks in directions different than common thinking for other, perhaps more applicable perspectives – let alone coming up with newer, greater visions not yet perceived.

So one might wistfully dream of ancestors pondering the milky way, a sunset or the budding of springtime, wondering aloud about where life came from and how it all worked. But that romantic notion is rather unlikely to have happened **at all**, let alone commonly.

Our ancestors, stemming generation after generation from ever more primitive roots, were likely frozen philosophically to 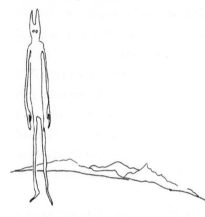 rigid, superstitious beliefs handed them, in turn, by their parents – not unlike we have been, except without the added influence of extensive exposure to alternative ideas. Whether hunter-gatherer or early farmer, that lifestyle depended on reliable sources of food, sustenance regarded as provisions from the gods. With well-being seemingly at stake, ancient peoples would have been very reluctant to question standard procedures for appeasing the gods, for those deities provided food as well as protection from natural dangers.

I suspect ancient times featured precious little open-minded speculation outside narrow confines of local ritual and religious imprint. Perhaps a few imaginative individuals visualized beyond cultural confines, but they likely learned quickly to keep their thoughts to themselves, less they suffer reprisals from authorities or fearful peers. Simple passing of arcane notions from shaman to apprentice hardly counts as philosophical inquiry. But – in terms of ancient professions – tribal healers and spiritualists, whatever the details of their mindset, were undoubtedly pros. Their corner on the market of their tribe's psychological needs certainly justified full-time support as a specialized career path.

The comparative age of ceramic production vs. philosophical inquiry, then, depends on what constitutes the latter.

Earthenware pottery, hardened in bonfires, goes back at least 30,000 years. Indeed, the earliest examples are Venus figures – ceramic images of females with exaggerated feminine features. Likely reflecting religious notions then, these ritual talismans indicate that abstract regard for reality had to predate creation of ceramic symbols for that regard.

So explaining how life works, however inaccurately, must go way back into man's prehistory. Just when it became a *profession* is another thing. Perhaps that status even predated payment for sex.

Anyway, effective exploration *outside current cultural notions* took place much more recently, just about within the margins of historical scope. (Whether open conjecture of consequence happened prior to writing would be difficult to ever confirm, lacking real evidence. Preserved clay tablets don't indicate much by way of free thought. And rebellious concepts wouldn't tend to be conserved through generational word-of-mouth lore without becoming mainline thinking or woven into myth.)

Of instances I could find which recorded "thinking outside the box", first was Abraham – provided ancient accounts passed along many generations are to be accepted at anything close to face value.

Along about 1900 BCE, this founder of the Hebrew line headed westwards from his southern Mesopotamian birthplace, ultimately establishing a new way of thinking along with a new residence and new tribal identity. His regard of El as the chief god was a significant step beyond contemporary polytheistic notions. His belief system, likely henotheistic (worshiping one god while acknowledging others exist) rather than monotheistic as later generations portrayed it, would certainly qualify as unconventional, particularly for that remote time frame.

What Abraham really thought, of course, is impossible to distinguish. Ancient Hebrew accounts were passed down more than a millennium before even being written down, then certainly revised to fit current thinking for another two and a half thousand years – all within various religious hierarchies never noted for objectivity. Still, given the long-term impact of Abraham's abandoning idol worship and multiple, special-purpose gods, he seems to have departed from dominant polytheistic, myth-based notions.

Subsequent Hebrew prophets after Abraham revised earlier thinking, but not by much. Still others began new branches of religion – they differed only in detail.

By 1350 BCE, Akhenaton, the unique Egyptian pharaoh of the 18th dynasty, moved away from rote thinking consistent with  cultural standards as well. After becoming head of the state, Amenhotep IV shifted gears in the Egyptian pantheon. He promoted Aton, a god associated with the Sun's light and its life-giving qualities (previously an aspect of Ra) to principal god.

Changing his name to Akhenaton (a title referring to spiritual aspects of Aton – after all, in Egypt a daily, regular and certainly life-enabling Sun dominated the sky), he strongly promoted revision of religious practices away from other gods towards a prominent , but **not quite exclusive**, single god.

That, of course, didn't go over well with the entrenched priesthood – or practically anybody else. Once he died, thus relinquishing authority without enough time for his ideas to solidify into Egyptian thinking, his notions were as vigorously obliterated as the grand buildings he'd established in reverence to Aton.

The only other philosophical dissident of truly ancient times seems to have been Zarathustra.

Thought to have lived about 1000 BCE, though perhaps earlier, Zoroaster (so called in the west) of Persia (modern Iran) certainly reformulated conventional notions of his time. He saw in Ahura Mazda, his principal god, a force for good against Ahriman, the bad guy in a perceived duality.

While Zoroaster's ideas are difficult to compare with precursors, Ahura Mazda seems to equate to the Vedic god (Hindu root) Varuna as evolved images from earlier, common Indo-European god-notions. As such, the good-evil/truth-lie conflict innate to Ahura Mazda and Ahriman – not featured in Rig Veda lore, despite the cognate of Ahura with Varuna's class "Asura" – seems to have been initiated by Zoroaster. This teaching certainly qualifies him as innovative – and rather perceptive, for life is value based, just as implied by the good vs. evil image.

His ideas, however, were revised considerably beyond his lifetime, an eventuality typical to most visionary teaching, as they became canned into a religion. Added were post-death judgment of a hypercritical god, relegation to heaven- or hell-type places, the Bounteous Immortals as heavenly occupants, etc. (Many of these ideas, core to the eventual religion, found their way from Zoroastrianism right into classical Christianity, with the last of those becoming angels and arch-angels.)

So I would include these three individuals of quite ancient times as progenitors of significantly new notions within their cultures.

But reducing many varied gods to two, one principal one or even one exclusive one isn't all that much of a change – as all causality was still attributed to conceptualized sources. It was only by approximately 500 BCE, with Lao Tzu in the Far East, Siddhartha Gautama in India and Greek philosophers in the west that individuals would significantly question prevalent cultural myth-based notions of god causality and begin looking at reality to make some sense of it.

Before shifting focus toward that, though, let's first finish the scorecard of early professional endeavors...

As to prostitution, the sex act per se goes unfathomably far back, way before Australopithecines, before the divergence of apes and man, way, way back to the first life form that used meiosis to recombine genes into a new life form. That might be as much as 1.4 billion years on Earth.

But paying for the pleasure is considerably more recent. That likely occurred shortly after two aspects of man evolved: one, objects representing value came to be exchanged for other goods or services, and two, human personality and its complexity had reached a degree where sex took on a calculable value, rather than being spontaneous or exclusive to an alpha male. So, how old are objects of value?

Tools and other useful implements have been crafted for ages – stone implements date to 2.5 million years ago and likely objects of other, easier to use materials long predate them. So it might be, who knows, three million years ago that some wily, but seemingly unattractive, Australopithecus Afarensis dude, having fashioned a nifty strap from some reeds, added a cockle shell or two and enticed an otherwise reluctant Lucy wannabe into what had previously been a non-negotiable, impulsive act. We may all be descendants of that coupling, given our bent to rely on rational thinking.

Pottery dates back a long way, but not nearly *that* far. However, pottery is arguably just an extension of complex tool making. So, conceptually, it can be looked upon as having the same roots back to that nifty strap – likely back somewhat farther to purely *useful* straps without fancy adornments needed to attract sex.

Developing adequate understanding for reality must have prompted language becoming complex enough to express abstract ideas, as opposed to simply referring to named objects and actions. (Both, of course, required **self-awareness** – recognizing, as even great apes do today, that the Self exists as an entity engaging an apparently external world of objects.)

I suspect things came in this general order: using tools (utilizing natural objects, like sticks and rocks, to accomplish goals), language (communication using spoken words as well as gestures), *making* tools (complex items created for a preconceived purpose), explaining reality (stories and myths that became endowed with attributed causality) and only then, use of the manufactured items for eliciting trades for other valued items (ultimately including sex).

But, finally, explaining reality in exchange for reward is not what I do. As such, unlike the long tradition of preachers, gurus, priests, shamans, self-help experts, imams, rabbis, spiritualists, scientists, philosophers and psychologists, who provide some degree of specialized insight (whether valid or not) in return for money, my expression is rather unique and quite new (and invariably valid). My offering never elicits personal gain in value. So the gesture is as new and fresh as the message.

Thus, I hereby relinquish any further competition with prostitution and pottery-making!

The Background

Of How We See Things

Much of how we regard reality hearkens back to religious thinking of ancient times. Two thousand years ago, practically every human in existence regarded some set of gods – perhaps a single one – as driving reality, i.e., directly causing things to happen in their real lives. (There were indeed many a pantheon to choose from – except *few people ever chose*, but rather accepted gods they'd had defined for them as children.) Implicit in that universal notion (or explicit in myth) was that deities had their own agenda for a design spec. This notion of gods out there controlling things had grown through time from early animism, an outlook common to pre-agricultural groups where soul qualities are attributed to animals, objects, etc., in the real world.

Our civilized ancestors commonly used time-honored means to augur what the gods had in store, as well as various methods to attempt to influence them: entreaties, burnt sacrifices, offerings of grain and virgins, rituals, devoted priests attributed special powers to persuade their deities. (Indeed, for long periods, those very same priests made proper use of the grain and virgins, given that the non-existent gods had need for neither. There must have been more than one miraculous "virgin" birth along the way, aided by priests dedicated to implementing fertility rites!) All of these were employed to cajole imagined sources of power, beseeching them to provide favorable events.

For much of the Roman Empire's span, Latin didn't even feature a word for religion! Notions of gods as innately causal were self-evident, not religious as we think of a theology, but so commonly shared, so deeply built into common thinking as to be obvious, simply a part of life.

Indeed, many today still hold to those archaic notions, accepting a religious paradigm as unquestionably true, praying more intently when prayers offered last week failed to elicit improvement.

But for much of our past, the common man's mindset featured multiple collections of deities and mythical accounts of their intent and nature. Held as truths, these were invariably passed along without question to offspring.

Occasionally, though, as civilization and language evolved in complexity, an individual would come along with greater awareness of life's real process – the inner-outer flow I've been illustrating – well beyond common superstitions and fantasies. But these visionaries had to express their perspectives within the confines of contemporary language and understanding, having to illustrate unusual ideas such that contemporaries might grasp and somehow make use of them. The difficulties they encountered were multiple and highly restrictive.

Principal among them is explaining concepts necessarily above and beyond the ken of peers.

Most people **in any time period** are firmly frozen into conventional thinking. As most individuals during childhood accept and find comfort in cherished, shared beliefs, the great majority in any cultural setting simply *don't want to change*. They are happy with standard rituals, which invariably appear valid to their indoctrinated minds and thus seem to work; they wouldn't want to risk retribution by offending their favored god or gods.

(Interesting point: as Christianity became entrenched in the Roman Empire following Constantine's acceptance, the last group to accept these newer ideas were country people, the conservative-thinking farmers, etc. The word "pagan" originally meant **country dweller** in Latin. Indeed, it is always the less liberal people, less exposed to different ideas, less accepting of new notions, who hang on to old thinking. In those times, a rural population accustomed to imploring Ceres [Demeter], goddess of harvest, for crop abundance certainly resisted switching to requesting the same from a single, all-purpose god. Didn't make sense. Wasn't what their parents believed and taught them.)

Exaggerating that effect, from ancient times to modern, entrenched priesthoods have always seen fit to discourage *any* deviance from prescribed thinking, often threatening eternal punishment if church-sanctioned explanations would be questioned. If theological fear didn't suffice, inflicting severe harm was the next option. Some 40,000 people were victims of Christian inquisition over centuries – painful death dealt via torture to those who would question the church interpretation

and authority. Religion-dominated societies never welcome – nor tolerate – visionaries who might threaten the secure status of any priesthood. (After all, where would the priests get their unending supply of grain and virgins from – or, in the case of deviate Catholic functionaries, innocent choirboys?)

To official Christendom, brotherly love has always been a wholly theoretical commodity that quickly dissipates upon threat to political power, control, church wealth and monopolization of hegemony over the ignorant populace. Many a mystic and, later, early scientist as well, faced or received severe punishment from the official Catholic bureaucracy for proposing blasphemous observations in the face of officially sanctioned fantasy.

So the dual problem inhibiting introduction of greater vision consisted of rigid, conservative thinking and an encased bureaucracy that benefitted from that status quo.

Beyond that, even, sages, attempting to voice new perspectives invariably had trouble finding words to express greater vision. Words, as noted, carve an integrated Reality into little pieces to begin with. And no ancient culture provided an adequately sophisticated vocabulary to allow the depiction of complex elements of mind, aspects of consciousness and specific psychological mechanisms to others – notions that weren't yet conceived of by then so as to begin to accrue names.

But difficulty in communication only comes up if indeed the innate restriction of mind-to-language thought conversion – immediate channeling of thoughts into words which every human inadvertently constructs while learning to speak during childhood – even allowed a highly open-minded individual to see the inner-outer Oneness with much clarity in the first place. We tend to think in words, rapidly assigning meaningful thought into grammatical structures. Grasping ideas outside the scope of accepted words is difficult enough. Formulating deeply introspective insights into reality beyond normative, common notions requires exceptional vision and open-mindedness.

In that regard, try to observe the world around you or take some action without automatically translating the initial meaning into words. Clearly the thought-value must always come first to mind, the innate meaning to objects or action perceived, before it is formulated into words. But word formation based on intent is so automatic by adulthood that separating proto-notion from constructed-language thought of it is very difficult.

Similarly, in formulating spoken statements, you first think, often quite instantaneously, of complex concepts, only then rendering them into words. At some point of early childhood, prior to learning language, you thought, recognized and understood things without channeling those impressions into words. But the ability to imagine without immediately and automatically phrasing the thought wanes well before adulthood.

Recognizing the difficulty of thinking in concepts without formulating them into words, try to take the next step: thinking of concepts for which *no words exist*. Exactly that challenge – to first think creatively or perceive aspects of reality outside standard notions – awaits the true visionary. Then, lurking in the wings, should you actually perceive reality beyond standard definitions, appears the problem of trying to explain that vision to others lacking it using only conventional words!

The greatest of ancient visionaries, unable to communicate superior perspectives directly with rather unsophisticated, certainly uneducated and likely resistant audiences, would have to depict their advanced concepts otherwise. They did so either by illustrating them as stories, i.e., incorporating the meaning into allegories or parables, or explaining to listeners how to attain their enhanced understanding: what course of study or practice was necessary to attain the greater realization...

From the East

Into Your Mind

Li-Er, known as Lao Tzu, meaning the "Old Philosopher", living some two and a half millennia ago, recognized life's flow and composed a series of illustrations in his Chinese vernacular to depict what he called the Tao, or "way" – something of a flow in life that, ineffable in itself, couldn't be explained but was there to be perceived if you could do so. His means to communicate that was by picturing it in various ways, helping the sincere seeker to see it by showing what it *wasn't*, how it might be observed in practice, etc.

In those times and in Lao Tzu's culture, there were neither words that covered aspects of psychological attribution nor images to depict them in writing. Lao Tzu was certainly aware of the interconnectedness of things wherein life flows in distinct patterns as engaged by any individual. He was certainly cognizant of interactive effects between each person and experienced reality. His means to communicate that awareness is unique, absolutely pertinent and highly meaningful even today – 100 generations downstream.

But as perceptive a visionary as he was, Lao Tzu did not seem to recognize the malleability of reality: how it modifies in outward effect in response to one's inner change. He certainly recognized the connection, and very likely understood that the very act of reading his *Tao De Ching* – thereby conceptualizing his accounts – would intrinsically spur change. But, without a background culture featuring adequate recognition of psychological attributes – and lacking a language complex enough – he could hardly make the next step: relating the Tao, the outward, flowing manifestation of life, to specific, causal, inner elements.

(Of course, without Lao Tzu's valued nudge towards greater awareness early on along my own path, I wouldn't be here two and a half millennia later, doing so either.)

Likewise, at about the same time, Siddhartha Gautama came to an advanced level of awareness while living in what is now northern India. Growing beyond Hindu notions to see life more clearly than his peers, Gautama's vision allowed him to refine that age-old basis of his culture's world view, bringing greater clarity to some fairly accurate notions of that ancient discipline.

The "Buddha", or enlightened one, was one of humanity's first to recognize the interrelatedness of all things. He emphasized, quite accurate in essence as well as practical in application, that karma is best regarded, not as carryover of negative implications from previous incarnations into this one, but as one's current nature *now*. His teachings influenced the evolution of eastern culture from his time on to ours. With eastern approaches recently gaining considerable recognition in the west, his influence has spread even wider.

But Gautama's limitation is significant as well. Although his teaching was well advanced for its time, he didn't quite pierce the illusion to recognize details of cause and effect in inner-outer pattern generation. Doubtless limited by impediments to clear vision – and communicating that perception – I've mentioned above, the Buddha integrated some flawed notions into his message.

Principally, Gautama's observation of life's flow as voiced in the Four Noble Truths is inaccurate. They are – like so many paradigmatic depictions of life – only truths from the limited scope of his bounded view...

The Buddha looked at life as saturated with suffering, seeing pain and despair in all aspects of life: birth, aging, illness, death. He interpreted intense desire, i.e., craving, to be the cause of that, such that only ending desire could lead to cessation of suffering. He offered the Noble Eightfold Path as the discipline that would lead to an end to attachment and resultant craving – thus snuffing out suffering and the need to continue the otherwise endless cycle of incarnating into miserable lifetimes.

The rationale for that, behind the scenes, was traditional Hindu recognition of personal existence as a series of incarnations from which negative actions and intent in one lifetime would carry over into the next as a trail of **karma** – where it would be re-encountered as negative aspects of life, leading to suffering. Life was seen (still is in the Hindu realm) as troubled principally because each of us is working through negative karma accumulated during previous lifetimes. So the ultimate goal of Gautama's Noble Path was to restructure negative gestures into positive ones, thus avoiding adding any new *"Kriyamana"* karma to one's store to plague subsequent incarnations.

Thus, the Noble Eightfold Path included elements such as Right View and Right Speech, Right Action and Effort, Right Speech and Intention, etc. – with the implicit recommendation that when one's impulse yields negative thinking or action, it should be countermanded by peaceful, positive thoughts or deeds. Properly practiced as recommended, the Buddha implied, the outcome of one's actions would be constructive and accepting, rather than harmful to others as underscored by greed and hatred, or aggressive, involving blame and hostility.

Within the context of his view, Gautama's suggested path would seem to be absolutely, well, *Right*. But limitations to his world view forged shortcomings to his message.

(To fully recognize shortcomings of any teaching, it is prerequisite to surpass the initiating source in clarity of awareness of life's functionality. Acceptance of the source – any great teacher or discipline – as the final, uppermost expert in understanding only serves to restrict one's own growth. This invariable outcome results from the mind's propensity to attribute validity to accepted beliefs and definitions – rather than recognizing the artificiality of such mind constructs. I could only see the short-comings of Lao Tzu's or Gautama's perspectives by having moved beyond them.)

Indeed, in this reality, life does involve suffering in many aspects – physical pain from illness and injury, emotional suffering from rejection and disregard, further misery from failure. But it also provides – or at least allows for – enormous reward in many of its aspects: creativity and accomplishment in countless avenues of life, love and acceptance by family and cherished others, budding health and good feelings, the wonders of nature and earth's beauty, of music and literature, performing arts of dance and theater, raising and nurturing of children, sports and competition, intellectual pursuits, philosophy, law and communication of stimulating ideas, to name a few. Absolutely, as the Buddha intimately recognized, a process of cause-and-effect operates at all times. But functional causality operates *now* in this moment as real events and relationships emerge into experience – but based on one's personal nature in this very time frame, not on a past which, in reality, does not exist.

The Buddha was right that karma was best regarded as one's nature in the present rather than looked upon as an accumu-lation out of the past. And he was absolutely correct that reality is always changing. But he didn't recognize the inner-outer connection as originating in, thus caused by, meaningful inner aspects of mind. Nor did he perceive that **change**, innate to life's process, revolves around reliably recurring patterns in personal experience. Rather, he interpreted causality inaccurately as stemming directly from actions or even *thoughts* – things that could be rationally corrected before emerging and thus appar-ently adding to collected karma.

And therein, **the Buddha was wrong.** His Eightfold Path will not get the adherent to the Promised Land, that state of **Nirvana** wherein one's life works right because one *is* right, because thought and action *are not causal* such that negativity cannot be corrected at that level. Both thought and action stem from deeper inner structures, elements of value and meaning lodged in the core consciousness of the experiencer. They must be addressed – and ultimately dispelled – there in the intangible subconscious in order to remove the negating or neutralizing effect.

Considering Gautama's approach, imagine encountering a threatening situation where your immediate response brews aggressive speech or damaging action toward the perceived offender. But, following the Noble Path, you intercept the negative thinking and substitute positive, pleasant thoughts in place of action detrimental to the source of that threat; having tempered that initial response, you say nothing and walk away. What would you have accomplished?

Because real events reflect your own nature, you have not disengaged the inner propensity to attract conflict, but only stifled a natural response to a current, manifested instance of it. You have also, in fact, by following the Buddha's recommendation, just laid yet another level of rational override on top of your natural response – heaped upon all the other rules and compromises already absorbed in order to fit into cultural norms of action. Because nothing changed appreciably inwardly, other such negative encounters *will happen again*.

When I discuss the inner-outer connection, I emphasize the need to cull out inner mechanisms at the root of outer problems – upon which inner cleansing the resultant patterns change for the better *so that you won't encounter such undesirable events later*.

Clearly Gautama was not aware of the deeper elements of underlying value and meaning residing in the complex, though intangible, subconscious. He saw causality as stemming from accumulated, judged action from previous incarnations, documented in some fashion in compiled akashic records somewhere. Such is not really the case. Rather the total scope of value and meaning that you comprise rests in a complex mindset held within your psyche, *in this now moment* – discernable if you go looking. That cumulative mindset combines to manifest real events and relationships, emerging as experiences that comprise the value content of its inner origin.

Still, Gautama moved the Hindu implication along somewhat, providing some clarification and insight to a long tradition that was already quite sensitive to the continuity of consciousness. It is certainly noteworthy to recognize his major contribution to mankind's recognition of its own nature.

But now it's time to move beyond limitations posed by Buddhist, Taoist, Hindu and other mystical traditions – for many a visionary has incarnated along the way since then, echoing similar notions to Lao Tzu and the Buddha. While many later sages certainly added meaningful insight to the general picture, they invariably misconstrued thought as being directly causal – a significant, though subtle distortion.

Let me be very clear on that point: *thought* is only causal *to the degree that*, with proper focus, it can be directed to pinpoint, discern and revise overall content in the complex subconscious. Only through that deeper gesture can thought influence the patterned flow of one's experienced reality.

In the same vein, as reviewed in Angle Two, thought is looked upon by eastern disciplines as the "crazy monkey", thus elevated to the status as the bad guy that clutters attention and disrupts awareness of the Oneness with which life flows. The principal gist of meditation as practiced in yogic disciplines is quelling thought by releasing it and replacing it with a mantra – thus freeing awareness to directly perceive the flow.

But, again, I emphasize: *thought is not causal.* The flow of intrusive and even reactive thoughts that occur during daily life – as opposed to specific, purposeful and quite voluntary thinking involved in creative activity or normal engagement of life's chores – results from conceptual separation of Self from Reality and the many ways one has learned to manipulate the world. That intrusive thinking will not subside by stifling thought, but rather by eliminating the notion of separation and the need to manipulate real-world elements that stem from it. Likewise, thoughts reacting to negative situations – what to do, how to respond, how to handle it – will not subside until *negative situations cease to occur* upon elimination of the inner conflict that attracted them.

To the degree that eastern traditions, influenced by Lao Tzu and Gautama, picture the Self as timeless, spanning many lifetimes and engaged in meaningful interaction with a cohesive reality, they are very helpful to personal advancement and that of mankind.

But to the extent that eastern mystical disciplines, stemming from longstanding meditation techniques via many movements and variations, seek enlightenment purely through active manipulation of thought – repressing it or overriding it with other thoughts – they miss the point. Deferring reverently to great teachers of the past precludes moving beyond the teachers' level of awareness.

From Western Thinking

Deeper Into Your Mind

Another 500 years passed before Jesus of Nazareth came along to engage yet another portion of budding humanity. Addressing a principally western audience here, I must emphasize the effect his lifetime had on the evolution of western thinking.

Becoming aware of life's inner-outer flow, ceasing to regard others as causes in your life and perceiving the flow and pattern-imparting in personal experience, you see in Jesus' teaching and healing an early awareness how life works – even as unreliably as the New Testament's Synoptic Gospels report. Parables recorded there, illustrating a "Kingdom of Heaven" – to be found *within* – reveal remarkable insight as to life's innate flow.

Jesus encountered a culture steeped in ancient lore and dogma. He tried to carry his peers from a belief in Yahweh god who was something of a small-minded, self-centered war god – a deity, which, like **all others**, only existed in the imagination of its believers – to some minimal but improved recognition of life's innate flow.

But mankind wasn't ready then. (And, if his crucifixion is accepted at face value, Jesus hadn't cleared out his own inner conflict.) So, as events played out, rather than his message of love and healing, based on perceiving this Kingdom *within*, becoming incorporated into a Jesus movement, Paul came along and changed everything. Based on his **own** vision of a Jesus-image speaking from the heavens during his swoon on the way to Damascus, Paul changed Jesus into a mythical savior figure: believe in him as this God-on-Earth figure and everything will be just fine.

Of course, everything *isn't* fine for even the truest of believers. Because the billion Christians populating the "modern" world have bought into the fantasy of Paul's myths, they can't see the reality they face daily. They continue blindly to promulgate mankind's longstanding woes – poverty, inequity, illness, prejudice, sexual inhibitions, drug reliance, environmental degradation, etc.

Much of the western mindset is built on Christian thinking. Whether or not one grows up in a religious environment, Christianity and western culture co-existed for so long that many archaic notions from that religion and its pagan precursors still dominate western thinking.

That realization leads to this vital recognition: as our ancestors along the trail of evolving western culture absorbed newer ideas, *they never really got rid of the old ones!!*

When Christianity was promoted to state religion by Constantine in the early fourth century, the subsequent spread of its tenets never eliminated older thinking. Many pagan rites were simply incorporated into Christian ritual. Easter, spring fertility rites offered to the Germanic god Ēostre became the rebirth of Jesus, complete with eggs and rabbits as fertility symbols; Christmas fit nicely into year-end gift-giving celebrations of Saturnalia and winter solstice celebrations, with Yule trees symbolizing growth coming with the sun turning from its lowest arc across the sky.

Later, as western culture moved toward scientific consideration, common thinking never abandoned superstitions like lucky charms, magic numbers, witchcraft and grossly generalized horoscopes. Indeed, common cultural notions still include many primitive attributions of causality, often in direct conflict with each other, as an immediate effect of this inability to shed archaic ideas.

But still other concepts woven into western notions – and thereby into your background understanding – draw from thinking less shackled by rote belief in a causal god, the standard feature to the mindset we've inherited.

The first significant divergence in the west from pure attribution of causality to gods came from Greek city-states roughly contemporaneous with Lao Tzu and the Buddha. It was there, due to unique advancements of civilization that yielded democratic ideals rather than the standard kingdom, that freedom of thinking allowed speculation beyond the god-in-chief model.

It's worthy to note that gods, their nature and their imagined interaction with man basically parallel local conditions and political situations throughout the ages they evolved. Egyptian gods, Osiris and Isis, plus the reborn Horus, were generally supportive and dependable, reflecting the regularity with which the Nile flooded yearly, adding silt to its shores and allowing farming reliably. Its myth featured rebirth and the sun as prominent elements reflecting dependable natural cycles.

In the Mesopotamian region, the Tigris and Euphrates flooded as well, but those events could be spontaneous, coming unpredictably from storms far off to the north. The capricious gods reflected that, with conflict woven into myths involving Enlil, later Marduk and Assur.

But in both cases and most pantheons of ancient times, gods' relationship with humans was of an authoritarian nature, very much like privileged classes ruling over the common man. Indeed, often the ruling figure inflated *himself* to divine status or god-sired offspring.

In the Greek cultures a half millennium BCE, old Indo-European gods had evolved into a rambunctious crew, with rich myth featuring spirited escapades among the unique characters of that pantheon. But expanding Greek colonies, extensive trade and the independence of many Greek city-states (as opposed to central, dictatorial powers) nurtured freer thinking and philosophical speculation.

So the unique intellectual climate of the eastern Mediterranean saw man's first meaningful attempt to explore reality and speculate about its nature. From Thales and Anaximander, looking for the base material of which all things consist, through Pythagoras and his followers, finding numbers at the base of being, to Heraclitus, likening nature's essence to fire based on its character as ever in flux, curious, seeking men began to regard reality as more than just a mystical creation of unfounded deities.

By 400 BCE, Athens became the prime locale of serious philosophy. It was Plato, coming on the heels of Socrates and leading to Aristotle's somewhat differing views, who launched significant rational exploration into what is going on here.

That examination, spurring intellectual consideration across nearly two and a half millennia, eminently deserves detailed regard.

While certainly religion formed and still forms much of our western view of ourselves and reality, it was only courageous prodding by many brilliant thinkers across time that we, as a culture, moved beyond simplistic allegiance to conceptualized gods toward better understanding. While vital that each sincere seeker remove shards of archaic thinking remaining in his/her subconscious, finding and understanding many other ideas planted there is equally important. Some need to be cherished, others deleted. But the source of them, the luminous individuals who perceived elements of nature beyond stock images of their time, should be understood as well.

As Isaac Newton famously noted, "If I have seen further, it is only by standing on the shoulders of giants." In viewing the world and ourselves in this time we call "modern", we all ride the shoulders of giants. Yet, the horizon to be seen lies still farther when *we ourselves* grow to that status and greater, standing indeed on their shoulders – rather than wallowing at their feet.

From Clear Awareness

Much Deeper

I don't deem myself a philosopher in a traditional sense. My view of reality expressed here and elsewhere is not logically derived from complex explanations put forth by the great, earlier thinkers I am about to regard, neither arrived at in agreement with them, nor launched in opposition. Indeed, I do my best to illustrate reality without even establishing a delineated model for others to agree or argue with. Specifically, all such rational paradigms *must be discarded* to clearly perceive the innate flow I repeatedly illustrate.

But I do regard life here. Looking in depth at previous philosophical notations concerning reality helps illustrate my perspective in two very important ways. First, it point outs various liberating insights introduced by great thinkers along the way – a most fascinating illustration to those who seek understanding, particularly because older, less accurate elements of belief were not typically eliminated as new ones took hold. And second, it highlights shortcomings – real fallacy and invalid claims – that influenced western thinking, often adding inaccurate notions to our modern mindset.

So I will proceed to review various fields of inquiry philosophy generally addresses. The best list of such items I have found comes from the book, *Basic Teachings of the Great Philosophers,* by S. E. Frost, Jr., so I follow his well-thought order.

The principal enabler to my journey was the early recognition of how susceptible the mind is to its own accepted notions. That conceptual bias takes hold at all levels of understanding. The very act of **recognizing that** allowed me to specifically focus on and eliminate illusory notions from my mindset – indeed to raze my belief structure completely, step by step over time. Many elements I detected and eliminated, common to our culture, were entirely founded on definitions – simple mental constructs planted in my psyche at an early age.

The greatest of philosophers, with towering, inventive intellects, seem never to have reduced conceptualizations adequately to get beyond appearances to perceive the Oneness with which reality works – but only built on favored ideas. As such, their conclusions were invariably tainted by subtle, fallacious assumptions woven into cultural notions and language itself.

As we will see, the mind-matter *apparent* duality, the main obstacle inhibiting perception of Reality's functional Oneness, caught the greatest of thinkers in the barbs of its conceptual fence. Some simply accepted the duality; many bought into a conceptualized, third-person god as principal metaphysical source to the real; others came to disregard the mind aspect as inconsequential in light of the matter side, establishing science as a rule set. Transcending conceptual impediments, I perceive the **Oneness** *of mind and matter* directly. Indeed, I illustrate precise psychic mechanisms that relate to meaningful encountered aspects of reality.

This metaphysical awareness was beyond the greatest philosophers in the trail of man's intellectual growth. But that unfettered standpoint forms my basis for regarding my predecessors' conjecture.

In one of the many books on philosophy I've encountered, the author noted that most great philosophical breakthroughs, once noted by the visionary philosopher, seem quite obvious. Prior to the brilliant observation, however, nobody had noticed the effect, so it wasn't featured in common thinking.

The founding fathers of the United States, for example, while constructing the Articles of Confederation and later the Constitution, explicitly referenced John Locke, British philosopher of a century earlier. Locke had noted that royalty, in the greater scheme of things, should have no innate call to higher status than anybody else simply due to noble birth. This thought reverberated through the inspired construction of the Constitution, such that it permeates our American attitude. Yet, prior to Locke, common thinking attributed kings and nobles inherent, god-given attributes of privilege. It took the vision of a Locke to see through that definition and formulate a creative new way of seeing the real world.

Few in my time perceive the intrinsic tie they have, by virtue of their own nature, to qualities embodied in and reflected in their real lives. In coming times, though, many more will until that perceptive nature becomes commonplace. Whatever role I play in that transition, I welcome – because mankind won't evolve past its propensity for pollution, poverty, war, drugs, abuse and hypocrisy until individuals on a wide scale do.

So, although I don't regard myself as a philosopher, I will relent long enough to function as one. That is, I will play with ideas for a while – but only to the degree that it helps get my point across: how the Oneness of life function works. The typical philosopher eventually gets lost in his ideas, moving ever farther away from life into the realm of imagination and conceptualization to where that thinker ceases to distinguish the two, losing sight of the former as it disappears behind the latter.

I won't. I only ever deal with reality. And I will repeatedly expose thinking that substitutes notions about how reality functions for how life really works.

Oh, and philosophy can be excruciatingly boring as greater and greater complexity is woven into mind models of reality. I'll solve that, too, by not treading deeply into the muck of excessive explanation of points inherently invalid to begin with.

So, on to the realm of philosophy – and you won't mind if I

reconstruct it along the way...

Point One: The Nature of the Universe

Philosophy at Its Best

The great mystics noted above, trying to communicate clearer vision, and the handful of revisionists – prophets, lesser visionaries and such – who shifted standard thinking only slightly, did precious little over the ages to wrest common thinking away from cherished gods.

Long after Zoroaster personified life's apparent struggle between good and evil as god-myth, tradition through time reduced that notion to a judgmental god, sitting up there (generally "up", as the heavens, clouded and blue or dotted with points of light, some moving, were unfathomable in concept), waiting to declare you, upon death, as having passed or failed your incarnation. Beyond Lao Tzu's reflections on the **Tao**, warning against rational opposition to life's flow, religion evolved from his insights came to discredit *any action whatsoever* as fruitless – thus rendering followers to extended meditation, frittering away an incarnation in non-activity.

Although Jesus could attain and present remarkable insights into the Kingdom of Heaven within, how it was at hand *now*, was within reach *now*, Paul and other far less visionary successors turned him into the mythical son of a virgin and god, while promoting a grand and glorious state *later*.

What surely had been a significant statement for mankind became a Monopoly-board quest: believe their bunk and be ultimately rewarded. Christianity ended up with the same primitive post-death judgment myth bandied about by Zoroastrians – complete with their Amesha Spentas (Bounteous Immortals), renamed Angels.

(By the way, ever wonder what Gabriel has been up to for the last 1400 years? He seemed pretty busy for several centuries during Biblical times, then had quite a gig, regularly delivering info to Mohammed. But, where is he now? Unemployed? Retired? Reincarnated, perhaps?)

So, over time, while religionists, the professional, philosophically closed-minded cut of mankind, clung to archaic, soap-opera maneuverings of aloof gods – resisting at all costs any degree of awareness for life's function proffered by visionaries – some few thinkers now and again chipped away at old notions.

Often at great peril to their own well-being, facing major threats posed by authoritarian religionists (or religious authoritarians) through centuries of intolerance to expression outside narrow confines, philosophers from the Greeks onward added enormous richness to our mindset. Some were remarkably close to perceiving the flow, others well off the mark. But both groups, however incorrect their notions, in emphasizing discourse and exploration, moved mankind away from standardized blinders and conformity to false but unquestioned ideas toward better understanding.

While personally, my path didn't feature much direct input from these great thinkers – I have only explored western philosophy in any depth subsequent to Clear Awareness – without them and the freedom of exploration they established, I would never, in this time frame, have been able to even undertake the journey. This culture, if relying only on religion and conformity, would still be scarcely out of the stone age, riding horses and maybe, but not for certain, scraping by on primitive agriculture.

So, how does life work? How does this complex reality we face daily function? That's easy. God (or a bunch of them) made everything (and still controls things) and you'd better buckle down, bow to the priesthood, accede to authorities and shut up with your questions.

That simplistic view, with a grand array of variations,

dominated man's view of reality for ages. For much of mankind, even now, six or eight thousand years into civilization – *it still does!!*

2600 years ago, three men of Miletus, a colony of Ionian Greeks on the western shore of Asia Minor, began speculating on what the world they encountered was made of. To Thales (c. 524 – 546 BCE), that seemed to be water and later to Anaximines (also 6th century BCE), air. Anaximander (c. 610 – c. 550 BCE), though, saw matter as parts of a living mass, a whole, that had, through motion, broken into pieces – not a bad precursor to the Big Bang theory of science, given the limited background of speculation he had to build on. Indeed, though it may now seem trite to imagine that all matter consists of simple substances like air or water, to *even consider* what constitutes matter in the first place was a major leap!

Thinking must have caught on, given the right climate. Pythagoras (c. 580 – c. 500 BCE), living in Greek colonies of southern Italy, and his school moved toward **numbers** as the commonality of things. (Interesting precursor to the computer age wherein all data is reduced to binary representation!)

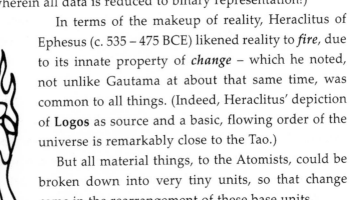

In terms of the makeup of reality, Heraclitus of Ephesus (c. 535 – 475 BCE) likened reality to *fire*, due to its innate property of *change* – which he noted, not unlike Gautama at about that same time, was common to all things. (Indeed, Heraclitus' depiction of **Logos** as source and a basic, flowing order of the universe is remarkably close to the Tao.)

But all material things, to the Atomists, could be broken down into very tiny units, so that change came in the rearrangement of these base units.

Given the limited basis of common cultural thinking out of which these men grew, with little notion of structure or substance, simply undertaking to regard the nature of reality is already impressive. But by 400 BCE, with

Plato (427 – 347 BCE) and his early exposure to Socrates (c. 469 – 399 BCE) in Athens, philosophy grew from elementary regard to conceived insight.

Socrates focused on the realm of ethics, morality and inter-action, on the very practice of dialectic and argument. He greatly influenced philosophy – but principally through his student, Plato, as he left no writings of his own.

But indeed Plato looked beyond reality's nuts and bolts towards the *qualities* of life, including its conceivable function-ality. He recognized the illusory nature of reality, illustrating it brilliantly in his Allegory of the Cave. In conceptualizing the essence of things, he placed their base nature *behind* real objects of substance. Plato saw beyond each real item an ideal "form" of which all real objects were simply instances, not substantial at all, but mere copies of the perfect ideal.

(Many fascinating perspectives are available for all thinkers referenced here. For readers unfamiliar with them who want to learn more about these philosophers' ideas, do look them up. I can only regard specific features of their messages pertinent to the point in focus – indeed, this is *not* a detailed philosophical analysis so much as an illustration of evolving ideas and how they may or may not be pertinent to reality and the western mindset.)

Aristotle (384 – 322 BCE) could not separate the ideal, this form or "universal" from the object itself, but saw them appearing always together, there, *in* the real object. In bringing together both Plato's ideal and the Atomists' real substance, he felt that both matter and form were found together in the real item.

These differing core notions from two of mankind's greatest thinkers eventually established alternate ways of perceiving reality that would influence all subsequent debate. When Christianity later firmly gripped western thinking, it tried desperately to reconcile belief in the Christian god with

Aristotelian and/or Platonic understanding. It presented its conceptualized "God" as the principal creator, the unmoved Mover, the First Cause or *"Demiurge"* conceived by Plato. It looked, in effect, to define the "form" behind the object, not as an innate ideal, but as a thought in this deity's mind.

From ancient Greek times, rife with imaginative thinkers and various schools of philosophy – e.g., the Skeptics (questioning the ability to actually *know* anything), Stoics (through ethical regard, they maintained self-control and superimposed happiness in the face of seeming powerlessness) and Epicureans (focusing life on contentment and happiness) – until Christianity's emergence as a dominant religion, there had been considerable insight into many aspects of life. Aristotle's wide contribution to logic, math, metaphysics, ethics, etc., formed a body of thinking that strongly influenced early Islam as well as all subsequent western thinking. Plato's ideas re-echoed as Neo-Platonism in Plotinus' teaching in the third century CE.

But from Augustine of Hippo (354 – 430) onward, that is, from about 400 CE through 1600, much of the quest for understanding reality and man's engagement of it froze solid – stuck to the side of frigid religious thinking. (Of course, once Christianity gained the inside track based on political clout, subsequent to Constantine anointing it state religion, it didn't need to reconcile its fantasy with any other ideas – although by the mid-13th century, Thomas Aquinas was still trying.)

Where Plato had sought an expression to illustrate the value-essence of a thing, seeing its **ideal** as a **form** apart from the real, apparent object, Augustine placed that value squarely in the mind of a grand and glorious conceptualized entity. And for much of the ensuing millennium and more, western man no longer considered examining reality to any great degree for understanding, but looked to recycled ideas and their attendant illusions for his favored definitions.

On rare occasions through the Middle Ages, an original

thinker did appear on the scene, but Thomas Aquinas wasn't one of them. It's always obvious, from my standpoint perceiving life's interactive Oneness, to see the specific pointed intent of any thinker trying to retrofit cherished ideas into arguments supporting pre-accepted notions. Thomas, likely an intelligent and well-educated individual (for his time), had to twist and contort to fit a view of reasonable breadth into the narrow god fantasy that constituted his conviction.

(One sees that effect regularly in current times as evangelical Christians or political Republicans construct a banal argument to promote one of their fantasies, a non-workable premise or a favored stance on anything meant to enrich a special interest. Their policy statement is generally a real twist of meaning, convoluted if not fallacious in construction but always repeated continuously such that it works on those predisposed to think the same way or unable to see the fallacy. So it is successful sometimes – particularly in localized, typically rural regions – at nurturing enough support to be implemented, even though the policy, when applied, never works.)

When original thinking does finally reemerge, Francis Bacon (1561 – 1626) and René Descartes (1596 – 1650) began to move regard of reality into a more considered light. Bacon pushed toward empiricism: understanding what's out there necessitates **exploring** what's out there in some depth. Descartes leaned toward rational regard, i.e., reasoning, for reliable under-standing. Bacon's move toward scientific inquiry was continued by Thomas Hobbes, while men such as Galileo began the practice in earnest – often enough to the consternation of the powerful church. Descartes, a mathematician as well as philosopher, saw the universe as mechanical, finding in substance and motion, even in mind, definable qualities – though he couldn't release the concept of God behind it all, nor could he adequately requite mind vs. matter.

For Benedict Spinoza (1632 – 1677), by the mid-17th century, the God notion became osmotic – spreading throughout all things. Where Christian thinking has always tended to view its God as a character removed from the universe he created, Spinoza's pantheistic view saw god embedded in all things within the universe.

About that time in England, John Locke (1632 – 1704) began to question how we can really know what is out there, given the limitations of our senses. Understanding the world, Locke noted, is limited by how we can perceive it. Still Locke recognized *something* out there, but settled his ultimate image into a duality, not unlike Descartes, of *matter and mind*, two disconnected aspects. For countryman George Berkeley (1685 – 1753), by the early 18th century, the material world was only a consequence of ideas – thoughts in the mind of the perceiver or of God. Thus, it didn't really exist, **except** as perceived. Shortly, David Hume (1711 – 1776), ever the skeptic, was to eliminate all but the ideas *themselves*, dumping God **along with** matter. Whatever ideas were proposed, he tended to refute. To him, all that existed were *the ideas themselves*.

Meanwhile, a significant body of German thinking was evolving as well, along some similar lines, but with different flavor – much, I might note, as German Lager differs from English Ale. In regards to consideration of the Nature of the Universe, the Deutsch side will be considered shortly. But as to Reality…

When humans, however wise and intelligent, look at Reality for the purpose of understanding what is out there and how it works, the tendency has always been to consider from the tip of the nose outward, used to, as most of us are, peering out from a substantiated Self, locked into the visual field from a vantage point seemingly lodged within the eyes. Those thinkers regarding objects and their interactive motions in trying to make sense of reality, typically neglect two significant elements innate to the very process of regarding: one, that the Self is ever-present in the scene of consideration, and, two, that any consequent interpretation of what exists in the field of sensory encounter rests on a considerable background of understanding.

From Thales through Plato and on to the most recent inquisitive toddler, we all come to see the encountered world not as it is – a problem Locke and others have noted on a physical level regarding limits of sensory perception – and not even really **how it seems to be** to that perception. Rather, people see and understand reality *as they were taught to*. Aristotle, Locke, Kant and all others passed through childhood, absorbing cultural definitions replete with their underlying assumptions. Principal within those assumptions, encompassing all modes of interpretation, is an almost default *separation* of objects from the central, perceiving self, the integral position the observer looks out from.

Plato saw an object as simply an imperfect instance of the ideal *form* that exists in some fashion behind it. But indeed that form was, in the gist of his statement, only an idea itself, a notion hosted in the *mind of Plato* that defined it. Certainly, a brilliant thinker, his consideration of that object entailed recognizing the object as an isolated entity itself. Pondering an ideal image behind it, somewhere or other, was merely a conceptualization reached by, first, disregarding the self in the picture, second, disregarding the context in which that object existed, and third, conjuring up something not really there by defining its boundaries.

Furthermore, the "form", that item's idealized essence, existed only in the imagination *of Plato*, lodged there as a conceptualized notion, a named thing he had once learned to perceive while a child.

Aristotle saw things differently, but similar in approach. He regarded the ideal, the *form*, as though it were *within the object* itself. The expression is different, carrying an alternate philosophical ramification, but the gesture by the man was equivalent, indicating a concrete nature to the object in itself (whether hypothetical or real) but neglecting the observer and context in his conjecture – and significantly, interpreting that and any object as inherently existing unconnected to the observer.

The two interpretations split off within subsequent philosophy a long-term differentiation of regard. In the eyes of Descartes and Bacon, one view ultimately disregarded the existence of the *form* altogether, while totally ignoring the ever-present observer. In the other line of thinking, the thought-image, that form ideal behind real instances of objects became a mind-image placed in the imagined mind of a fantasized God.

Reality Beyond the Notion

In Reality, all objects within the field of perception are elements of a *cohesive whole*, not isolated units of self-contained, bounded matter. Gestures by these early thinkers, however fascinatingly conceived and brilliantly depicted, are only ever word descriptions that represent a visually isolated item. The object itself, its essence and base of existence, all find being only within the meaning of that item's use within its context, its functional nature particularly in terms of its impact on the observer.

So both lines of thought, Platonic and Aristotelian, which each evolved into more elaborate mind-imagery during centuries of debate and enhanced conceptualization, were founded on the *illusion* that an object, any object within the field of perceived reality, exists intrinsically and can be discussed as such – ultimately to be detailed, measured, categorized and otherwise compartmentalized.

Further, that situation – regard of an object as an isolated entity – has led to elaborate paradigms at the foundation of majestic schemes of thinking that are really only **grandiose ideas**, not clarifying the absolute function of Reality, but merely building ever grander schemes of more convoluted conceptualization.

Greatest among these bloated depictions are god-definitions. Just as Plato and Aristotle initiated ideas – notions seeming to them and many others thereafter as valid – subsequent generations interwove those philosophers' original arguments into their traditional projection of creative power out to imagined sources: the fantasy of one or more deities.

The gist of Aristotle's line of thinking, affixing *form* – an object's idealized notion – into that object itself, led to empirical regard for reality as a collection of isolated objects. Fostered by Bacon in concept, philosophy headed full bore onto a track it's never really left – the default assumption of science that reality consists of a collection of particles and the interacting bodies they comprise. True, modern philosophy appreciates an approach that incorporates human values and ethics into its

model. But essentially much of that is done more because it is emotionally pleasing than because the model supports it.

In any case, both notions, that of a god-driven reality and that of an isolated object reality – one embodied in western religions, the other in science – while intimately intertwined in modern man's self regard and psychological resting point, are both inherently *false*.

The dichotomy of mind and matter, an apparent separation of object from mind-image of the perceiver, is not an essence, a cornerstone attribute of reality noted by many philosophers from Descartes onward, but only an impression formulated in the mind that has learned it along with many other features of traditional western understanding. The mind – mine, yours or anybody else's, from the dullest clod to the most brilliant thinker – is intimately connected to all phenomena it encounters, linked in meaning tied to the real element's role in the experience of the mind engaging it. That intimate, inviolable tie, with its inner roots and outer, corresponding consequences in imprinted, recurring patterns, has been abundantly illustrated in Angle Two.

To regard, quickly and finally, that longstanding tradition of one or more gods driving reality: a thorough examination, however pointedly it seeks one, never finds such a divine entity anywhere but in the imagination. For all the untold volumes of ancient lore, of philosophical explanation, of sacrosanct dogma and myth-strewn legend, of art and music and poetry dedicated to conceptualized deities, no single god is found anywhere outside the thoughts of a true believer.

In exploring the teachings of great philosophers and their religious environments, I've encountered many a rational argument for and against the existence of a god.

Arguments *against* typically question how a benign god could allow or include evil and widespread suffering in man's experience, particularly impacting devout believers who do all required of them by sacred dictates and theology, yet suffer physically and emotionally. Other lines of thinking question how an omnipotent, all-powerful creator god, who must know all consequences of all its creation, could judge its human creations for performance – based on attributes that deity would have incorporated in them in the first place.

Typical arguments *for* the existence of a god generally pinpoint the Christian creator god (named God) replete with assumed attributes of ultimate, unbounded power and knowledge. They look at the enormous complexity of reality – its many interactive, interdependent elements – and postulate it could only have come into being by design, instigated by creative intelligence. Fair enough conclusion, as indeed, Reality embodies complex, interwoven meaning – including enormously complex biological function at all levels – in its many elements. But that intelligent source is invariably – and fallaciously – presumed to be *some other entity* than the Self, some grand and glorious, preconceived deity.

Both arguments, blind to the background, artificial set of assumptions they rest on, consist of superficial mind games, worded pseudo-rationales that seem to address a critical issue, but really only promote a foregone point of view of the proposer, whether skeptic or believer.

One need only regard the real world faced daily with adequate personal insight to observe its interrelated function and its tie back to the one doing the observing, the Self – you, for instance – who encounters it. As illustrated throughout earlier parts of this book, meaningful patterns are repeatedly created by each individual throughout a lifetime. The patterns always reflect propensities of the psyche, such that change introduced within the mindset yields subsequent, responsive change to the quality of experienced events and relationships.

In that process, all objects and other participants in experiential encounters combine to produce outcomes that embody specific values. Inwardly, the psyche contains a broad array of memories, potential and expressed feelings, specific mechanisms reflective of definitions held, impressions absorbed and processed and an array of other intangible elements all of which contain pointed propensities for those same values. There exist thus, two realms of encounter: the outer and inner. Both aspects embody the *same set of values*. And in a constant, corresponding flow, unfolding day-in and day-out, the outer manifests to realize, and thus fulfill, the value scheme of the inner.

Classically, these two have been interpreted as a *mind-matter duality*. Few have seen their connection, and most of those who have did so in fleeting glimpses rather than ongoing perception. Invariably, those fleeting glimpses have been contorted and compromised by deeply seeded bias of pre-held religious notions.

But the two relate in essential and specific ways I've illustrated. In neither is found an external power source. In the realm of matter, the outer, visible universe, no substantial, third-person entity floats out there approximating a deity – and with various instruments, man can peer into vast portions of the cosmos. In the realm of mind, the inner, the only god to be encountered is one anticipated based on preconceived notions, generally in some humanized form, and pictured in that absolutely flexible portrait field of *imagination*.

So including a deity as external cause in any philosophical paradigm requires a pre-conceived, previously accepted notion of that entity, and only exists as a fully imagined idea, merely made apparent by the belief itself.

And the supposed *objective* nature of the outer realm – pictured by science – is rendered to appear so, again, only by notions hosted within the psyche depicting it in that fashion. Matter lacks the apparent substance it would seem to consist of: sub-atomic particles have no solid body. They are mostly open space containing probability-oriented energy fields with associated forces capable of reflecting light – which also has no appreciable real essence to it. The substance-energy field outer reality consists of is simply not the collection of hard, integral objects it appears to be – an illusory appearance generated, again, by held beliefs.

Rather, the outer, the real, consists of malleable quantities absolutely interconnected in precisely the fashion that realizes inner propensities of the perceiving conscious entity. The outer and inner are inherently conjoined, with the outer a result, a manifested effect, of the inner complex of value and meaning.

What Is

What really exists, then, is a Consciousness/Reality Singularity wherein values held within manifest outwardly in a constant flow of events and relationships that fulfill inner propensities.

It is that simple.

The vast physical universe exists as an unbounded background on which to play out those events. It consists of matter, which is *not* the objective, inert, energy-mass, particle-based solidity it appears to be. Rather, substance emerges constantly into this "effect" continuum, the physical realm; it consists of significant entities from a sub-atomic scale through atomic and molecular scales on up to huge collections in stars and galaxies. But each focal item appears only when defined as an object and looked on as an entity unto itself. It functions in absolute collaboration with its context, fulfilling inner elements of the engaging individual, in meaningful episodes. Each element, though – isolated artificially by considering it separately – entails consciousness in its unique way and functionality within its local and overall context.

OK, so it wasn't quite that simple. Remember, I'm trying to phrase this in understandable terms when you are used to viewing matter and reality in conventional terms wherein consciousness is an attribute of brain function.

Three critical points there:

1. Consciousness permeates all matter, with quality, scope and effect dependent on scale and context.
2. Quality-essence of matter varies greatly according to hierarchical level.
   - Each body cell has its own individual consciousness, yet you ride the collective as an overall consciousness. Likewise, each molecule has its conscious properties, as does each atom, quark, string or however else they

might be subdivided.

- ✓ You don't know what each cell knows even though each of them in your body is fully aware of its role and its environment.
- ✓ They don't know the details of your life's content, but they respond intimately to your mindset, functioning in concert properly responding to trust and confidence, failing or dying in response to fear, conflict, powerlessness and other inner negation.

- Reality **consists of** an interrelated Oneness but in pure *being* corresponds in philosophical terms to *neither...*
  - ✓ *Monism*, where reality is regarded as a single substance – although it functions as such and is connected, it is collective in effect, not purely, simplistically a single entity.
  - ✓ Nor *Pantheism* in classical philosophical terms. No separate, conscious super-self functionally overrides your personal engagement. So the very notion of an **external** god of which all the universe consists or is a part is fallacious.

- You engage Reality in a higher, more complex hierarchical perspective than, for example, yeast cells or squirrels. But the functionality is equivalent: each entity engages a real situation, equipped to thrive, able to sense and evaluate all necessary elements of its environment, driven to succeed and bound to die.

3. Matter does not exist as purely objective stuff, but as values manifesting in a now moment, oriented to fulfill metaphysical propensities of the experiencer.

Of course, while quite simple in function, life's complexity outtrumps simplicity due to vast, interwoven intricacy of the mind encountering a realm replete with enormous potential of activity and engagement incorporated into all facets of life. And the apparent complexity evokes manifold increase through many invalid beliefs, definitions and assumptions the mind may hold that not only cloud the view, but weave insidious elements into the mix.

Most people would readily accept that dreams consist of meaningful elements within the symbolic dream context. The kaleidoscope of morphing objects and settings rather obviously reflects meaning and value residing within the psyche. Few, though, speculate that dream figures consist of atoms and interactive objects that obey the laws of physics. My point is that Reality itself functions much more like a dream, with its constituent elements – events and relationships – symbolically reflecting the Self, than anything remotely like an objective realm with isolated, bounded matter interacting without intrinsic meaning.

Not Recognizing What Is – Only Seeing What Is Thought To Be

In general, the Greeks, that first batch of curious seekers to actually regard reality, missed the inner-outer connection – although Heraclitus, with his *Logos* as a determinative flow, came close.

Noted thinkers who followed the early Greeks tended to get caught up in ideas, had trouble communicating their elevated perspective and/or simply had no sincere, significant audience to address...

- **Jesus'** highly insightful message about the Kingdom of Heaven within was ignored by Paul and other small-minded – if well-meaning, which they certainly weren't always – followers in succeeding centuries. They failed to grasp his meaning and launched a movement that negated the very gist of his intent. The religion formed around Jesus' conjectural divine status draws heavily from Zoroastrianism, basically ignoring what the real human said. (Jesus of Nazareth, Galilee, 4 BCE – 30 CE)

- **Plotinus** came a long way, seeing the Oneness in multiple episodes. His accounts, compiled from essays into the *Enneads*, illustrated a supreme, transcendent "One". (Plotinus, probably of Egypt, 204 – 270 CE)
  - ✓ But Plotinus didn't relate the *One* back to the experiencing Self as source.
  - ✓ His orientation and expression were too reflective of Plato, too reverent to and tied up in that older message, and, in any case, lacked impact on subsequent thinking.

- **Augustine**, far too embedded in Christian fallacy, only helped solidify fantasy into what would become centuries-long cluelessness. (Augustine of Hippo, 354 – 430)
  - ✓ A great, if confined, thinker, Augustine was an early example of "Scholasticism", a movement within medieval universities employing *reason* to insert the square peg of theology into the round hole of philosophy.
  - ✓ I have to wonder how he could have contributed to western thinking if not so constrained by Christian shackles.

- Ditto **Anselm**. Noted for his fight with the crown of England, his ontological argument for the existence of God was like others noted above – prefixed to support something imaginary that was already accepted. Anselm at least embraced reason for some support of church doctrine, but couldn't get past his own mind-image of the Christian deity to actually deal with reality.

(Anselm of Canterbury, 1033 – 1109)

- **Roscelin** helped end *universals* (that is, *forms*, Plato's mind-image ideal behind real objects) and establish a path towards objective notions. Also, Roscelin was involved in controversy over his thoughts on the Christian Trinity – a longstanding debate about whether the Father, Son and Holy Spirit were one and the same substance or separate entities. He held the latter view and got bitten by church dogma. (Roscelin of Compiègne, c. 1045 – c. 1120)
    - ✓ Any debate before or after Roscelin about the existence of forms as anything but names is really moot: neither Realists nor Nominalists are correct. In essence, independent objects are as illusory as imagined forms behind them.
    - ✓ Of course, all three Trinity elements are only ideas, having *neither* substance nor intrinsic significance.
- **Abélard** affected medieval thinking, though it seems as much through his romantic liaison with his student Héloïse as via his outlook. But he did succeed in reducing acceptance of Realism – something of an accomplishment – and gained a reputation as a debater of his philosophical positions. (Pierre Abélard, 1079 – 1142)
    - ✓ Debate prowess is only reflective of quick intellect, as debate can **never take place** about *how reality functions* – only about **ideas** as to how life works. Reality works as it does, an inner-outer flow of meaning, regardless of how it is perceived by any given person. Dialectic intercourse can only bandy about synthetic notions built on conceptualizations.
    - ✓ And dexterity at debate does not solidify veracity of an argument: good debaters can convincingly present either side.

- **Averroës** advocated "existence precedes essence" as a tenet. While Averroës was an impressive contributor to several areas of thought – astronomy, physics, politics, medicine – his philosophical stance was steeped in incorrect assumptions. His claims that religion and philosophy have no inherent conflict were overly idealistic. (Ibn Rushd, Andalusia [Muslim Spain], 1126 – 1198)
  - ✓ Of course, religion looks to preconceived definitions as a starting point, while, at least theoretically, philosophy looks for valid observation or rational argument from which to draw meaning.
  - ✓ As to whether essence or existence comes first, the argument is not unlike the chicken-egg quandary, but with less playfulness. The emergence of real effects is ongoing, as is the mind that encounters them. As mind changes, so reality follows. But neither "precedes" the other, nor could in an ongoing *now* moment of continuous manifestation and encounter. *Meaning*, i.e., value encased in unfolding events and relationships, does emerge into the outer as response to the inner, *after* its conceptual establishment within. But once manifested, it is experienced; any consequence of change in the psyche following that encounter can just as easily be seen as coming after. Both thus exist continuously and can only be viewed as qualitatively preceding *each other*.
- **Maimonides**, a Jewish philosopher whose ideas, influential within Judaism, were more widely accepted after his death, offered negative arguments to support the existence of his god. Such "Apophatic" theology describes what god supposedly *isn't*, rather than define what he, or more accurately, *it*, is. (Moses ben Maimon,

Cordoba/Egypt, 1135 – 1204)

✓ Interesting approach and an easy way out for not appearing obviously incorrect – one can always phrase things to leave murky positive images without claiming them true.

✓ But his and similar arguments are not taken far enough. No god depicted, either positively via grand claims or negatively through unspecified implications, really exists. Whatever mind games are played with logical or grammatical ploys, the god held by Maimonides inhabited his psychic imagery, not this reality.

• **Thomas Aquinas** was highly influential in refining Catholic theology – but mostly after he died. His ideas, expressed much in defense of standard dogma against the growing popularity of Averroism and a rebirth of Aristotelianism (although he himself seemed rather Aristotelian in whatever thinking he did outside the Christian-god paradigm), were early on deemed not in line with standardized thinking, but later became accepted – thus *influencing* that standard image – to the degree that he was made a saint. (Thomas of Aquin, c. 1225 – 1274)

✓ Dying seems to be helpful in establishing one's points. Personally, I intend to pursue the alternative strategy first, but keep death as a viable backup plan.

✓ Overall, Thomas's thinking was religious in nature – so dominated by the third-person creator source that his influence only served to refine the illusion. Curiously, though, while Thomas spent his life recycling the Christian conceptualized god, he had an epiphany very late in life, a mystic experience upon which he realized that all he had written had been, in his own characterization, "mere straw". He would have done well to have lived long enough to sweep out the straw.

✓ By accepting Thomas's ideas as valid enhancements of official understanding, the church tacitly acknowledged that everything it propounded for centuries prior *was inaccurate!*

- **Eckhart** had a certain vision of the "unity", but projected that into an external god-image. Still, in a fashion, Eckhart was looking for God-ness within the Self, rather than way up and out there somewhere. His thinking was thus not consigned to mainline church dogma, and he had gumption to actually express some of his ideas during his Dominican career. Ultimately and predictably, the church's political clout in his time led to significant backlash. (Eckhart von Hochheim, "Meister Eckhart", c. 1260 – 1328)

- **Duns Scotus** of the Franciscan order put forth a quite complex proof that God exists and an argument, not quite equal in convolution, for Mary's Immaculate Conception. A line of thinking, Scotism, grew out of his writings, though this notions are akin to previous ideas rather than original. (John Duns Scotus, Scotland, 1266 – 1308)

  ✓ Not to be confused with the Virgin Birth of Jesus, Mary is fantasized as having been conceived in her mother's womb, although through intercourse, without the stain of original sin – despite absolutely no mention of this in the Gospels. (Traditional religionists seem to have a big problem with sex.)

  ✓ It's interesting to imagine how these logical arguments played out in medieval minds, but the gesture is impressive in itself: how a preconceived notion (also immaculately preconceived, I suppose) can spur an intelligent individual to concoct the justification of its validity – when it is only based on a fantasy. In any case, typical of philosophical output of his age, his arguments – ideas far removed from reality – recycle foregone conclusions into proofs of premises.

- **Wycliffe** strongly protested various excesses of the Catholic Church and its popes, expressing ideas not so much inconsistent with Biblical presentation, but out of line with official sanctioned thinking. While his extensive teachings and determined intent for reformation had a lasting effect, particularly on later events as western thinking began to outgrow medieval dogma, Wycliffe's core thinking revolved around standard Christian definitions. He was determined in his approach to follow the Bible rather than narrowly confined interpretation of it. (John Wycliffe, c. 1326 – 1384)
  - ✓ He would have been far better off, philosophically if not politically, to regard *life* and jettison the Bible *along with* fossilized dogma of Catholic thinking.
  - ✓ What stood as ultimate truths to Wycliffe were only complex notions, definitions he had accepted, just as with most thinkers of his (or any) time period. Still, any rebellion against dictatorial thinking was a significant step.
- **William** of Ockham, strongly Nominalist (didn't accept forms), rather pioneered the launch toward real science by advocating that only **items** exist – not universals, forms, nor essences. His famous "Razor" precludes explanations that carry excess entities beyond the minimum needed to explain something's nature. However, his basis was, true to his time, God. (William of Ockham, c. 1290 – 1348)

✓ Proper application of his insight would have eliminated God, too. What exists is the Self and a reality
that consists of realized, meaningful elements of the
Self – no god, independent objects, forms, universals,
existences or essences, all of which are either ideas or
deceivingly parsed pieces of a contiguous whole
reality.

✓ Ockham also advocated an early notion of separation
of church and state, a vital situation for any
individual to outgrow church nonsense without
facing official retribution – which indeed, he
personally did via excommunication.

Not a whole lot of visionary, deeply insightful thinking there,
through those centuries. I suppose, had I been living in agrarian
Western Europe with little intellectual stimulus, faced with
torture or ostracism, encountering few open-minded peers and
no infrastructure through which to communicate, I might not
have been so ready to voice my clearer perspectives either.
Hmmm... More than that, I couldn't have incarnated in that
environment – or wouldn't have lasted long, had I done so.
Pointing out in front of my local preacher where Christianity
was obviously wrong, as I did in a talk for a luncheon group at
the age of about 12, would have likely curtailed my venture early
on.

While Greek philosophers had searched for greater understanding, thereby opening mankind to an examination beyond
traditional myth, the best of them inadvertently set up definitions that, for better or worse, greatly influenced subsequent
thought for centuries. Both Plato, with his reference to an ideal
form existing for each iteration of real-world thing, and
Aristotle, who integrated the form notion into each object itself,
established ideas that subsequent thinkers – such as those listed

above – adopted in several ways:

- They tried to twist their traditional belief-based, myth-structured notions of religion to fit one or the other of those philosophers' notions.
  - ✓ Generations attempted to justify Christianity within Platonic bounds, imagining his forms to be thoughts in their conceptualized god's mind.
  - ✓ Even Islam, early on, incurred attempts to rectify its propositions to Aristotle's.
- They expanded on the original idea to create more complex definitions.
  - ✓ Plato's forms became "universals", taking on their own meaning in ever expanding conceptualizations.
  - ✓ *Essence*, which to Plato originates in forms, only to find *existence* in iteration – real things imperfectly copying their forms – while to Aristotle essence lies within things themselves, came to be debated as preceding existence or resulting from it. (Neither, as I mentioned, is accurate.)
  - ✓ The integral ideal of Aristotle implied validity to objects as inherently existing, isolated things, thus leading ultimately to science, which ignores the inner realm of consciousness in favor of exclusive regard of the outer.
- They rebutted one or the other idea, creating in the process other paradigms of growing conceptual complexity.

To examine any explanation describing how life works, this simple but exceptionally profound insight is vital: if it rests on a *single point* for its overall veracity, when that point is invalid, the *whole idea* is rendered fallacy.

Consider Islam as an example. As all religions, Islam claims to explain reality – asserting exclusivity as well. It describes a creator god, claiming the Koran as direct revelation from that deity, inimitable and unquestionable in its entirety due to the perfection of its divine source.

Given the absolute nature of that claim and Allah's presumed perfection, even a *single* inaccurate or demonstrably invalid proposition within the text renders the work **false** – in its entirety. Yet, the Koran includes **many** blatant internal contradictions: declarations in one sura that disagree with those in others, mistakes in mathematics, incorrect attributions, political statements coming obviously from Mohammed rather than from Allah – and many other flaws.

In appraising validity, proclamations of value found there are **immaterial**. That a billion people hold the Koran in esteem is **irrelevant**. Self-contradicting statements reveal that the Koran is not the expression of a perfect source! Such flaws render absolute doubt not only on the book, but on its god and the whole religion. An intellect that can't get simple facts straight could hardly have created such a vast, interconnected universe.

Similarly, however brilliantly Plato and Aristotle regarded various aspects of life, however well-versed and intellectually astute have been subsequent philosophers and scientists in enhancing Platonic and Aristotelian notions, however many movements, supporters, believers, air-tight arguments and rational thought structures have evolved from their initial notions, if their proposed paradigm for reality rests on an invalid assumption, all rational construction layered atop crumbles in cascading *invalidity*.

Likewise, propositions of external entities, deities of any sort – who don't really exist, but only seem to because some humans believe so – have tainted man's regard of reality for ages, Allah, God and a thousand others included. But proving to closed-minded believers that no such god exists is impossible: their core understanding – along with self-esteem, value structure and world view – rests on **just that notion,** one learned early in life and thus undergirded by bubbly good feelings of motherly care and infallibility. That god-notion, calcified by fear and petrified by definitions that preclude questioning, can be so affixed that it isn't even worth the effort to attempt rebuttal.

But firm dedication to conceptualized gods is superseded by an even deeper-seated definition to which more sincere seekers fall prey.

The illusion of an objective reality rests fully on the core notion that real objects and living entities are innate, existing unto themselves. An objective reality, whether its component objects sport forms separate and apart from them or contained within, underlies as a key assumption the philosophical model of all propositions from Plato's time until now. That's the case, although more subtle, even when some stated paradigms recognize the interrelated nature of all things. The very application of a word to an object – conceptually attaching a voiced or written symbolic representation of an object to the item itself – embedded since early toddling time, has built a core implication *that the object inherently exists* as a base understanding into the world view of the vast majority of mankind.

In this regard, to render western philosophy's greatest components invalid in a single sweep – epistemology, empiricism, axiology, natural science to a degree, psychology in its implication of separation, all attempts at theology, certainly both Nominalism and Realism, mathematics in its practical implications and much more – I need only reveal the innate fallacy of that core implication: that reality is objective in nature.

It isn't.

Consciousness and Reality are inherently connected, like the ends of a magnet or two sides of a coin: one can't exist without the other. And the connection is found at a level of values – not raw substance – for Reality engenders meaning, as interpreted by the Consciousness that encounters it.

So all of the above thinkers, key visionaries in mankind's evolving understanding, are wrong in the images they concocted and propounded: first, because most bought into traditional cultural notions that third-person gods exist (or affixed an alternate name for one), and second, because they regarded the world as a realm full of real objects.

Any god or gods imagined as causing real events are built on beliefs and reinforced by the mind's tendency to confirm its pre-accepted definitions. Hence, any philosophical model featuring such a source is simply invalid. Ditto for objective paradigms.

Consciousness *creates* the reality it encounters. All objects, people, actions and events fit into that cohesive flow as encountered by any individual. And its meaningful outcome is caused, not by some external creator, but by value expectancies innate to the experiencer.

Before I move on to the track of German philosophy, where this innate Consciousness-Reality interdependence found some recognition, I would add another key point:

I cannot argue the invalidity of broad branches of philosophy

to the intellectual realm of academic adherents who, through long ivy-covered tradition, hold to the various studies that I abruptly neuter here. They won't be sensitive to illustrations of Oneness in a real sense – as opposed to convoluted academic banter – any more than religionists gleefully respond to my dismissal of their favorite, fantasized deity.

Argument, indeed, doesn't fall within my technique of communication.

All reasoned argument *itself* – as an endeavor of discourse intended to clarify things – falls within the confines of common belief systems and complex logical constructs shared by individual philosophers voicing it and those listening. We all learn to see the world through base constructs of cultural notions, parental indoctrination and language bias. So any and all conclusions reached as to reality's function arise from world views held by individuals engaging it. That personally held philosophy rests on accepted paradigms contained in belief structures that resulted from early definition establishment and subsequent learning.

So any argument, to be convincing within a philosophical discussion, would have to stand upon common underlying notions. My point is that those underlying conceptual props, common to western thinking and on which all modern philosophical conjecture stands, *are themselves fallacious*, a status which thus renders the superstructures invalid!

In coming to perceive that Oneness with which reality unfolds, via an extended inner journey lasting decades, I scoured my psyche of all the common cultural notions that most contemporaries still hold. So I don't present **arguments** based on common logic, leveraging my conclusions vs. others' firmly founded impressions. I simply explain how life looks from the standpoint of Clear Awareness – seeing reality *without the belief system* to interfere with perception.

Ein Wurst und ein Bier – and Some Good Ideas

Heir to English-speaking tradition and its accompanying mindset, I've kept focus thus far mostly on the track of philosophy that ran from Greek through British thinkers, with some French and other continental contribution. Through the course of the Renaissance, from the 14th through the 17th centuries, as education became more common, spurred by exploration and trade, etc., thinking opened up considerably. While Europe was maturing in many facets of civilized interaction (like wars), pointed query for exploring and explaining reality became possible.

But, for whatever products, services, conflict and attitudes were shared across language barriers, complex philosophical regard was somewhat isolated. Absent translation of significant works between English-, French- and German-speaking countries – and all the others – there seems to have been little collaboration among universities in various countries, so that ideas weren't so readily exchanged – until later, when various schools of thought could actually communicate. (Of course, the outcome then wasn't necessarily pure exchange of enlightened perspectives, but multiplied argument over inaccurate conceptualizations.)

So isolated, philosophy took a track in Germany that explored some aspects of reality not quite broached by other schools. Entering this realm, it is important to note a different cultural attitude among various European peoples – characteristics observable in America from the influence various European ethnic groups left in traditions, etc., but whose impact has been diluted by a grand wash of so many different cultural influences in American tradition.

The German culture by its own tradition – so far as one can rely on generalities to illustrate a broad situation – has always valued knowledge and respected academia and expertise. Within the German ethic common thinking relies on rules, promoting an implicit group-effort to achieve order – and implement efforts towards improvement to *accomplish* that ordered situation.

This mentality has led Germany to great accomplishments in technology, music and many other avenues of life. It has also ushered a few negatives into the unfolding of history.

But for whatever minuses on the account books, the plusses are significant. It's impossible to imagine music, technology, science, structured economic systems or the quality of beer, without the German people and their collective mindset. The traditional German attitude toward philosophy falls in line with those major contributions on the plus side.

In a fashion, the American culture idolizes mediocrity. The base attitude of prizing equality seems to translate unconsciously into promoting the middle range of things while disdaining excellence. Perhaps that rests on the rebelliousness that launched our country, as hordes of middle- and lower-class ethnic immigrants brought their attitudes with them. Perhaps striving toward superiority as an inherent trait defiles equality as a goal. For whatever reason, the American media and thus public discourse is dominated by subjects devoid of intellectually stimulating and life-enhancing themes. Movies highlight big explosions and superficial good-guy/bad-guy conflict where neither group is really distinguishable from the other. Superior intellectual gesture is looked upon as elitist, where meaningless flaunting of beauty and money – which really *is* elitist – is prized.

In Germany, though, by tradition, the focus of attitude is somewhat elevated. Academia and education in general is traditionally prized and highly valued such that superior thinking is held in high esteem and excellent academics are nurtured, not wrangled into bureaucratic ineptitude by loud-mouthed, unsophisticated parents – as in America.

The rigid Germanic ethic, of course, provides some humor. Years ago, while living in Munich, following a few fine, naturally brewed Bavarian beers, I would head home late at night. Walking along quiet, deserted streets, without a car in sight, I would marvel at Germans who stopped at *Don't Walk* lights at crosswalks. Of course, I would just cross the street. They followed the rule; I judged the reality that rule was meant to cover in other, more crowded, situations and ignored the sign.

But that commitment to order, to establishing the best rules then following them, has yielded considerable advancement in man's understanding, tempering whatever considerable downside resulted from following rules that sometimes weren't ideal.

In any case, philosophy, as a reasoned and complex exploration of man's state of being, has enjoyed considerable prestige in the German culture through time. Martin Luther, by the early 16th century, had established an independence of appropriate action over church hierarchical dictates and launched in the act a greater focus on the native, daily language – rather than Latin – as an acceptable means of intellectual expression. While Luther's new church remained fixed on the same old notions, he did initiate movement toward freer thinking that carried considerable influence on philosophical inquiry down the road.

Leibnitz, already by 1700, had established a line of Philosophy in Germany that was to imprint considerable influence on western thinking. With the invention of the calculus as a mathematical function – independent of, but at about the same time as Newton in England – and significant contributions in many fields, Gottfried Wilhelm von Leibnitz (1646 – 1716) established his credentials in brilliance. But the "monads" he envisioned as dividing points for real elements in a dynamic, living universe had two notable shortcomings: first, they were too mathematical; second, they don't exist. And, equally flawed, some semblance of the Christian god still sat at the top as monad-in-chief.

Picturing reality as the creation of a perfect god, Leibnitz projected that this must be the best of all possible worlds. Given extensive, rampant ills in the world, he was ridiculed, even parodied by Voltaire in *Candide*, for this blindly optimistic sort of evaluation.

If this great thinker took his mathematical perfection a bit too far into blatant idealism, he did touch however dimly on a significant insight. Of course, no free-floating god out there conjures things into existence with his eternal magic wand. And of course, reality as experienced by the vast majority of humanity is not the bubbly swatch of great health and success normally deemed good. But what occurs to the direct encounter by each individual is the pure manifestation of his/her total being. As such, the ideal is personified by the inner-outer process itself. Perfection occurs in regard to *the process*, however, *not* the outcome: you encounter exactly what you are, a qualitative mix of good and bad reflecting precisely your own inner conflict and struggle.

But as such, the process provides each incarnating entity – you included – enormous potential for growth via meaningful experience. So this reality, in a very significant way, *is* the best of all worlds – but can be realized as such in qualitative effect as well as process **only** when the open-minded person recognizes his/her enveloping creative power and begins to use it. In recognizing that real events and relationships stem from within, any individual can begin to hone the inner realm to shape the outer consistent with desires so that perfection of process can be converted into quality of experience.

Decades later, by the late 18th century, Immanuel Kant (1724 – 1804), while recognizing limitations to what **could be known** (and in the process conceptualizing – thus establishing – limitations to his own perception) projected *Reason* itself as the means to work through experience to understand the world. He encountered the longstanding debate between empiricists, looking for understanding through examining the real world, and rationalists, looking to clarify reality through reasoned argument, and found some common ground.

Kant recognized to a degree the effect I often illustrate – how held beliefs and definitions affect one's perception of reality. In his doctrine *Transcendental Idealism*, Kant differentiates in reference to objects meaning **drawn by the observer** concerning the nature of the object vs. the innate nature of the object *unto* *itself*. He recognized that one can never make sense of the world through straightforward recognition of things, i.e., simple sensory perception, but through the process of **"synthesis"**, or absorbing meaning via learned rules. Thus, as Kant saw it, one can never transcend limits of one's own cognition to really know, as stated in the original German, the *"Ding an sich"*, i.e., the object in itself, but is limited to the perception-interpretation outcome of recognition.

Kant proceeded to reflect on morality in regard to one's relationship to reality, coming to recommend beneficial action, whether a god exists or not, as a moral imperative. (We encounter that later in other sections.)

Of course, Kant's consideration of *knowing* in conjunction with that *which is out there to be known* is quite complex in regarding cognition, how it works and what is to be made of it. But the subtle effect in play which eluded him pertinent to understanding is the interactive nature of the encountered reality itself – and its dependence on **quality** in reference to its manifested impact on the experiencer.

Because Reality is an interrelated Oneness, not a collection of independent items, the elaborate system conceived by Kant, based in significant ways on prior philosophical models and later to be enhanced or rejected by other philosophers, fails to grasp the whole picture. In regarding a thing as an isolated entity (*whether or not* it has meaning unto itself at any level), he limits its essential nature to **either**: first, a perceived value based on recognition-interpretation or, second, an importance it

holds – a transcendental essence – innate to itself that *cannot* be discerned, due to sensory limitations or interpretational bias.

But Reality flows as a contiguous Singularity, an awareness of which is precluded by adherence to long traditions of objective regard – a heritage replete to our western mindset. This integrated nature – each object fitting into its surroundings in ways meaningful to the observer – carries implications considerably beyond the two factors recognized by Kant. Reality, then, in *how it works* renders both of his images incorrect.

Not only is interpretation of the nature of an object affected by learned rules and definitions, but by the meaning that item represents *in its context* – through the impact it has via the role it plays in the observer's life. It may have some philosophically distinct essence in itself, due to its composition or manufacture or whatever, but this objective nature is *irrelevant* in the scheme of Reality. Attempting to discern some transcendental, deep meaning an object harbors for the advantage of enlightened discovery would be a moot gesture. (Yet much of philosophical discourse focuses on this!) Meaning of significance is found only ever within the consciousness of the perceiver, not in some duly recorded, secretive/mystical internal database within the object.

Life itself as seen in the qualitative Reality that manifests in the course of one's daily encounters is based on meaning. The objective paradigm employed subtly by Kant and much of the line of western philosophy misses the *gist* of Reality while attempting to define (if not divine) its *structure* in minute detail. The value of any object is reflected within the utility by which it functions within its framework and meaning that entire scenario embodies.

Johann Gottlieb Fichte (1762 – 1814) seemed to move Kant's perspectives on phenomena and noumena – things as they appear and ideas beyond them, respectively – to a focus on the Self, *"Das ich"*, or "the I". He saw this *I*, not as a thing in itself, but as an activity that "posits" itself into the real setting.

Fichte seems in this expression from his *Wissenschaftslehre* (Science of Knowledge) to perceive the essential nature of the Self within the context of its own being, as actually exists here –

with inner meaning being manifested in outer phenomena. Indeed, each of us projects the Self into this real setting, using the life format to accomplish, grow, love, fight, adventure, build, create, musicize or any other of a thousand potential endeavors. But, while he begins to grasp the innate being of the Self and its unique status, his views evolved throughout his life towards this *I*-self as rooted in a source: an absolute being.

That gesture, of course, renders the integral, self-generating *I* as more of an *it*, groveling conceptually at the foot of the trusty, age-old Supreme Being that has haunted man's journey and hindered his progress since the original Sky God and Venus provider. While he looks for the *I* to discover its own freedom within its process, he precludes that happening by mistakenly imagining the Self as an outgrowth of some greater, postulated entity.

Indeed, freedom comes only when that external overlord, the imagined deity, and all its psychological ramifications are eliminated from the conceptualized picture. So long as one holds philosophical tenets of some other entity being final judge and implementer, the Self *cannot manifest innate desires and fulfill intent*, because any external, controlling god would *necessarily have a different agenda*. And that god would be imagined as the one making it so – an inaccurate impression that **can only** contribute conflict to one's manifested reality.

So the Self, positing its nature into a real setting, as Fichte would have put it, could never realize freedom while entertaining an external deity and weaving that imagined being's expected intent into life's situations.

Hegel expands on the notion of **freedom**, equating it with a level of consciousness capable of making a choice. A younger contemporary of Fichte, coming on the heels of Kant, Georg Wilhelm Friedrich Hegel (1770 – 1831) saw in the train of man's history a progression of the "consciousness of freedom". Included in the notion of freedom here is the personal recognition of choice: moving beyond the status of being controlled by outside forces, but rather coming to a personal realization that, *through reason*, one can gain dominion over those external forces.

Reason, per se, isn't really the answer, but noting the progression is significant. As observed, ancients projected causality out to gods. Specialized deities, including the Fates, were seen to determine the outcome of all things. At that point, there was virtually no freedom to encounter life and proceed to accomplish one's desires. Hegel felt that, in ancient times, only emperors had any degree of freedom. (I might add to that priests, save to the degree that they actually bought into their mythological fantasies.) The common man, as Hegel recognized, was frozen into an involuntary role, living a continuum of activity in which he had no determinative power, no choice.

Much of mankind *today* still maintains the conceptual shackles of his ancestors, projecting power to outside sources and forces, frozen into a fearful, powerless lifestyle. Only now, his pantheon of deities has been largely replaced by a basically defrocked god and a collection of attributed forces: bacteria, the economy, the government, conditions, providence, the rich, plus, of course, luck, fate and chance.

Hegel's view and that of his other contemporary, Friedrich Schelling (1775 – 1854) center on an absolute source, a god or conceptual substitute, thus furthering the lack of freedom Hegel so insightfully noted. They couldn't acknowledge that their god-source and other forces grow, once again, out of the illusion of separation of self from reality – because they, themselves, weren't aware of the integral Oneness of Self with Reality. One encounters restrictions to freedom *only* by holding within the psyche notions of separation and inherent mechanisms of struggle and conflict.

In Schopenhauer, German philosophy absorbed eastern influence, while continuing along a path paved by Kant. Critical of Kant and particularly of Hegel, Arthur Schopenhauer (1788 – 1860) drew from the Buddha's teachings to temper his picture, incorporating in a pessimistic vein Gautama's focus on suffering and release from it, but continued in effect along that trail of general Idealism (that reality is ultimately based on ideas).

Of course, Idealism had many detractors along the way. Johann Herbart (1776 – 1841) and more significantly, Rudolph Hermann Lotze (1817 – 1881) pushed things towards the growing movement of natural science, while others pulled in the direction of a more spiritual, god-based, philosophy.

Søren Kierkegaard (1813 – 1855), Danish philosopher, was highly critical of Hegel in particular. He observed not mankind's advancement, but rather a human condition rife with ambiguity and uncertainty, basically absurd in effect. He had difficulties with forced religion – the Danish government in the mid-19th century imposed church membership and required contributions – as totally against the spirit of Christianity. But he didn't detect invalidity within the Christian model. From my standpoint, Kierkegaard looks more at life's qualities than its nature, so he didn't contribute to clarifying its function – rather furthering old religious notation as a given.

(And by the way, Kierkegaard's life reflected in significant ways the absurdity he imagined in the process: early on he rejected the love of his life based on concocted rational grounds and rued the decision in emotional turmoil for the rest of his life.)

Ultimately, though, considering those two directions, the outcome is obvious in our polarized modern world: science and religion dominate the scene. Philosophy, however much it chipped away at those notions, ultimately became aligned with the scientific view, furthering the early direction of Lotze and the long previous offshoot of Descartes and Bacon.

But German philosophy still had a twist or two worth regarding. Karl Heinrich Marx (1818 – 1883), in the mid-19th century, latched onto Hegelian ideas and tried to apply them to the working classes. While the line of German Idealism generally focused on the human condition, a fulfilling life, sense of self-worth and social improvement, Marx sought to apply Hegel's ideas to foster life improvement for a whole class.

While vilified in the western world (a realm often given to gross oversimplification and propaganda-induced conclusions) as a precursor to the major Communist movement that dominated world conflict in the 20th century, Marx doubtless had man's best interest in mind when looking to improve the large, mostly downtrodden classes of his time.

The difficulty he and all would-be reformers face is this: **no operative social or political system** *can impose improvement* on individuals (and thus groups) *beyond their capacity to realize it personally.*

Communism, theoretically an equalization of all classes, looks great on paper: grand, idealistic (in the sense of naïve and unrealistic) goals for brotherhood and equality, shared effort for a better future. But in practice, Communism breaks down in actualized quality as real people play life's roles. Some prosper and gain control (Party members), living good lives; others fail and muddle along.

In capitalist countries, some succeed, make a lot of money (the wealthy), prosper and live good lives as reasonably free; many don't.

Both systems function similarly, but with the downside to communism that, with no personal motivation to succeed, workers, not among elite party members, accomplish as little as possible.

Regardless of its form, people find their niche in any political system because **each individual is engendering his/her own real life.** In reality, all political/governmental systems *result from* the collective mindset of its constituent population; no system actually *causes* the collective outcome, be it prosperity or drudgery, based on its structure.

(Marx didn't really contribute to recognizing the Nature of Reality, as engaged in this section, but his heritage lends itself to that key point. It also illustrated how philosophy can impact the real world, as the rise of Communism was a highly significant feature of the emergence of the "modern" world.

(I put "modern" in quotes there, as the advancement of technology and communications hasn't yet truly modernized man, despite self-aggrandized notions of even a *postmodern* phase. Maintaining ancient rituals, myths and gods along with now popularized materialism, rampant prejudice and fallacious scientific objectivity, mankind won't remotely approach a status truly worthy of the appraisal *modern* until enough people recognize life's Oneness to impact major, collective events as well as their own lives.)

A Glimpse at Mind Design

"God is dead!" Thus spoke Nietzsche in the late 19th century. Of course, that didn't imply that the old El-Yahweh mix hijacked and reconstructed by Paul and the Christian movement had passed away to Elysian Fields of a higher order. That deified brew of divergent features such as forgiveness and yet punishment, love and yet judgment, perfection and yet inflicted misery, *never existed in the first place* – as Nietzsche certainly realized.

Friedrich Nietzsche (1844 – 1900) saw a world always changing. He recognized in both Christianity and Democracy a herd mentality, wherein the masses were driven into a submissive slave mentality, obedient to authorities who resisted even considering such change. Insightful for certain, his critique on societal morality failed to pierce the default psychological isolation innate to both doctrines, indeed, woven deeply into the mindset of his time – and far from gone even now. But at least he recognized it.

In Nietzsche, unique to philosophers I've explored up to this point, I see a sincere and profound recognition of the short-comings of mainline thinking to his time. His stark criticism of Christianity stands in striking contrast to the unquestioning inclusion of and shallow acquiescence to traditional religious notions of most philosophers up to his time.

"There are no facts, only interpretations," he wrote often in his notes. While there is much in his writing that merits explo-ration (and certainly quite a bit worth ignoring), two key themes stand out. In his later publications, he projected an *"Übermensch"*. Not accurately translated as "Superman" in English, his intent here referenced qualities lacking in the standardized version of the modern individual and looked for, anticipated, even **hoped for** in a new and improved version: one that wouldn't lord over others, but function in superior style, with greater sympathy, empathy and effectiveness. And certainly without the archaic beliefs and programmed, rote thinking of his typical peer.

Likewise, his expression *"Wille zur Macht"*, often translated as "Will to Power", extends beyond the ken of the typical inter-preter or reporting philosopher/writer who would describe its meaning, for that phrase in English loses his gist. Nietzsche could see man's inherent limitations and expounded consid-erably on those as evidenced in politics, daily life, the arts, and certainly religion and metaphysics of his day. Without doubt, he could sense the potential for a much higher level of existence – though realization of the track to that level, *how to get there*, was not within his purview. His work brilliantly cut at man's patent shortcomings and in voicing that, along with the conse-quent effect it had on his time and the 20th century, would help nudge humanity upwards.

But in his Übermensch notion, along with his reflective, insightful impressions on meaningful aspects of life, Nietzsche glimpsed the nature of an individual who has attained the peace and fulfillment replete with the status of Clear Awareness. The **Will** he refers to is not, in essence, geared towards power *over* encountered reality – as one might suspect from the outside, unaware of the Oneness – indeed as Nietzsche perhaps pictured it. Nor is it requiring of transcendence, yet another of his anathemas – for the metaphysics that he so clearly disdained, lumping it in with religion, was very hokey in his time.

No, the *Wille zur Macht* is simply, but profoundly, the unrelenting intent to be what one is and succeed in life, in relationships, in health without compromise and without prerequisite struggle and conflict so characteristic of standard Homo Sapiens' lot. This, too, anticipates the life status of Clear Awareness illustrated here – the "revaluation" he was looking for.

With Friedrich Nietzsche, then, German philosophy began to push about as far as the intellect can go in recognizing a status inherently greater than the innate limitations of the intellect itself. By that I mean that rational thought, so prevalent in philosophical regard of the world, can scarcely recognize the full, functional engagement of Self with Reality when the broad array of complex definitions, expressions, arguments, paradigm-building and conclusion-drawing it rests on basically *inhibits* awareness of the Self rather than clarifying it.

Following Nietzsche, Edmund Husserl (1859 – 1938) ushered things into the 20th century by looking again at the nature of objects and the observer of them in **Phenomenology**. But far from earlier attempts at clarifying the nature of objects themselves, the gist here regarded consciousness in its apprehension of objects. And this line of thinking, carried on through Martin Heidegger (1889 – 1976), became a branch of epistemology, noting that knowledge gained from encounter with reality is so strongly influenced by social, historical and other conditioning that it can't ever be objective.

That, of course, is what I've been emphasizing all along. But recognizing the limitations doesn't ever seem to deter philosophers from deriving firm conclusions from synthetic, illusory precepts.

Anyway, German philosophy seemed to culminate with Ludwig Wittgenstein (1889 – 1951). The first half of the 20th century saw significant contributions by a man who had studied under Bertrand Russell (1872 – 1970) in England, but moved towards his own statement with *Tractatus* and later *Philosophical Investigations*.

Wittgenstein, certainly aided by an early mystic experience, recognized inherent shortcomings to language in expressing ideas with any degree of real reflection on the essence of the real world they were meant to depict. He looked at reality as consisting of facts – not things – and delved quite deeply into analysis of the basis of those facts and limitations in regarding them via language.

With these later influences along the line of German thinking, philosophy stretched beyond Nietzsche, reaching, it would seem, real limits to accurate rational recognition of the integrated nature of Self-Reality.

Again: the rational, calculating mind, drawing conclusions about life based on its learned precepts, building complex explanations and arguments for or against tenets that fit within already-accepted notions, can only get so far in the quest for understanding before it runs into a boundary of its own making. At some point, complexity of conceptualization breaks down into fractured idea-images that lend themselves only to further argument, to added analysis of what appear to be truthful insights, but which are really only shiny, artfully polished ideas – bearing lesser, not greater, pertinence to reality and its flow.

And Onwards, To and Through the Present

While continental philosophy cruised down the autobahn of German thinking – with some contribution of Auguste Comte (1798 – 1857), the French founder of Positivism – other elements of man's regard for reality were contributing to advancement in British thinking and man's outlook in general.

(According to Positivism, only sense experience can be relied upon for authentic knowledge – basically untrue, for the senses are easily fooled by beliefs on which interpretation rests.)

The push toward empiricism (actually exploring and testing the world to see how it works) created the major trend in astronomy and mathematics that would greatly influence the track of man's advancement. Nicolaus Copernicus (1473 – 1543), Johannes Kepler (1571 – 1630) and Galileo Galilei (1564 – 1642) had restructured man's regard for the universe, moving it from an ancient, Earth-centered domain of the gods, wandering about the heavens, to a reliable, mechanical realm.

Following the track set by many ancient Greek thinkers and Descartes, Isaac Newton (1643 – 1727) and Leibnitz moved along man's quantified regard of functional reality – with later contributions from Euler, Gauss and many others – as they expanded mathematics.

By the 19th century, Charles Darwin (1809 – 1882) and Alfred Russel Wallace (1823 – 1913), recognizing the constant process of change that has marked the evolving planet, and responding to growing evidence from the fossil record and natural sciences, proposed Natural Selection as the driving process behind that change. Indeed, later British philosophy, with John Stuart Mill (1806 – 1873) adding falsification as a critical component to the scientific method and Herbert Spencer (1820 – 1903) seeing the human mind as subject to identifiable natural laws, contributed as well. Add to that the enduring work of Bertrand Russell, with contributions to many areas of understanding, principally in

Analytic Philosophy.

William James (1842 – 1910), helping to put North America onto the philosophical map, touched on psychology and mysticism. Through his reliance on Pragmatism, James tried to reconcile claims of science with religion and morality.

(According to Pragmatism, a proposition or claim is true if it works adequately – which isn't valid, actually, as a proposition may function as anticipated, but for other reasons not apparent to the observer.)

Western philosophy has offered a long line of brilliant thinkers, men who have shaped our approaches to regarding reality, men whose ideas carried us away from strict reliance on control of the gods to a classification of natural systems, a deep, intricate technological basis in science and math and many views on morality and cultural life in many, many dimensions.

From the later 20th century into this millennium, philosophy seems to have abandoned any exploration beyond fixed ideas and regressed into a social and academic mish-mash of debate and recycling of established, agreed-upon ideas. The USA alone churns out hundreds of doctorates of philosophy yearly, stamping out like an assembly line people who think and only *can* think all in the same vein – or at least within a finite set of small, identical capillaries. Over a thousand philosophical societies flourish in North America, with hundreds of books and papers issued continually.

The current scene features two major factions of philosophy: Analytical and Continental. The former, at home in the English-speaking realm, focuses on intricate, well-argued points concerning specific, narrow topics. The latter inhabits minds of European philosophers – something of an outgrowth of earlier German Idealism, particularly evolving from Husserl onward. It generally spotlights larger scale focus than the narrow Analytical side. It seems more personal, more focused on meaning and impact in real life – and generally looks beyond science as the ultimate model for understanding.

Not surprisingly, the two schools look disparagingly on each other's approach.

As for **The Nature of Reality,** the focus of this section, modern regard *in general* – notwithstanding the genre of philosophy, which is essentially irrelevant in daily exchange of ideas – has stultified around two basic models: the scientific and the speculative, this latter being my characterization of how anything outside science is regarded based on the exclusivity of the scientific paradigm. Metaphysics has matured considerably since the time of James where the parlor séance provided fodder for consideration.

But the purely objective focus of science attracts near fixation of modern thinking outside religion and the far more open-minded exploration of consciousness. Its objective paradigm and technique are even seen in the Analytic approach to philosophy. In academic corners, it seems, the old debates of Platonists vs. Aristotelians, of rationalists vs. empiricists, over the nature or existence of God, of this idea vs. that one simply *carry on* – with solutions being highly intricate studies of minutiae, far more pertinent to ideas than to reality.

But here's the problem, beyond my interlude earlier: *the mind is easily and invariably fooled by its firmly held tenets.*

As a member of Mensa, a high-IQ social organization, I frequently encounter smart people. But intelligence doesn't guarantee any degree of insight, of wisdom or open-minded exploration. Some brilliant people are strongly religious, others strictly atheist. A brilliant mind, while enabling the possessor to manipulate complex information with dexterity well beyond the average, doesn't in any way guard against absorption of illusory, fallacious truths as base understanding. But it *can* allow – perhaps even promote – virtually unlimited expounding on details that fall within whatever paradigm is accepted, regardless of invalidity of underlying assumptions.

Before enhancing my illustration of the Nature of Reality beyond the **What Is** section above I would make a few points:

- An advanced degree in Philosophy doesn't make somebody a Philosopher.
  - ✓ A real Philosopher in the mold of the great ones sees reality beyond conventional limitations, not within the confines of ever greater detail of stated bounds.
  - ✓ A student of other people's ideas, able to spit out grand arguments and supports for a mode of thinking, able to write up a thesis acceptable to another body of degreed pseudo-philosophers is an *academic*, not a real Philosopher.
  - ✓ There have been very few true Philosophers, individuals whose insightful ideas broadened man's recognition of his real nature, and *practically none* in quite some time.
- Brilliance in argument or complex thinking neither guarantees nor even implies veracity.
  - ✓ Complex ideas, however brilliantly argued and supported, fizzle into nothingness when even one core assumption is fallacious or *any* supporting point invalid.
  - ✓ Any depicted structure for reality is only as valid as its most rudimentary assumption, however subtle, however widely shared, is accurate.
- **No complex definition or paradigm reflects reality.**
  - ✓ The Consciousness-Reality Oneness is an exceptionally simple process. The more complex a model, even one that features the functional Singularity, the

farther from legitimate it is.

- ✓ Any depiction of reality rendering it to words is already, by virtue of the act, no longer a *clear equivalent* of reality itself; no additional detail can revise this symbolic rendering into perfect accuracy.
- ✓ As often repeated here, the individual must come to see the functional Oneness of Reality/Consciousness personally to grasp the real nature of being – no paradigm can substitute.

- The field of Philosophy has evolved into functional irrelevance (not, however into a state of *meaninglessness* – if anything, it is *too full* of meaning, all of it synthetic), existing as its own haughty realm within academic circles, with little relevance to or influence on modern thinking.

With the ever-increasing influence within our culture of science on one hand and religion on the other, philosophy should play a valuable role in opening minds to new perspectives. But for centuries, the few people capable of vision were too tied up in religion to see anything beyond their archaic images. From Descartes on, as science (along with math) gained sophistication and acceptance, leading to a grand expansion of technology and communications, it came to dominate philosophy and more or less compete with religion as a popular base view of life.

Philosophy now haggles over endless, complex details concerning generally accepted major notions: that reality exists as an objective realm, that the mind has real restrictions in discerning exactly what is out there, what moral and ethical codes must be agree on, that metaphysics and meaning should play a role in the world, but that role is debatable, etc. (Actually, more like: etc., etc., etc., etc.)

Indeed, in significant ways, Philosophy is as dead as God in Nietzsche's view: sequestered (if not embalmed) in academic halls, relegated to endless debate over ideas. Innovative thinking in the tradition of Plato and Aristotle, Locke and Descartes, Kant and Hegel, is gone in the twilight enlightenment of intellectuals who can't see past science's confines – blinded as they must be by their own artificial brilliance.

Being

The Nature of Reality is simple, inviolable and straightforward: Consciousness creates the Reality it engages.

Each perceiving Self is contained, not in quantified aggregations of particles and energy, but in meaning and value held in its unbounded, intangible, timeless mind. Those particles and energy manifest into form in response to inner essence. Real impact: you are intimately, uncompromisingly connected to the real world you encounter.

Change is a requisite feature of unfolding particulars manifested in real events and relationships experienced by the Self, but that change occurs in specifics, in details, while patterns persist reflective of the composite nature of the Conscious Self. The outer, "real" universe – matter itself – consists, then, not of solid, isolated particles and composite objects made of them, but of plastic energy-fields whose manifestation into perceived combinations follows exact meaning. And that emerging meaning *lies rooted in the psyche* – never happening by chance, never following divine dictates, never impelled by external-world forces or sources, but only driven by propensities reliant on meaning held in the mind of the experiencer.

Illusions form in the field of perception of each experiencing Self, created by synthetic notions – beliefs and definitions – absorbed as true. Such illusions can be simple, e.g., the workings of a god held to exist, or quite complex, such as the most convoluted of epistemological or positivistic explanations.

But whatever the scope of the illusions, the means to directly and immediately perceive the Oneness beyond them in its unrelenting flow is to **explicitly** *rid the mind*, one by one, of all explanations that create illusory notions – not build up ever greater ones.

The Self is unbounded. It occupies a space referred to as "here" with no outer edge in any direction and only ever exists in a "now" time frame. It encounters, waking or sleeping, incarnated or not, a perceived environment driven by the essential translation – a functional transformation – of its inner values manifesting into real events that embody them. This Self imprints its own value-status on the immediate environment it engages, such that only events and relationships can occur and develop which correspond to its inner propensity.

The real universe visible to the senses *exists*, but not inherently, detached from the consciousness that perceives it. And it doesn't consist of solid stuff, frozen in its form and simply moving about in this now-moment. It exists as an ongoing *resultant* configuration, an effect, unfolding in substance and meaning in response to the inner realm, functioning as a stage, replete with set and props, on which to engage and work out elements of one's own nature.

Let me illustrate that: picture a whip being lashed forwards so that, as its wave energy concentrates at the very end, that tip exceeds the speed of sound as it smacks itself, releasing a cracking sound. Imagine, though, that, due to the limited nature of your vision, you can only see items approaching the speed of sound. So you only perceive *the tip* just as it cracks – not the whole whip with the hand holding it. From your perspective it appears, moves slightly and makes a loud *crack*, but for no apparent reason. So you look for some explanation – maybe attributing it to magic or divine edict, perhaps to an explosive property of that visible tip.

Reality – each particle, each collection of particles that

comprise objects and people – is like the *end* of that whip. It emerges into the visual field with properties resulting from elements *you don't see*. The mindset in this analogy is like the whip itself – its characteristics determine the nature of the snap. Intent is like the hand that wields it. In the whip analogy, you observe a small object appearing, moving and making noise, yet remain oblivious to the wave action behind it or the hand initiating the movement.

In the real world, similarly, you only ever encounter the result: emerging configurations of objects that play out meaningful events and relationships, but whose root source within the mind is invisible.

The tip of the whip wouldn't be there, moving and snapping exactly as it does, without the shaft, the energized movement and the hand. And events wouldn't emerge exactly as they do without the inner-outer flow responding specifically to the mindset's content and personal intent driving it.

As an accumulation of experience, a grand collection of encountered events and relationships, a lifetime is engaged for a purpose – for all life is built upon purpose and meaning. Yet the purpose itself can vary from entertainment to encountering challenge to achieving growth to creating artistry, with fulfillment (or, alternately, negation or neutralization) of the will being expressed in any of life's abundant modes.

The nature of the Self is reflected in that collage of life experience. But the Self can be seen in its latent state within the subconscious mind, wherein emotional potential, creative urge, energetic undertaking and other probabilities reside in hopes, dreams and desires. But there, **within**, those shaping, figurative drivers share breathing space with doubt, fear, conflict, notions of separation and struggle. Thus, as the total essence of Self manifests in the outer realm, success blends with failure, illness with health and rejection with love, to form real, ongoing situations reflecting qualitatively the whole scope of inner values.

The real world, with objects and other people, replete with all mathematical and scientific rules, all real and imagined conditions and situations, emerges as background to the play-out of meaning in events and relationships. Mass events, the vast visible universe, potential and experienced disasters, widespread effects – all these, while significant, can be seen in their most actualized nature only as they impact each experiencing Self with, in terms of desire and intent, fulfillment, negation or neutralization of them.

Plato imagined a "form", a perfect ideal behind each real iteration of object or person, while Aristotle integrated forms within things. Both are distorted notions, for neither is correct, but only imagined effects.

Objects exist, not in themselves, as Kant might have put it, but only *ever in context with the rest of reality in emerging values*. Trying to make sense of a single object, pulling it out of the context in which it serves its meaning, only leads to illusory conclusions – like observing the whip's tip without the rest of the whip and the hand that lashes it. (This, of course, is the entire focus of empiricism, of science in general – to look only at seemingly real objects and ignore the contextual implications. Like religion, where any imagined god seems real, or any other accepted paradigm, scientific endeavor looks for causality in its defined external sources, and therein creates illusory forces – all of which seem valid to the indoctrinated believer.)

No god ever existed in outer Reality, to be observed, touched, dealt with – only ever in the furtive imagination of believers. And *no object ever existed out of context or without meaning*.

Causality stems only from within, as Reality responds *exclusively* to the total mind content of the experiencer. All aspects of apparent being, all manifestations engaged as daily experience, are only ever *effects*, never causes. (Aspects of reality appearing as conventional causes are really only triggers, playing out their appearance consistent with held beliefs that attribute artificial causality to them.)

So, metaphysics rests on meaning, not on super-natural effects (of which there *cannot be any* – for nothing exists outside the scope of the inner-outer Oneness) or any religious consideration. Indeed, all religious definition is fantasy.

All conscious entities who *ever* existed, *still do* – but the specific, incarnate identity of loved ones doesn't remain tied to old character. The Self incarnates as often as desired in order to accomplish its goals – which, again, can be many and varied. But incarnating, as all of existence, is based on meaning and value – and certainly isn't limited to an Earth-based setting.

Exploring the real world, the multi-featured Earth, as an empirical study, is a grand gesture. Science is absolutely correct to do so, as it leads to far greater richness of experience and advancement in culture. Delving into each detail of particle functionality and exploring each parsec of space establishes ever greater, more varied backgrounds for living life. Technological advancement adds enormous richness and potential to accomplishment. But scientific and mathematic "truths" only exist within the confines and context of personal existence.

So, at its core, The Nature of Reality is found in meaning manifested by the personal engagement of a conscious entity. The real world, as encountered personally, embodies meaning held in the complex, virtually unbounded subconscious of the engaging individual.

Because Reality reflects meaning held within Consciousness, in order to understand the function of Reality, it is vital to understand the workings of the mind – as illustrated in Angle Two.

Based on that picture of reality as a responsive, interactive display of personal meaning rooted in the Self, let's consider other important problems tackled by philosophers through the ages...

Point Two: Man's Place in the Universe

Evaluating the Evaluator

Not surprisingly, estimation by philosophers of man's **situation** within reality coincides reliably with how each construes reality.

The early Epicureans, looking to maximize pleasure during life, regarded the universe as something of a playground for engaging in enjoyable, rewarding activities. The Stoics, as Determinists (seeing events of the world unfolding as a consequence of a long chain of previous episodes inevitably yielding this particular status) looked to self-control to overcome emotional involvement in things, almost *expecting* them to be negative in effect – and apparently taking some pride in their ability to weather the ordeal.

Plato, with his orientation to ideas, regarded man as unique in his ability to think, limited only by the physical body, which as **matter**, was considered a separate essence. Aristotle likewise cherished reason and man's unique abilities within nature to be able to reason – thus placing man in a distinguished role.

Through the long phase when religion dominated western tradition, man's status was inevitably evaluated in light of, relationship with or comparison to a third-person, conceptualized deity. For some, man's status was severely diminished by the notion of the "Fall of Man" – stemming from Adam's consumption of the fruit of the knowledge of good and evil, heretofore forbidden.

This rather fascinating old story – Adam and Eve in the Garden of Eden – serves as one of Genesis' two creation fables. God had created Adam from dust and Eve from his rib, removed while he slept and "closed up with flesh" – apparently quite effectively, as he seems not to have noticed. God – likely a deity named "El" or a precursor, though it is impossible to know **what** god was featured when this story was first concocted in the distant, dim past (though one wonders who was there taking notes to report the event when Adam, Eve and the talking serpent, all illiterate, were the only ones around) – then gave them permission to eat any of the fruits available, *except* that from the tree with the fruit of knowledge of good and evil.

The unnamed serpent, apparently with little to do but cause trouble – coincidentally speaking the same language pre-programmed into Adam and Eve upon creation as adults – talked Eve into eating that fruit, promising wisdom equivalent to that of the god. As it sounded like a good deal, she ate some and gave some to Adam – thus violating the Tenant's Agreement in the lease on Eden. Not only did they immediately incur *shame* in the process, suddenly finding exposure of their genitals – even  though nobody else was around, presumably in the whole world – guilt-inducing, but they also got summarily evicted.

While, astoundingly, many people actually take this yarn literally, looked upon as myth, it wraps a significant idea into its cartoon-character plot. Early, nomadic man lived well off the "fruits" of nature – abundant seeds, grains, leaves and roots as well as game within most settings. His instinctive, intuitive immersion in a reflective reality prompted him, as hunter-gatherer, to sustain himself quite well. But increasingly, likely beginning well before agriculture, man began to rely on rational thinking to deal with the world. The spirit-nature attributed to wild game – so vividly depicted in cave paintings of 17,000 years ago and before – became lost in his view, along with a measure of honor previously bestowed on pristine nature. The "knowledge of good and evil" stands for rational thinking – the need to dominate nature, conquer it, not live within and in tune with its bounteous sustainability. And Eden is a state of mind – trusting reality, not needing to rape it.

Shame, in sexual terms, is an archaic notion, as are guilt and sin in that same regard. Those attitudes were built into religion along the way by priesthoods filled with sexually inhibited or deviate thinkers. Still, the metaphor for shifting into rational override of intuitive interaction with an innately connected reality is impressively woven into this creation myth.

While some, then, applied these negative connotations to man's status based on his "Fall", others regarded man as prized and honored, a unique creation of their god.

Whatever status might be overtly attributed to man, the unavoidable subtle effect of conceptualizing any god *at all* is to evaluate man – that is, *each individual,* for the collective of mankind consists of many single entities – as a far lesser being.

Most people in modern western cultures can drive automobiles. Learning to control a motorized vehicle isn't too difficult, so driving a car to get around is commonplace. Far more complex is actually manufacturing one. From the design phase, with much of that resting on decades of technological research and development, through prototyping and engineering to improve performance and efficiency, to the manufacture, sales and repair phases, building autos is very complicated. Very few people could even begin to build a car from scratch.

Body function, however, is far more complex than a motorized vehicle: interaction between cells for exchange of nutrients and oxygen, self-regulating secretion of hormones and other substances, complex nerve communication, digestion of foodstuffs, operation of the sense organs, function of reproduction capabilities – all that goes on continuously, nearly flawlessly for up to a century.

If creation of that Self-vehicle was done by some external creator god – along with the vastly more complex Earth environment in which it, in context of trillions of other life forms, functions – that entity would have to be incomparably, many multiple orders of magnitude, more intelligent, powerful and effective than any person. That's the implication in a god-projection: that humans are inferior beings, creations, mere assembly line products, at the beck and whim of this majestic, yet invisible, being which created them.

So, for whatever the rational arguments of Abelard and Thomas, of Augustine and a long line of popes, the gist of Christian (as well as any other god-propagated model) thinking is that we are beings of *very insignificant worth* compared to the manufacturer.

Science reduces personal value even more. Within that paradigm, compared to the unimaginably vast universe, containing billions of galaxies within tens of billions of light-years visible in all directions, you are an indecipherably insignificant speck, ever so slightly removed from pure nothingness – a state, indeed, finally achieved upon death when brain-based consciousness fades from existence.

And science, of course, is the track honed by Francis Bacon, reinforced through the great mathematicians and astronomers, then enhanced by Hobbes and others into a modern, purely materialistic view.

Philosophers have found both those images lacking and unsatisfying, not surprisingly, as both render the Self to miniscule, near-meaningless proportions. Locke saw man, with his ability to reason, as unique and special, where Berkeley felt that the universe only exists in the mind of man – not a bad conclusion, except that he brings god into the picture, too, allowing that conceptualized entity to be the ultimate source of our sensation. Hume seems to have dumped both the god *and* the universe, placing all effects within the mind – claiming that all recognition takes place there.

Kant, while doubting that the mind can accurately recognize the universe's real nature beyond distorted ideas extracted from sensory input, allowed that man should endeavor to do so. Jean-Jacques Rousseau (1712 – 1778) had rejected the mechanical model for man, looking somehow for meaning, specifically in freedom from the isolation science seemed to place him in. Kant seemed (to me) to be trying to justify some innate meaning to man's existence in a realm that he appeared to all but acknowledge *lacked it* – the objective universe science was depicting, a mechanical, material one without metaphysical root.

Fichte, Hegel and other German thinkers through Schopenhauer looked to freedom as a goal or ultimate destiny of man, based on his will. But Nietzsche accurately saw that as fruitless in a universe that didn't care.

Without a valid view of the Consciousness/Reality integration based on meaning, the latter group of philosophers have had to invent character elements such as ethics and morality – or at least extract them from ancient Greek dialog – to create a meaningful picture. As the scientific view took ever greater hold of man, it simply washed away rational arguments – sterilizing western thinking like its antiseptic approach attributing illness to microbe infection.

With ever greater reliance on technology and rational control – politically, in health issues and education, socially and otherwise – with widespread media exposure inundating the common, unthinking man in sundry means to control and manipulate a seemingly remote reality and with the only apparent alternative being a fantasized god, inept and impotent in light of human suffering, philosophical arguments come across as plaintive wailing in the foggy night. Based on core failure to recognize the innate connection of the human individual with the Reality he encounters, any rational argument seeking to attribute meaning to *either* this puny, temporal biological unit on a lonely planet or an equally puny creation of a great god wafts flaccidly in a futile, insensitive universe.

But seeing the real engagement of life by each conscious entity in terms of the Oneness *with which it emanates,* you recognize that no other consciously focused Self who ever existed has more significance than **you do,** *right now.* Therein your value grows exponentially. Man's Place in the Universe equates to **YOUR** place in existence, embodied, living, manifesting, creating, interacting, perceiving, reacting mostly with love, joy, fun and humor, adding to the grand experience of the growth of human culture and advancement of civilization. You don't have to imagine or theorize such a status, much less cram it into a paradigm that doesn't allow for it, *just recognize it!*

Some nearly did. Hegel saw the advancement, Fichte the freedom incorporated into the human spirit. Nietzsche lamented the downside of man's failures. All of these ultimately lie rooted in broad non-recognition for the immersion each of us has in this interactive bath of real effects.

Exalting a non-existent god only accomplishes depletion of self-worth within one's own self-image. Blind to the Self's metaphysical connections, acknowledging only the outer realm, science further diminishes the self to a rudimentary status of meaningless transience.

But those are **only ideas** – complex, well founded philosophically in reason and argument, but mere notions resting in the illusory cradle of traditional and modern thinking. And that crib of infantile impressions glides back and forth, seemingly without end, bumping and squeaking on those two lumpy rockers, science and religion.

Having matured and outgrown the cradle, you realize your role as a human occupying a unique niche in the universe, as valid and meaningful as any who ever undertook an incarnation: *a consciousness secondary to none.* Your existence is no less important than that of any human who ever lived – and **to you in particular**, the importance of your being far exceeds any other!

So Man's Place in the Universe is utterly vital and energetic. Philosophers trying to argue for that high status within the context of science and religion are doing so with the dim lighting of limited understanding. Philosophers who disregard Man's meaning in deference to science sit in the florescent glow of their own synthetic luminosity, scarcely perceiving a ghost of man's accomplishment.

Without man, this playground is empty and all the equipment unused.

So Man's Place in the Universe, in *this* Universe, is integral and foremost. Without man as a complex consciousness on the perceiving end, the *matter* side doesn't matter.

Point Three: What are Good and Evil?

How Does it Feel?

Once again, the view of this traditional philosophical query rests entirely on what sense is made out of this reality in the first place.

Clearly, you are well equipped naturally to gauge goodness and its opposite. The former, when encountered in unfolding events and relationships, elicits joy and ebullience, satisfaction and feelings of warmth and fulfillment. The latter brings pain and depression, feelings of rejection, drawing tears and withdrawal from an emotional base, fear or anger as a response.

To the untainted mind, it is obvious that **good** results upon fulfillment of desire, such as success in endeavors, a healthy body and rewarding relationships resulting from one's daily efforts. And evil would be the term applied when one's status, encountered events and relationships, etc., negate intent or neutralize desires. Similarly, initiating gestures enhancing others'  lives would also, to the clearly functioning mind, be deemed "good", bringing them joy and warm feelings. Likewise, doing damage to others' interests or bodies would, viewed clearly, be evil in both intent and action.

But, within the scope of standard regard, it isn't that simple. An action taken that results in benefit to one person can bring pain and suffering to another. An outcome that improves the life of some can, by direct consequence, wreak devastation to the environment, polluting the air and inflicting irreversible damage to the landscape.

Philosophers through time wrestled with that conundrum. Socrates invested considerable focus on such issues, concluding that the highest good was knowledge. He reasoned that a knowledgeable person would only take actions resulting in widespread benefit.

Plato, though, looking at reality as a collection of objects which are only imperfect instances of the ideal form behind them, saw **goodness** specifically in that **ideal realm**, *thus rendering the real world as flawed* – the epitome of evil. Yet, so Plato thought, the rational aspect of man can gain dominion over the flawed realm of substance – so man's ability to reason provides the opportunity to impart goodness into life. But, unlike the Epicureans in their pursuit of sensual pleasure, per se, as the goal, for Plato pleasure was fulfillment of a good life gained by reasoned regard and ethical action.

Aristotle, too, seemed to equate reason and the application of rationally considered action with goodness. He looked for a "Virtuous Mean" position in any of life's gestures lying between the extremes, the Vices: one of Deficiency and the other of Excess. Modesty, for example, lies between brazenness and bashfulness. He also extracted pleasure from the ultimate Good, attributing that highest status to self-realization.

While religion dominated philosophy from Augustine through Aquinas and beyond, good and evil were generally broken down in attribution to god and matter. Seeing in the grand conceptualized creator unquestioned, unlimited goodness, evil was relegated to the mundane physical plane and its various potentials. Christianity specifically has always had trouble justifying their ideas with rampant evil effects in the world: how can a monumentally good god create a world so full of suffering? Added to that might be, how can aspects of life that feel so pleasurable (sex as prime example) be evil in *any* estimation.

One classic copout, of course, is attributing evil to yet another mythical figure, Satan, the Devil. That embodiment of malevolence – a notion extracted directly from Zoroastrianism, with its ongoing conflict of Ahura Mazda vs. Ahriman – of course, simply avoids the question. Either Satan is a god of equal creative power, in which case Christianity is a duality, or he falls under the auspices of the great God – which reverts right back to the initial question: why so much evil is permitted by the boss.

The answer, of course, is simple. Religion in general and Christianity specifically *don't describe Reality*. They build up a set of synthetic notions removed from life's real function, subsequently only ever dealing with their concocted fantasy.

Later philosophers migrated into differing notions to explain *good* vs. *evil*. Descartes, moving toward rational thinking while hanging on to (capital "G") God, attributed sin to human action (another copout, as God was deemed to have created man). Spinoza, emphasizing reason based on intelligent regard, credited (or perhaps debited) lack of knowledge for sin.

John Locke had an interesting thought, though. Locke,

thinking that humans begin life with a clean slate of understanding and that all understanding comes from
experience/learning, figured that conceptions of what constitutes good or evil came from outside understanding. In this
regard, he noted the point that I repeatedly emphasize: parents
impress on us ideas embodying right or wrong action from the
get-go. They only seem innate, natural and even proper because
they were learned so early.

Locke is exceptionally insightful in that regard, though his
approach is limited. Indeed, we do pick up confines of cultural
regard, i.e., standards and allowed behavior, from parental and
societal influence. But Locke missed this: we bring our essential
nature *with us* into an incarnation. The details fall into place
rapidly, as we've more or less "chosen" an incarnation to fulfill
specific goals while realizing our core nature.

Recognizing pain and pleasure as part of the scheme of
things – man's resultant lot in his engagement of life – and
seeing that a particular experience might not universally bring
the same response, Locke incorrectly (but interestingly)
concludes that various laws were in effect, including divine and
man-made. This led to a not uncommon conclusion in the
direction of morality: doing beneficial deeds would bring the
highest reward to the individual as personal fulfillment.

Of course, in the real world it doesn't work that way. Often
enough the most rotten, self-serving people reap great reward
via success and pleasure, while the most moral, ethical languish
in poverty and pain.

Kant recommended moral action as well, although his idea of
reality seemed not to *require* beneficial behavior. Subsequent
German philosophers, wrestling with the good/evil dichotomy,
seem lost in arguments of rationalization meant to support
caring acts.

Others along the way analyzed *the good* based on more
scientific, quantitative terms: choices that would yield conse-

quences benefitting more people are better than actions which would help fewer.

Before shedding some light on a longstanding rational inquiry meant to discern a meaningful moral conclusion – a venture traditionally undertaken by examining life within an inherently flawed paradigm – I would add a highly significant effect here.

In the *good* vs. *evil* consideration, centuries of religionists and philosophers never seem to have recognized a third potential outcome: *nothingness*. Based on intent to fulfill one's

will in the course of life, regarding desire for positive outcome in various aspects, just about everybody would like health, success and acceptance in real life. Good results when those happen in significant measure ongoing. Bad, that *evil* alternative, manifests when, ongoing or even for short periods, health fails into misery and suffering, endeavors fail with disappointment and relationships crumble in painful rejection by friends, potential lovers or society in general, as in warfare, depression or famine.

But that third potential outcome doesn't fall into either category: *neither good occurs, nor bad*. The will is neither fulfilled nor negated – just *nothing happens*: that business venture just doesn't take off; relationships are bland; health is OK, with no glaring problems, but energy is low, motivation lacking. In this third, often subtle vein, one's desires just *don't get fulfilled*, relegating life to ongoing struggle for fulfillment.

This extraordinarily common occurrence seems never to have been noticed by philosophers in any such examination of good vs. evil. Yet, in life, nothing happening can be as detrimental to quality of living as any negative outcome – and far more common. It leaves intent and *focus on fulfilling that intent* dangling in an unresponsive state of incompletion – perhaps for an entire lifetime.

In general, the influence of religion over millennia has distorted what would otherwise be a rather elementary, straightforward evaluation. The number of humans killed, maimed and tortured in the name of religious piety – ostensibly to serve that wondrous god – over centuries is inestimably vast and absurdly hypocritical. The judgment of sex and its free engagement – an act that not only brings pleasure and feelings of acceptance at its very root, but is vital for human continuity – as sinful and thus evil by religious traditions stands as a monument to the twisted reasoning that results from holding artificial tenets as real. Perhaps worst of all, though, the general restriction of one's being and doing what is innately, intuitively felt as correct and right – due to artificial moral judgments and fear of divine retribution – has grossly restricted accomplishment and fulfillment in countless lives for ages.

On the philosophy side, long-winded, rational arguments, with synthetic conjecture of moral definition and ethical standards – all expressed within the confines of invalid overall understanding – has done little over the ages to temper the advancement of archaic, often brutal treatment by small-minded religious adherents and the great preponderance of humans who don't think at all.

Only when understanding that *you yourself*, not others, not some god out there or evil source across from you, not the government, the police, the rich, germs, luck, your mother-in-law, conditions or anything else, but *only you*, are at the root of all encountered problems, do you stop looking on all those external sources negatively. You see them as playing roles reflective of your own nature, not as causes to be destroyed or conquered, as restrictions to be struggled against.

As you clear away inner conflict and struggle, mechanisms of the psyche leading to engagement with opposing interests, you realize that *evil,* **per se**, *doesn't really exist.* Evil is only an attribute tied to events and outcomes that embody pain, failure, rejection and such as real consequences of inner turmoil. And those real outcomes in life all reflect values, notably *conflict,* held within your own intrinsic nature.

Absent awareness of the inner-outer connection, however, evil – like causality in general – gets attributed to illusory sources or diabolical forces. But none of them really exist.

What exists, **in Reality**, are you and a lot of people with varying interests and intents – incarnated entities currently occupying a shared Reality. You and all others – this author included – attract those specific types into personal engagement appropriate to inner need. So long as self-defeating elements occupy your mindset, you attract people with interests not in line with your own. They may seem rotten, evil and intent on doing harm – but they are just engaging life with *their own* set of distorted understandings and *their own* conflict and struggle. To the degree that personal fear and powerlessness allow, they may damage your interests.

Only after releasing negating and neutralizing inner elements, **do you stop encountering those qualities in others!!**

Religionists in western settings, though, distort the whole scheme of things by misinterpreting aspects of life based on archaic notions and primitive definitions. Just as they attribute causality to imagined sources, so do they also project evil onto others – and to mythical entities.

And philosophers, all the while, conceptualize complex sets of definitions for goodness or evil based on their own substrata of accepted understanding – all of which is as synthetic as the religionists, just more complicated.

Point Four: The Nature of God

You Name It

Mankind has harbored, in fears and entreaties, some sort of god or pantheon of them for tens of thousands of years.

It's hard to imagine the typical Homo Erectus mindset (1.5 million years ago) or that of Homo Habilis (2 million BCE), much less the dim reckoning powers toward external forces that went on in the mind of a late Australopith (3 million BCE). But whenever our progenitors began to communicate, create tools and reason, their lore and lifestyle likely led to attributing causality – movement of herds, germination of edible seeds and roots – to the elements, the seasons, ultimately to heavenly bodies moving across the sky. Of those, more prominent than the "wanderers" (planets) which all became associated with gods, were the sun and moon – most notably the former, as old sol's seasonal wending of height arcing across the sky always preceded the seasons.

If our ancestors were aware of anything at any point along man's trail of evolution, it was seasonal fluctuation of the sun – for that brought herd migration and herb, berry and root availability.

That notion of external control – something *out there* making this all happen – was passed along, generation to generation, woven into cultural notions, built into evolving language and ultimately, after long and convoluted evolution, handed to us as we learned cultural basics.

As noted, based on years navigating the psyche, once I removed conceptual residue of old beliefs in the Christian god, never did I encounter any shred of a deity within the inner realm – no single hint or indicator of external agenda-setting. In relating real issues to their inner roots, once I'd eliminated those psychic attributes, their effect of negating or neutralizing my intent ended as well. That change echoed no external forces, required no entreaties to gods, diversion of qi, blending of yin and yang or *anything else*.

Indeed, of the only two realms of engagement I am aware of, *only two* fields of encounter to which I have conscious exposure – the *outer* space of objects, people and daily encounters and the *inner* of mind-image, of dream and unbounded imagination – any god-like entity separate from me, yet somehow causal in this Reality, would have to occupy one or the other, probably both. Should this inductive force exist in some other dimension, it would be irrelevant to my existence, *as I occupy these*. Invariably, inevitably, 100% of the time, when I have revised specific elements of my own psyche, Reality has changed qualitatively in direct correspondence, improving in exactly those areas I revised.

So with no god existing in the inner realm, he would have to occupy the outer. Yet nowhere in space is even an inkling of a deity-like being. Many used to be thought to reside up in the "heavens", the clouds or beyond, even in the mountains, like Sinai or Olympus.

Smoky volcanoes and cloud-tipped, snow-covered peaks could stimulate the vivid, fearful imaginations of our ancestors to come up with grand fantasy. And the outcome of such thoughts became stories, then myths, then timeless truths, passed along to wide-eyed children of each succeeding generation, evolving along the way into grandiose stories of war gods and judgments, of humans spawned by gods and miracles beyond question.

Remember, our ancestors of long past times when myths of god arose and evolved held not even scant understanding of the vastness of space, the nature of cloud formation, volcanic activity spurred by plate tectonics, weather patterns or natural growing cycles. And they were certainly unaware of the inner-outer connection of psyche-reality. The "heavens" they imagined as god's abode, after the mountains, sky and universe were better understood, reverted to this ethereal *other place* – never specified, just imagined.

Convoluted Attribution of Divinity

Philosophers began long ago to outgrow those rambling imaginings – but still, external causality found its way from godhood to other fancy expressions: First Cause, Logos, Unmoved Mover. These were reasoned by brilliant men, Plato and Aristotle among them, looking for some *initial* source to get Reality primed and flowing, if not simply created in the first place. From their standpoint, it **must have been so**: all things *must be* made by something or somebody else – where would they otherwise come from?

Plato fashioned the initiator as the "Demiurge", a word whose meaning simply indicates a skilled artisan, but which implied a creator god, generally attributed as having good intent. Plotinus, many centuries later, was to revise the implication to more of a *divine mind* as originator, attributing his allusion of "**the One**" to that source as its initial emanation.

But Aristotle, looking at reality in more material terms, saw the universe as always having existed, only **put into motion** by a god figure. His "Prime Mover" was stirring the pot but hadn't cooked the soup.

These ideas, initiated as they were by brilliant thinkers whose innovative views on other aspects of life carried great weight, subsequently impacted all western thinking.

As Christianity took root and spread, many of its base ideas were unclear, interpreted differently in various regions and hotly debated for centuries before they became standardized. Considerable effort was made to fit the Christian creator god into this role of *demiurge* or *prime mover*, thus legitimizing the notion – and the Christian movement with it – in light of the high regard for those philosophers. As god was deemed ultimately holy to the highest degree of perfection, it was handy to attribute the dirty work of creation, including some pretty miserable attributes of suffering in the real world, to some other agent. The Christian deity *did* cook the soup, they felt, but shouldn't be held responsible for all ingredients.

Enter *Logos*. For Heraclitus, that word, drawn from a Greek root that could indicate a word, thought, saying or such, had come to indicate a principle that governs reality: something of a flow that one would need to recognize. The Stoics then took that idea and applied it as the vitalizing force of their god, a sort of **directive** guiding the universe.

And eventually Philo of Alexandria (20 BCE – 50 CE), a Jewish philosopher, drew on notions of the Logos in trying to synchronize Judaism with Greek thinking. For him, Logos equated to the "word of God" and thus divine wisdom. Somehow this line of thinking made its way into the Gospel of John, the fourth gospel in the New Testament – the one that abandons Jesus as a healer/teacher figure and promotes his mystical god-nature. In so doing, John basically aligns *Logos* with the *being* of the deity. That gospel famously begins:

In the beginning was the Word, and the Word was with God, and the Word was God. He (meaning Jesus) *was with God in the beginning.*

Later, John 1:14 adds:

The Word became flesh and lived for a while among us.

John, of course (whoever he was, writing about the year 110, certainly wasn't John the original disciple of Jesus), didn't compose in English. The word "Word", in John's original Greek, is *Logos*, not indicating a single particle of speech, but this long-evolved collage of a *principle* governing reality through something ascribed to divine wisdom. But it reflects – or perhaps establishes – the thinking by that time that the notion of a grand God also *included within* its essence the *Son* (Jesus, basically functioning as Logos) as well as the *Holy Spirit* (yet another notion rooted in John).

And that three-pronged conception evolved by the fourth century into a full-bore doctrine that God – big "G" deity – was actually three divine persons, alternately considered *modes*, all in one. He was, at once, the *Father* (his role in sending his Son as savior), the *Son* (the Logos who incarnated as Jesus) and the *Holy Spirit* (this one rather difficult to pin down). That multiple nature of the Christian God has been long argued, following its original conflicted establishment through heated debate and numerous rifts. Indeed, even today some denominations of Christianity don't buy into the notion that one entity can be three.

To address that evolving scene: names and their application can always be confusing, creating illusion of being where something doesn't really exist. False impressions are common enough when naming a tangible object – its essence becomes bounded by the description, carving it deceptively out of its context. But when intangible, ethereal entities are invented by superstitious ancient people through overzealous conjecture or overblown piety – then enforced through church authority – the deception can take on major proportions, even increasing through time.

The Trinity – never mentioned or even really proposed in the New Testament – was first concocted by Tertullian around 200 CE, describing (actually "defining" would be more accurate, as to *describe* anything, it has to exist in the first place) the Christian deity as being three persons, but one substance. It was later formalized by the Council of Nicaea in 325, when much of the early church doctrine was established in a Creed at the behest of the Emperor Constantine.

Of course, once the operative bishops hashed out what was acceptable from the wide-ranging variety of documents, accounts and inconsistent doctrines available from various regions, eliminating what they deemed incorrect, it quickly hardened into being the *only acceptable "truth"*.

(Disagreeing with officially sanctioned doctrine from then onward made one a *heretic*. Originally stemming from a word meaning simply to choose, as in "choose a different interpretation of invariably contradictory church declarations", it quickly became a weapon against anyone who would question church authority and standardized thinking. As such, the word took on very negative connotations, implying blasphemy and consequential unimaginable horrors, when it only meant to choose to see things differently than the sanctioned church doctrine.)

From that point forward, the Trinity further evolved over time as various others honed it to edit out the more blatant absurdities and inconsistencies. But over generations it simply became accepted – particularly to those unable to think for themselves and recognize it as a fantasy.

Indeed, that evolution is typical for any sort of religious conjecture in any culture in man's past: it becomes ever deeper ingrained as the indoctrinated world view of subsequent generations. Thinking and customs build themselves around established definitions.

The Trinity itself doesn't exist; indeed, all three components are fabrications. The "Father", an image steeped in Jesus' depiction of a loving, father-like deity compared to the old, tired war-god, Yahweh, not only **doesn't** exist but *couldn't*. Qualities attributed to that deity are mutually exclusive and couldn't possibly co-exist in any intelligent entity, particularly one so vastly powerful as to have created a universe billions of light-years across containing untold trillions of stars and associated matter. The "Son", rather than co-existent, is equally non-existent. The notion stems from mythical offspring of gods and traditional Aramaic phraseology, whitewashed by Paul and later dreamers into epic, divine proportions. The "Holy Spirit" or

Ghost is utter concocted fantasy.

Indeed, the integrated, interactive Oneness with which life flows indicates that the universe is *being*-generated, not **action**-generated. Thus, no entity can create *anything outside itself*. You, in the overall expression of your life, are self-contained, a flow of meaning from inner psychic structures to outer manifestations embodying that same meaning.

So, in terms of creating reality, while no Trinity exists, no grand and glorious external puppeteer pulls strings to induce events, one very real god actually exists – and *you are it*. Of course, you don't conjure up Reality solely in line with your will, but reflective of the whole inner picture – where not only the will exists, but also many elements that function to negate or neutralize it.

Thus, the Nature of God is evinced in the comprehensive nature of *you*, as embodied in your complex psyche. Perhaps I should capitalize that to make it official: *You* with a capital "Y".

The Trinity, i.e., three-in-one god of Christianity – the Father, Son and Holy Spirit? Pure conceptualization. Allah, the most merciful? Nothing more than an idea. Zeus, Yahweh, Ra, Thor, Isis, Aesir, Huaca – you name it – Ahura Mazda, Parvati, Horus, Sama, Anat, Amma, Apollo, Assur, Durjaya, Aken, Seth, Maheo, El, Perende, Loba, Haukim, Chalmecati, Chikara, Na Ngutu, Dagan, Wotan, Saturn, Maju, Aya, Wakan Tanka, Venus, Freyja, Mithras, Adonis, Aranyani, Gaia, Il, Arjuna, Baal, Atl, Kitanitowit, Nagini, Elohim – shall I go on? These and a thousand more are/were all gods imagined by humans somewhere within historical times. Each had attributes, but they were characteristics assigned not by sacred revelation by privileged luminaries, but by individuals who believed in them and/or benefited by propagating the notion.

Your imagined god, should you still host one in mind, named or not, is no different.

Point Five: Fate vs. Free Will

Have It Your Way

Long debated in cousin genres of philosophy and religion is the notion of Free Will.

If a powerful creator god who made me along with all other things knows *everything*, it would include **all events to come.** So, how can I have anything approximating free will? With all things past and future fixed and carved in ethereal granite, then what difference does it make what I do? It would have all been preset and I'm just playing out a role, like an automaton, plodding through life with no freedom whatsoever. Whatever direction I go, whatever I accomplish, it was foreordained.

Traditionally Christianity averts this conundrum by positing *free will* as a condition imposed by their god, such that any individual is free to choose his/her path. The problem with that, of course, is how could (or indeed, why would) a god then judge any given individual negatively when he himself initially supplied the situation and the rational characteristics which would dictate the invariable outcome, rigidly preordained or not?

In a meaningful reality, can an individual really exercise free will? Or are outcomes set by fate or other forces – or even processes – such that choices are illusory, thus rendering intent ineffective and powerless?

The original Greek thinkers tended to conclude **fate** was a feature of reality.

Heraclitus, with his recognition of inevitable flux within unfolding reality, looked at that **Logos** as a set law that imposed a certain cascade of cause and effect that nobody could violate. Socrates, though, felt that knowledge provided man a means to some degree of self-determinacy. Plato attributed to man even more freedom to choose, with resultant quality of existence depending on one's ability to choose wisely. But Aristotle shaded freedom with morality – allowing man the freedom to make poor choices, relying all the while on reason.

Basically, it seems, throughout that early Greek period, thinking acknowledged a consistency within reality, a tendency functionally in the direction of fate. But it allotted reason the capability to overcome whatever law applied.

To the Stoics, conquering desire itself provided freedom. Disengaging any emotional response to disappointment seemed to them to short-circuit any pain reality might bestow.

As philosophy developed, however, the consideration of free will broke into various analyses: *Determinism, Fatalism* and *Libertarianism* comprise three explanations beyond the notion that unfolding events are frozen in content divinely.

In Determinism, reality is held to proceed with a set series of cause-and-effect cascades, such that, given the state of things **right now**, what ensues is fixed. Looking at the current status as an *effect* of all prior happenings, and given a certain momentum of things and the existing state of mind of all participants, Determinism says that future events will unfold in basically a preset pattern – a course which things *are bound* to take.

This differs from Fatalism in that the inevitable deterministic pattern is spurred by this cascading causality – processes in play now cause the next set, which then cause the next eventualities, etc. – as opposed to a logical system that simply holds a foregone, inevitable outcome.

Fatalism stems from the traditional notion of *fate*, in turn derived of the old mythical Greek entities, the Fates (or Moirae, Parcae to the Romans). As one spun life's thread, another measured it, then the third snipped it. Philosophically, Fatalism posits that decision-making carries no value as whatever will be, will be – regardless of any path chosen.

Libertarianism takes the opposite approach: emerging events from this moment forward depend **entirely** on decisions made through exercise of free will. Behind that notion is the thought that an action taken now literally, absolutely *causes* a subsequent effect.

Viewed from each of these points of view, reality takes on a different appearance. Each, of course, once accepted, seems to confirm itself. From this point on, if I have free will, I can decide to continue writing this book, filling in additional words – or get up and go take a walk. I have many other options at any given moment; the one I choose then creates an effect yielding a whole new set of choices. The Fatalist would say that my actions are all predestined – the option I indeed take is inevitable. The Determinist would agree only insofar as outcome, looking at the status of all things in the cascade of causality as predetermining what decision I make. The Libertarian simply looks at my choice as free.

Philosophers stood in one camp or the other, sometimes with toes striding the line.

Augustine saw no free will, attributing to Adam the only real choice – and he made a bad one, sticking us all with negative consequences. Abelard, though, thought that without free will, sin couldn't exist – that god had shipped us from the factory with free choice as standard equipment: we were thus free to sin as desired, but bear the consequences. Thomas Aquinas saw only the grace of his deity as mitigating those consequences.

One thing men **did** do as time went on was free *themselves* from the church – at least some did to varying degrees. Bacon drew a line between religion and philosophy, but attributed to religion *set laws* – divine directives that would have crossed his line, whether he noticed it or not. Descartes' mechanical universe still featured God tinkering at the control panel: while the body was part of the machine, stuck in a cause-and-effect realm, the mind/soul has some freedom. But his notions are convoluted and contradictive, seeming, as many explanations do, to try to justify the apparent within scope of that pesky, preconceived god-notion.

Spinoza, meanwhile, pantheisticizing the universe as god *embodied* (big body), allotted freedom to that deity alone, with man only fooled into thinking he is free.

Locke saw the question as insignificant, with the **will** based on god-endowed needs and desires. If those are preset, the will *itself* is only a consequence. Hume also noted the cause-and-effect relationship between desires and actions taken to fulfill them.

French thinking during the Enlightenment moved towards the scientific, attributing choices to natural laws, making man a slightly more complex beast in seeking to fulfill his needs – until Rousseau declared for moral considerations as part of the picture. Kant, however, on the German side, continued hedging his bets.

Seeing a rather determinative universe, Kant still promoted acting **as though** one were free based on moral grounds. He felt that proving free will was impossible, but one should proceed as though it were the case. That notion evolved down through Fichte and Schelling, however, and on to Hegel to where freedom became the ideal, something of a goal, rather than an observed situation or not.

With the movement of man's regard being towards the objective, scientific world view, one devoid of meaning and consequential morality, it seems an innate yearning was pressing thinkers to grasp at freedom as a prize, like a ring on the philosophical merry-go-round.

Of course, on the real scene of evolving society, much of these musings by thinkers is lost to the common mindset.

Religion in the theology of Christianity, if taken literally, doesn't allow freely willed action of any valued consequence. God created everything and will judge you negatively with eternal punishment if you deviate from his prescribed set of actions – to which the church is exclusively privy and, in light of such assuredness, is eternally ready to **prejudge** you, and quite glad to do so. Particularly, however, should you hand over generous tithes and offerings, *any* religious organization is likely to pre-arrange a more favorable judgment.

That other pillar on which the modern mindset is erected, science, allows for any freely willed gesture that the brain can concoct. Consequences of such actions will fall within deterministic bounds, however, as effects are only regarded as outcomes of actions taken, which are considered causes. And your actions are determined by your current status – thus limited in effectiveness by the scheme of things.

You might expect me to say at this point that neither religion nor science is correct, that philosophical conclusions through time are equally distorted by their underlying assumptions and that my point of view is correct – which I will then go on to describe. Now, was that thought in your mind predetermined by your mindset and all previous encounters in life (like having read the earlier portions of this book), or was it a brilliant conclusion because you are capable now of thinking outside conventional confines? Was it pre-determined, or did you come up with the expectation freely?

Well, I for one am personally locked into this *ill-fated* status of having to clarify everything – preordained by cosmic forces to be personally *highly annoyed* at implausible, nonsensical views of reality! So I now choose to clarify things, leaving it to the conjecture of you and subsequent generations of philosophical analysts to interpret whether I was causing this eventuality or perhaps it was Ahura Mazda, in a comeback attempt, prompting me to take the side of truth against fallacy.

To understand free will vs. fate or even determinism, it is necessary to take a look at *causality*. Only clearly seeing the nature of causality itself allows recognition of whether free will can ever be exercised in affecting a desirable outcome, or alternately, that things happen regardless of attempts to impose one's will through action. Indeed, neither religion nor science – nor any of the philosophers I've explored – really understood causality. Lacking that perceptiveness, none of those sources could or ever would grasp the subtlety of free will.

Science looks at the real universe as though it were all that exists, relegating mind and all attributes of consciousness to superficial consequence. It looks on self-awareness as a brain function evolved to the extent it can reason and conclude, thus complex enough to recognize its own being. It regards action taken as causal, and whatever outcome results as effect. Of course, in a physical realm, moving bodies of any nature can be causal: if a comet collides with Jupiter, it *causes* a dark hole in its atmosphere. If an earthquake hits a region of Earth, it causes widespread devastation. Mix the right ingredients and bake it, you create a pie.

For science, then, causality equates to impelled motion, resulting from force pushing objects into motion. To the degree that an individual is capable of instigating movement, that person can be seen as causal – sort of. Because that physical brain is quantified in a scientific sense, with its training and logical capabilities at any moment rather fixed, conclusions it comes to that would initiate an action are pretty much *determi-*

native. So, science may *seem* to confirm free will, but conclusions drawn and actions taken are predictable (based on the present, which was just as predictable from past moments) and thus not really free.

Christianity is even more convoluted, allowing the conscious Self with its complex inner state to be a significant part of reality – but only a temporal creation of its grand Instigator, thus limited in nature to capabilities designated by the Manufacturer. You, as a human, are free to exercise intent – or try to – but watch out for consequences should you violate preset rules!

The closer either of these propositions is examined, the less viable they become.

In Reality, your existence as a conscious entity is the *basis* of the universe you engage – neither an inconsequential outcome of a long evolution via natural selection nor a miraculous instantaneous creation. The flow of events and relationships encountered daily is a cohesive, interactive manifestation reflecting the nature of your Self. Thus, Reality is not a consequence of **what went on before**, cascading through mindless existence of particles from a series of overt causes, nor a **scripted play** dictated by a lonely god apparently out for entertainment – or as a gesture of self-aggrandizement to accumulate futile worshippers.

But rather each of us is self-contained in terms of attributes and resultant essence. What you hold within the complex values of your psychic content becomes real – with those values played out by encounters and their intrinsic meaning as they affect you.

So, in terms of life and the impact of surrounding events on you personally, *you are the cause*. Agents that science considers causal due to their apparent initiation of action are really only triggers to events (or relationships) attracted into encounter.

However, within the specific quality of events you attract **right now** is a precise consequence of your nature. When you revise that qualitative value content held within the psyche, so will the features of subsequent real events change in response to the new mindset.

The flow of encountered reality, then, *does not depend* on the present state of things, unfolding as potential overt causes spur situations and cascade into further causes. Reality does not flow from one second into the next, wherein an objective universe of matter flows in traditional cause-and-effect repetitive surges. The objective reality implied by science and much of western default thinking is an illusion, fostered by languages formulated to describe it and widely accepted by people who are currently incapable of seeing through the illusion.

Nor does the flow depend on some third-party divinity meting out complex situations, tempting, rewarding or otherwise. That illusion is formed by believing in such an entity.

Your life is impelled by your inner nature – nothing else.

So, in terms of the topic of this point, how does the inner-outer Oneness impact the notion of Free Will and Fate?

Actually, both are in play – a remarkable trait of Reality that has always managed to fool even the most brilliant of thinkers. You have absolutely free will *to attempt* to do anything you choose, *to try* to accomplish any task or project, any gesture or effort. You can literally *try* anything. Of course, inherent limitations frame the situation: as a 48-year-old, slightly dumpy, 5' 7", non-athletic male, you are very unlikely to find success as a player in the National Basketball Association.

Free Will to try something does not imply freedom to accomplish it. But Free Will is yours.

What *ensues*, subsequent to your efforts, comprises neatly wrapped real encounters, situations and events that absolutely reflect *what you are*. Events are never results caused by what you *do*, but only *what you are*. All intent, any actions taken trying to realize that intent and the degree of success that actually results – all these fall within the confines of **your being**.

Action is only ever a subset of being. With peace and confidence as cornerstone inner characteristics, your plan will be viable, execution effective and success will result. Without them, no action possible will accomplish your goal.

In understanding the functionality of life, then, eliminate *the past* as causal – Determinism is invalid. Each previous event and status was only an effect of earlier states of mind. What unfolds in upcoming episodes results from your nature *now*.

And disregard the future – that imagined state never comes. Only a new now moment unfolds, and it absolutely reflects being.

So *actions* chosen to be taken are rather moot. *Outcomes* – all qualitative effects in life – only depend on content of mindset. Planned actions, situational factors and outcomes fall within the confines of your nature.

Real freedom, then, is found in the *ability to choose direction*. Your power to realize that choice, in turn, rests totally on your ability to revise the inner state to ultimately manifest the desired outcome – eliminating doubt, fear and conflict that would engender failure. Thus, your leverage for moving reality in desired directions *lies entirely within*. The real world is only an effect.

So your apparent current "power" as seen in your societal status and its authoritative measure, wealth, level of robust strength and vitality reflects your self-image. That conventional status-measurement isn't really power at all, but a simple resultant of your overall mindset.

Your real *creative power* is displayed in every moment of every day as your psyche dynamically imprints its nature on the real events and relationships of its manifested Reality.

And your entire *effective power* is the ability to regard psychic content and change it. Of course, you are only free to do so to the degree that you recognize your status as a conscious entity embedded in its own essence.

So, you have **free will** in two ways. You can freely make decisions and take actions daily any way you choose. But the outcome of those actions depends on neither cleverness of planning nor ability to implement it – but rests only on your nature for its fruition. That angle of free will only sets things up. The second, though, is causal: you have the freedom to *delve inward* to change elements of your mindset that lead to self-defeating outcomes.

But **Fate** has an element of validity, too! As an *apparent* process fate can be viewed as the pattern-making propensity you display in your nature: rejection, ill health and failure continue so long as your psyche hosts elements that engender such effects. Neither fixed nor imposed by external power sources, fate shifts as inner change occurs. Of course, you only experience one outcome: without accomplishing (or even attempting) inner revision, persistent patterns seem dictated by an external force approximating *fate* – appearing external when you don't understand life's inner-outer flow.

In terms then of traditional regard for Fate vs. Free Will, indeed *you have both*. But **you determine your fate** by freely choosing to orient creative power via focus of your effective power: changing the inner always results in outer revision.

Point Six: The Soul and Immortality

Being as a Status

I recall asking my devoutly Presbyterian mother what my *soul* was. I must have been about 6, and that word made little sense. In church they told stories about my soul and its consequences. And of course, that prayer asked the "Lord" to set this item of mine on a heavenly shelf somewhere during the night – and keep it up there, taking it only should I die while the sun was warming the other side of the planet.

Mom's answer was certainly steeped in religious definition. I can't recall details, but it was unsatisfying: I couldn't see or sense this thing in any way. And why was it named like that slab of leather on the bottom of my shoe? (Couldn't spell yet...)

Had my mother reviewed concepts of soul as evolved in Greek thinking, she would have realized how the notion changed from early times of Homer through the great philosophers and on to Christian thinking. No such ideas pertaining to the real Self emerged early on, accurate from the beginning and conceived in final form, but rather they twisted and swayed with winds of both popular and conjectural thinking.

Of course, Mom didn't ponder those things in reference to the soul – or any other aspect of her religion. She certainly shopped at various grocery stores for the best meat and veggies – or the best deal – but took her given religion with nary a question.

Facing death as the ever looming end station of life's journey, our ancestors – probably initially asking their mothers such questions – drew conclusions as to mortality, hosting varied thoughts about one's final demise. Fit into that dim picture was the implication of **what part** of individual consciousness, if any, survives that inevitable event.

The very oldest of stories, the epic of Gilgamesh, recorded on cuneiform tablets two millennia before the Greek philosophers, features the quest of that grand, powerful king of Uruk in Mesopotamia seeking a way to avert death. At the passing of his friend, Enkidu, Gilgamesh, in quest of immortality, sets off on a long journey to find Utanapishtim, who had been given a reprieve from dying by the god Enlil.

After a long – and rather confusing – journey, having found Utanapishtim, Gilgamesh was told of a thorny plant that, upon pricking his hand, would make him young again.

People weren't particularly fussy about story details back then. Gilgamesh, after diving deep into unspecified waters to retrieve the plant, does get his hand pricked. But he then says he has to eat it for it to work. Still, following this convoluted journey, days of sleeping and that long dive with heavy stones on his feet to fetch the plant – after all that – a snake simply carries it off.

Boom, gone – tough luck! Foiled by the deed of another bad serpent. At least this one didn't talk like Eden's – though it somehow could carry a plant! Anyway, Gilgamesh went home and the story ends. He presumably died at some point, along about 2700 BCE. I do wonder, though, what Utanapishtim has been doing since then – granted immortality, he, like Psyche, must still be around.

Centuries later, the Homeric poems about the Trojan war (12th century BCE) make first reference to the soul as something lost upon death, indicating it remains a shade in the under-world. That notion evolved, however, into the soul being the seat of meaningful traits – pleasures, sexual desire, courage and such – by the pre-Socratic period of Greek philosophy. Also by then, **soul** came generally to be a feature of all living things. Then began the debate over whether the soul survived death or not and with what carryover elements, what rational or emotional characteristics it maintained, etc.

Plato generally argued for the immortality of the soul, attributing reason, emotion and desire to that *non-physical* portion of one's being. But Aristotle, consistent in considering forms to be contained within real objects, doesn't see the soul as separate from the physical being such that its characteristics survive death – though he does allow for *some* portion of the psyche to do so. (To me, that indicates he couldn't differentiate common notions of the soul within his own subtle belief set from the broader picture his towering intellect was painting. Philosophers rarely admit to not knowing something.)

Christianity drew from older Jewish notions of souls as creations of its god, attributing to them the individuality that embodies the character and rationality of each person. While details certainly vary among many interpretations of Biblical illustration, generally the soul is what faces judgment by the deity following bodily death – some placing the soul in temporary states pending final judgment, others figuring the verdict comes immediately (apparently without even a processing backlog in times of war). Of course, that non-appealable decision puts the soul into a heavenly or hellish place, based on some variable criteria extrapolated by church administrations from foggy scriptural notions over centuries.

My mother drew her description from that lore. The general notion of an insubstantial, perceiving, thinking, rationalizing self, called near-synonymously psyche, mind, spirit or *soul* bounced around considerably in the eastern Mediterranean. With many Greek colonies there, trade and cultural interaction provided considerable mixing of ideas, not only with Jews, but with Persians, Hittites, Egyptians, Phoenicians, etc. But early notions evolved through time, as founding and Medieval Christian thinkers often tried to rectify their religious ideas with those of Plato and Aristotle.

But Mom's thoughts of soul were doubtless based on Protestant church dogma.

Had she referenced Buddhism and other eastern traditions, her explanation would have been different. Gautama didn't see a permanent Self even during life. In his view all things, including you-who-reads-these-words, are changing. The soul, to the Buddha, was impermanent and thus a mere illusion as an entity.

Had mother studied up on Kant, she would have perhaps concluded that one can neither prove nor disprove the existence of a non-material soul. That great German thinker couldn't quite grasp the soul as extant, but, given the need for a knower in order to accumulate knowledge in the first place, he allowed an immaterial soul *might* exist. (Still hedging his bets...) And subsequent German Idealists didn't bring much clarity – or even regard – to the notion of the soul or its survival of death.

While science was moving more toward a strictly objective reality and John Locke was contributing to the move, he had no trouble imagining a soul with or without substance. From his *Essay Concerning Human Understanding,* "... it is not harder to conceive how thinking should exist without matter, than how matter should think." Utterly brilliant observation...

But the movement toward science – and away from religion – as a basis of understanding reality has ultimately all but eliminated the notion of soul from philosophical discussion. With consciousness ostensibly based on brain function, the objective paradigm marks death an abrupt end to processing sensory input and drawing conclusions.

The difficulty and self-imposed shortcoming of all these traditions in regarding the soul and its continuity beyond bodily demise falls at its basis – the problem I had way back, age 6, when I queried Mom for meaning but got her rote acceptance of a canned notion: naming something. The soul, psyche, consciousness or whatever the Self is named is not a "thing", some limited-scope, contained quantity, which **you possess** – it's what *you are.* Naming anything forms a defined boundary around it, separating what it is from what it isn't.

It's difficult to see the sole of a shoe when standing on it. It's even trickier on a considerably larger scale to recognize the inherent, unbounded essence of what you are while you are so thoroughly, so permeatingly *being it.* There is no boundary to you – for the real world, in its unfolding events and situations, reflects your essence, just as your psyche embodies that essence in its complex of interwoven values.

So, the very act of *naming* any limited portion of your Self as **soul** or **spirit** destroys recognition of the whole, timeless being which that Self encompasses.

Thus, to recognize the innate existence of the soul and its

unending, unquenchable status of being, rather than entertain my descriptions and illustrations, **just look at your Self** *right now*. Untainted by a bevy of primitive beliefs and more modern rationalizations, of paradigms and attribution of causality, of external sources and forces driving the world, what you are is a conscious entity engaging a multi-dimensional reality on an ongoing basis. That's what you are.

That quality of being is inextinguishable. It is not immortal through time: *time doesn't exist*. But **you do!**

So the tradition of picturing a soul as some portion of the conscious Self that may or may not carry on beyond death – whether in some contextual realm of a deity or limited nature shorn of any portion of its capacity of awareness – coincides with a grand variety of limited, rationalized notions that compromise perception to conform to limited pre-concepts.

To distinguish the immortality of your very being, you need only delve inward to explore and revise as desired the inner echelon of your psyche. Given that *personal experience* of navigating the depths of Self and intimate recognition of real change that ensues consequent to having eliminated negating inner elements, you gain clarity in awareness of the vast complexity of your mindset and its interactive engagement with its own resultant manifestation as reality.

At that point, you see that the grand complexity of your nature – stemming from your earliest days of this lifetime – **could not possibly** have come into existence at birth. And that intricacy of being could not possibly rest on brain function.

So Locke was right to recognize in his fashion that the psyche, the soul – or more accurately, the Self – is immaterial. It exists as a conscious entity peering out into a field reflective of its own nature. But he was wrong to surmise that the mind can only gain knowledge through sensory input from the real world – and wrong to lean so heavily on empirical exploration for understanding.

Plato was partially right, attributing much of higher mind function to that timeless, non-physical **form** behind the real – but apparently didn't realize its full nature in a world of apparent objects.

The Buddha was absolutely correct to note that the perceiving Self is always changing. But his conclusion that this Self therefore doesn't really exist is incorrect. An entity need not be constant, i.e., qualitatively fixed, in order to be inviolably extant. From the standpoint of each individual, the only thing that really *does* exist is the **Self**. However much you change through life, you still experience life from the central position of the Self.

Christianity hedges toward accuracy in positing that the soul survives death. But it wallows in archaic fiction to imagine it was created at the beginning of a single lifetime by an external source, a judgmental deity. The real judgment each and every entity faces is considerably stricter than any deity would exert: *its own*. You, as all incarnated souls, judge yourself all the time – and will do so comprehensively beyond death. But that evaluation won't be on trite moral issues involving sex and subservience – but on love and caring, on growth and budding awareness. Then you'll incarnate again and grow some more...

So, Mom, in case you are watching or have reincarnated as a somewhat more open-minded soul than your previous go-round, I hope this glimpse at the timeless existence of the psyche has been of help to you on your journey.

Point Seven: Man and the State

Cause and Effect – in That Order

All previous points considered here commonly addressed by philosophers fell under the aegis of epistemology, the study of knowledge, or metaphysics, which examines the nature of reality. Considering the individual in relationship to the collective comes more under a third branch of philosophy: **political philosophy** – with some overlap into *ethics*.

(Yet another branch, *logic*, will be left out of this: I have yet to see any personal-governmental interaction involving logical thinking. Even the term *political philosophy* borders on oxymoronic – political statements more often intentionally distort reality than clarify it.)

To evaluate behavioral standards in terms of ethics and morality, philosophy treads, subtly yet gingerly, away from making sense of what's going on in reality and/or in the mind that perceives it toward viewing human interaction – a wholly different endeavor. Rational investigation, whatever the limitations, can directly explore reality and the mind. It will encounter illusions in either realm, for sure, but at least direct encounter minimizes interference.

But pondering such collective interrelationships as man with the state he has created moves philosophy into a realm where it only encounters complex *resultants*. For any culture's government is an *effect*, an unconsciously engendered, cumulative outcome that stems ultimately from the collective mindset of that culture's populace. It reflects in large scale that same aggregate mindset, mirroring qualitatively the overall interaction with reality staged at its base level by individuals.

As such, philosophical consideration at the group level only glosses over latent issues in the inner realm. It incorporates in the process an already inaccurate portrayal of human nature at its most fundamental level – entirely missing the engagement of personal reality by each individual reflective of that person's nature. And it subjects the inquiry to illusory distortion at many levels. Thus political philosophy, for all its optimistic intent, is doomed to flail away at deceptive problems with armchair, unrealistic solutions, all the while ignoring the underlying *real* roots – inner ones – behind overt issues.

That process began with the Greeks, as Socrates, regarding this point, argued that knowledge on a personal level led to consequent improvement in the state. The best minds should run the state, proposed Plato, while Aristotle thought the goal of the state was to produce good citizens. Grand and idealistic notions, all of them, with much more meaningful argument expressed than this superficial overview can include. But no state from then until now *ever* worked the way of the ideal; not a single one ever cared about a well-considered philosophy – including the grand and failed Marxist systems, which were, ignoring Hegel and Nietzsche, ultimately only about power and control with the sham about workers' glory no more than a façade.

Wishful thinking about model states, then, as philosophers are wont to conjure, is far removed from exploring the psyche or empirical inquiry into real objects. Sorry, Socrates, but knowledge, riding underlying, embedded conflict, only leads to more complex debate and more advanced weaponry.

Once past the fleeting Greek – particularly Athenian – experiment with democracy and the flirt of Rome as a budding republic, emperors cared little about philosophical regard and idealized states – they ran the show while commoners, fearful and ignorant (the two traits chaperone each other), knew their place. Once Christianity gripped the scene, though, their conceptualized God was injected into social relationships: the common individual, already secondary to nobility, dropped several notches in status – under the glorified, imagined creator

and aspiring operatives of church hierarchy.

Scholasticism, a movement dominating academic approaches from about 1100 into the 16th century, began by trying to reconcile Christian theology with the Greek philosophers – square pegs *do* go into round holes, if hammered hard enough. Abelard, Scotus, and Ockham were among the Scholastics, with the faction culminating in Thomas Aquinas. They sincerely tried to make sense out of Christian theology. Yet when it differed from Aristotle's take, they unceremoniously dumped the philosopher.

That wasn't altogether bad in terms of man and his government, except that resultant models were much worse than wistful yearning for a state that promoted the good of its citizens. Any state strongly dominated by small-minded adherents to an imagined god, looking for goodness and reward in that heaven *to come*, invariably features aspects detrimental to the well-being of its citizens and their life potential **now**. As such, the effect scarcely differs from one run by a self-serving king. States featuring both, as much of Europe did for centuries, may incorporate the worst of both worlds, with the only possible redemption that the crown could offset excesses of the church – and vice versa.

(Compare this dual, conflictual hierarchy to traditional Islamic governments, where the banality of religious tenets and enforcement of closed-minded imperatives have no secular alternative to mitigate their control. Or, with the scales tipped the other way, compare it to typical communist dictatorships where authoritative rulers stifle church power to oppose their dominating dictates. Both are/were exceptionally oppressive to common citizenry. By the same token, such dictatorial systems only emerge in cultures where people see themselves as powerless.)

Scholastics entertained reason, the basis of philosophy, only so long as it could be made to support religion's revelation object

– the existence of that supreme god. But that method of academic debate and inquiry – always geared toward its original precept – died out as philosophy shifted towards science, where reason did not have to justify revelation. European cultures resulting from fenced-in thinking languished for centuries with little progress. (Much as Islamic cultures do today and regimented communist societies did in recent generations.)

From the Renaissance onward, government was much debated – a significant change from absolute domination without question by church and secular hierarchies prior to that time. Lines of thinking centered on two tracks: equality vs. inequality among classes.

John Locke epitomized the first of those. While his older contemporary, Thomas Hobbes, rubber-stamped the divine right of the English monarchy to run the show, Locke put forth notions of equality among men – that all should be free and enjoy rights thereto. Far from harboring innate propensities toward war and control, man's core nature, Locke felt, leaned toward peace, helpfulness and good will.

With those ideas reinforced by Rousseau in France and the line of thinking of Fichte and others in Germany, upheaval of the old order was in store for western civilization. The American Revolution with its ultimate, unique republic and subsequent French Revolution came about because of such new attitudes being disseminated throughout a more aware populace.

Still, many continued to acknowledge inequality as the reality of life: that privileged classes were advantaged because domination was their nature – that all people are *not* created equal and the state shouldn't impose artificial standards to that effect on political systems. Nietzsche fell into this latter category as he recognized *reality*, rather than propounding the ideal in the face of the obvious.

Indeed, despite over two centuries of near rote repetition of the American ideal – that all men are created equal – so eloquently voiced by Thomas Jefferson and the founding fathers in echo of Locke, the *exact opposite* is really the case: **no two humans are alike**.

So philosophical schools varied from Niccolo Machiavelli's ideal state (c. 1500, that honored the rights of the individual) through the vive of Voltaire and the hobnobbing of Hobbes exhaustively considering a differentiated society where each could succeed to the extent of his/her abilities (and, of course, place in life) to the liberty of Locke, Schelling and John Stuart Mill where all could share socially in the common wealth. Each point of view was right, to a point – and wrong to a corresponding degree.

In reality, while no two people are the same, their differences come to the fore without the state being set up to either institutionalize or ignore those differences. Indeed, as the state functions in each culture and in all time, the core nature of each individual comes out, fitting each person into a complex life pattern that – as I've illustrated in so many ways – reflects their own base nature.

With that inner-outer connection in mind, manifested on a personal (and thus group) level, it becomes obvious that a long and detailed rationale for how government should work or *could*, or even **might** under ideal conditions, is a total intellectual fantasy. No political system can ever be imposed on a people whose collective mindset doesn't fit precisely into the scheme of things – because the government of any cultural group is a resultant of the collective mindset of the people, not the other way around.

Colonists in Revolutionary times were bound to eject the British Empire because their communal mindset was built on personal freedom: those who came here, primarily from Europe at first, were of a freer, more hopeful and independent nature than relatives who stayed back home. Their attitude was new and innovative. They couldn't retain the old ways of European monarchies and would inevitably break free – not because of some process of god-decreed fate, but because their core nature would manifest itself in real events.

Compare that to the overthrow of the Shah of Iran in 1979. Long oppressed by an authoritarian, often brutal regime, the populace jettisoned the Shah and, by national referendum, instituted a Shi'a Islamic government under the control of Ruhollah Khomeini, a Shia cleric of the rank Ayatollah (which refers to a general expertise in Islamic philosophy and law). Ultimately Khomeini instituted a starkly repressive supervision of the people to enforce Islamic standards – deviance from strict code was punished. With repression of political opposition and alternate religions on a scale approximating that of the Shah, clearly *little changed* in Iran but the window dressing: the powerlessness of the individual, a standard feature of the Islamic mindset, shifted from one ruthless dictator to another.

That same effect was evidenced at the fall of the Soviet Union's communist dictatorship: the traditional Russian mindset, rooted in centuries of authoritarian Czars and Soviet strongmen, couldn't support a democratic system. Eventually Russia reverted to a near-dictatorial head of state running their lives.

The government of any cultural group always reflects the collective mindset of its people, just as individually each person's life reflects the value set of the psyche. History and its political unfolding are only *consequences*, resultant effects of the mass inner nature of mankind and its various delineated subgroups.

The track of US history beyond the Revolution bears that out as well. Inner conflict, a long tradition within European roots of the western mindset, finds its manifestation in political attitudes of engaging parties as purely as in international situations. Historically, no sooner did the Great War wither upon US involvement than did seeds of World War II sprout yet another conflict to engage in. When that war ended, the Cold War confrontation of the Communist Bloc filled the inner need and supplied yet other wars – the Korean and Vietnam endeavors – in which to exercise American bravado, heroism and domination (all conflict-based). How long did it take after the crumbling of the Communist threat for Al Qaida and its terrorist techniques to win the latest audition for bad guy with which naïve, materialistic western values could engage? Not very...

Capitalism, Communism, Islamic ideals, Monarchy, Dictatorship – all these are equivalent in function: some people control lots of things and most don't. All are façades reflecting powerless masses, psychologically projecting their creative power to imagined gods and illusory power figures, including vain industrial and political forerunners who imagine – and act like – they *are* those gods. In reality, the gods don't exist and neither group is free, at peace or at ease.

Political Philosophy as a genre of consideration is a joke. Systems on all levels, from religious to political to social, result from the inner realm of the participants. No system, however free or restrictive, can be imposed on a people whose nature is not fundamentally attuned to its function.

The most recent raw example of such an attempt to do so was the folly of invading Iraq for the purpose (likely only stated as a ruse to justify control of oil supply) of imposing a democracy on the populace. Saddam Hussein, as all such totalitarian characters, was a *symptom* of a powerless, unfree people – not really the problem, but an indicator. In that instance, the problem was and remains: a widespread, archaic tribal and Islam-plagued mindset. That alone serves to neuter the hopes and dreams of Iraqis.

Indeed, no religion exists as *anything* but a set of ideas in the minds of its believers. Its effect plays out in the lives of those caught up in its dogma and illusion.

So philosophizing about improved systems for the purpose of accomplishing real political improvement equates to arguing with a television image. For any political system only functions as well as *the people within it*. When those people hold rampant inner conflict and struggle, even prizing those qualities as heroic and honorable, the government invariably makes poor decisions, wastes resources, neglects real issues, fosters corruption and promotes inequality; in general, it functions at a level far below its potential – just like its populace does.

The common mindset held by the vast majority of western citizens features the personal self as separate from the world it encounters and controlled by gods, natural events, potential infection, menacing neighbors, the wealthy and government – both nationally and locally. It promotes a need to control and manipulate other peoples, fight as needed, kill or maim as required to survive and prosper. So long as that inaccurate duality is maintained – the illusory separation of self from the real world – man will continue to unconsciously weave his inner propensity toward conflict and struggle into his manifest daily life, both on a scale of personal encounter and mass historical outcome.

Point Eight: Man and Education

Philosophical Cloning in Action

Education in some form has been a feature of man's approach to prepping upcoming generations for ages. From ancient times, when flint-knapping technique and herb recognition formed standard teaching, through the establishment of agriculture including evolving, specific techniques for farming and animal husbandry as well as clothing production, etc., daily living needs were principally taught in an informal, localized family scheme.

As civilization matured, more formal education began to coalesce around the emphasis of the cultural setting: Hebrew teaching centered around religion whereas Greek cities offered teachers in discourse and debate. Roman education featured a rounded approach, but included dialog for exchange (or adequate defense) of ideas, but phased toward Christian dogma with the entrenchment of Christianity and the oncoming, not coincidentally, of the Dark Ages.

Rather than trace the evolution of education, though, or illustrate philosophical approaches, I would comment here on the modern approach to education in the USA. Extensive education, having come to be regarded as mandatory and expected, is a cornerstone of preparation for most careers and even basic employment at non-skilled levels.

Given the bent toward technology and competitiveness, toward measure and categorization, much emphasis is put on testing students for reading, math and other delineated skills – particularly with graded evaluation as the primary measuring rod for relating performance, leading to graduation and advanced degrees.

But the caveat emerges that, if evaluation for comparison of skills becomes the only – or even dominating – criterion for determining focus on what to teach, qualitatively, education suffers. With overemphasis on math and reading, while both are important, passing along cultural qualities in the form of music, history and, indeed, philosophical, literary and even poetic regard for life suffers considerably.

In common American culture, the transient has long become favored over quality. Music and entertainment, often loud and offensive, with pieces popular only fleetingly, reflects a troubled mindset. While creative to a degree, and accessible to a much broader range of people via modern communication tools, modern art forms typically lack poetic beauty as a feature.

Significantly, the art, literature and music of a culture reflect the collective mindset. The educational emphasis on rote performance – rather than creative gesture – impoverishes quality in favor of quantity. It promotes the creation of like-thinking, philosophical clones in upcoming generations, addicted to the shallow pop culture of a throw-away mentality, rather than fostering a focus on quality of expression and loving, energetic engagement of life.

So, while there is adequate emphasis on education itself – perhaps even excessive in trying to extend advanced education to people whose character isn't so oriented – there is inadequate recognition of superior cultural aspects that could be incorporated into *what is learned*. The value of learning should hold sway over attaining a good grade or simply achieving a diploma or certificate. The richness of cultural tradition should supersede pure focus on current expression, as embodied in the latest movie, fashion, communication gimmick or music release.

Students, in general, scarcely see the long trail of cultural development that precedes their arrival, what it means (rather than simple historic dates and noted people), where it came from and where it's going. Few recognize significant contributors to their core cultural heritage, fewer still why that is *even significant.*

As an added factor of detriment, religion and fantasy-based distortion of history is commonly pushed for by more conservative voices, looking to bring standards down even further.

Education of coming generations is most vital. But failing to expose youth to creative, open-minded thinking, appreciation for the western heritage of art and quality music, recognition and respect for the depth of cultural heritage that underlies their very presence in a building dedicated to teaching can only guarantee that the same widespread ills plaguing our culture will remain in effect.

Of course, education passes along cultural understanding, communicating shared values to succeeding generations. But shortcomings and fallacies tag right along with technological prowess and preferred facts. So the growth of widespread awareness for the real functionality of reality, the Oneness of Self with Reality, will need to await general widespread growth of individual awareness before an orientation of education principles can likewise incorporate greater perceptiveness.

Point Nine: Mind and Matter

Outgrowing a Longstanding Illusory Division

As noted, this apparent dichotomy was long a stumbling point for philosophers: how to deal with two apparently different aspects of reality, a duality of nature at which any intelligent investigation ultimately arrived – mind and matter. The one was intangible yet complex, rational yet also intuitive; it seemed altogether different in nature from the other, which, whether solid or fluid, was visible and substantial – perhaps capable of knowing, i.e., hosting a mind, perhaps fully passive and unaware.

From early Greek times when "soul" qualities began to differentiate from real objects – a process that morphed over time from **all** things regarded as having soul to only the *animate* – a clear boundary between mind and object had already been distinguished. On that other track of our root cultural thinking, Judeo-Christian, the duality broke down differently: projected mind stuff, attributed to an imagined external deity, vs. the real – substance regarded as divinely created. Both tracks, and most subsequent views, ran right into that most mysterious of reality's seemingly dual attributes: the difference in quality between the tangible and the consciousness perceiving it.

Yet the more obvious links between mind and matter have long been noted...

The most overt of mind-matter connections comes through willed manipulation. To affect reality "out there", you need only plan an action then carry it out. Think about skipping a stone across a pond, then find a flat one and do it. Eat lunch; take a walk. The mind to matter flow at this current, real level is quite obvious.

But mind only seems connected to external reality *one step removed*; direct control only seems to extend over one's immediate appendages via the mind-body integration. Attempts to skip that stone directly via telekinesis will prove considerably trickier.

Still, the mind-body connection at this overt level is more than just manipulative. The typical male of this species need only think sexy thoughts to stimulate arousal (can't speak for females – that may well require an entire other book). Most of **either** sex could conjure up a real physical response, whether nausea or euphoria, by simply mulling over pertinent themes of disgust or joy – totally unrelated to the real world sensed at that moment. Music or remote events simply read about, pictures or imagined episodes that never really happened may elicit tears or thrills.

So the mind and body are obviously connected – and quite directly.

But those associations are immediate and physical. At that level, mind seems to connect to matter only via the body, either directly (and rather passively) through meaningful body response to emotional states or actively through muscle manipulation.

Plato, seeing this duality, had an interesting perspective. For him, mind was the real and far superior aspect, as matter seemed inert and obtuse. Mind made out of matter whatever it deemed fitting. Matter's *form*, the ideal behind each object's instance, was really that which existed in mind. So Plato's version of a duality was heavily weighted toward the mind as experiencer.

Quite different in approach, as we've seen, Aristotle melded the two. For him, as with **forms** being found within real objects, mind resided *within* matter – such that all objects, in responding to mind, resist its attempts to manipulate them.

Duality took on new dimensions as it evolved through the Christian era. Still split between mind and matter, absolute mind became rigidly projected out onto the conceptualized deity. And matter took on a dingy, shadowy sort of character.

Somehow in the dim, fearful minds of early Christians, flesh became sinful and tempting of transgression with its offering of pleasures through sex and feasting. Those negative attributes spilled over to *matter* in general, such that reality itself became base and heavy, particularly in comparison to the grandly idealized wonder of that higher spiritual place, heaven, in the time beyond death – when the mind wouldn't be plagued with its material-world anchor.

Augustine kicked off this travesty by projecting all goodness and truth into that perfect mind of his conceptualized god, God.

This line of thinking, mounting its idealized, divine mind on an ever higher pedestal, was bound to force the mind of man, by inevitable comparison, down into the pits. Seen as flawed and weak, man's intellect was rendered abysmal, insignificant in comparison to revealed, church-based truths – questioning them by mortals was forbidden and punishable. Anselm strongly supported this attitude, imposing that each individual, if incapable of understanding the vaunted church version of truth, should simply accept it and thus bypass his/her own innate human frailty.

Abelard at least allowed man to reason – but only on his own conviction that reason would support Christian doctrine.

Thomas Aquinas cracked the door open slightly, though, by allowing man some power to think for himself, to reason. As time went on, the door opened ever more widely. As the likes of Francis Bacon, Galileo, Copernicus, Newton and others pushed it in, it was never again to close. (At least not in the west, despite recent Evangelical Christian efforts to revert to neolithicism. The Islamic world went the other way: open to lively discussion in early times after the initial spread of Mohammed's word, it closed ever more tightly to any deviance from prescribed thinking as time went on.)

But exploring matter either by empirical examination or through mathematical relationships and reason, inquiries ushered by Bacon and Descartes, respectively, only slowly eased negative attributes layered on the evils of flesh and the temporal nature of life itself. Descartes, for example, could not get past an absolute duality, even in the face of common interaction – like skipping the stone above. Nor could he shed the third-person divine mind as behind it all.

Others rationalized the duality into their own pet notions. Hobbes, ever the materialist, thought that mind function was merely things happening in the brain. Berkeley tipped off the other end of the scale: everything existed only in mind. To

Hume, in fact, *absolutely* everything including all matter and mind, scarcely existed – only a series of impressions were apparent, from which no valid conclusions could be drawn.

John Locke, though, sat in the middle of the duality; allowing for both thought and the real, he recognized that they interact, but couldn't close the two prongs of the fork into a circle.

On the German side, Kant subscribed to a world outside the mind, but disallowed, given the shortcomings of senses and limits of awareness, that its nature could be known for certain.

That innate meaning, the *Ding an sich* – Thing unto Itself – was outside potential ken in his view. Significantly, he did recognize the innate connection of mind and matter, noting that they needed each other to exist. Fichte and Hegel moved toward the mind as all-inclusive, as though there were nothing outside it, although the former posed the ultimate as *universal mind*, not the immediate focus of personal consciousness. Hegel seemed more centered on the individual self as creative perceiver and source, moving along the path of German Idealism. This line emphasizes mind as the key element projecting or creating the reality – in the form of matter – which it encounters.

The other principal line of thinking, a vein of Realism, from Kant's time onward, interpreted matter as existing inherently regardless of our perception of it or relationship to it, with a notion that mind is some form of matter – or results from it. Along this line, Positivism allows that knowledge must be based on sense-derived experience and positive verification, while Pragmatism set the focus on workability. This latter, developed by William James, John Dewey (1859 – 1952) and ultimately

George Santayana (1863 – 1952), gave precedence in acceptability to propositions with practical consequences.

Movement in that direction – away from Idealism – typified the evolution of philosophy, as the objective viewpoint of science came to dominate things. But it led to other problems in a special, but highly important, nook of philosophical inquiry: the mind-body problem.

However obvious it is that mind can impel action, or even through imagination spur bodily response, simply noting that it can do so *doesn't explain how* that concept-to-event is even possible! When looked at in more depth, from virtually any common philosophical angle, the very nature of consciousness, of mind-body interface and related phenomena becomes very difficult to explain.

Generally, in a world view dominated by the overriding significance of the corporal aspect, mind function would have to be explained as a physical process of some sort. That becomes very difficult, as complexities of mind hardly reduce to physical quantification: as noted already in Angle One, memory, feelings and abstract thinking have no discernable physical component. Given some transcending nature of consciousness, explaining simple movement of the limbs via common *will* becomes problematic in itself, based on the general scientific view that the physical domain is "causally closed". By that, it is imagined that all impetus to movement can be traced back to an initiation in the real world – not into the realm of immaterial intent, that of mind.

So the long trail of philosophical examination always comes back to the same point of confusion, that same seeming duality when seen through any of multiple philosophical paradigms.

But all of those proposed models for reality – and a plethora of them weave their way among various branches of thinking – break down at the level of their own illusory bases. And that conceptual hindrance comes from mistaken understanding of the basis of matter itself within the context of conscious regard for it...

Matter is not solid substance, consisting of purely physical particles, as it has long been pictured in default western imagination – indeed ever more consistently conceptualized as the objective notion of science took greater hold over modern thinking. And mind is not so much response-based and reactive, superficial in survival terms, nor shallow in regard to overtly conscious consideration. Both mind and matter, in order to reflect the whole picture, must be seen at their core: each consists of **values**, of interactive functional meaning-based elements.

When seen in larger scope, wherein each life unfolds intertwined with meaning, i.e., significance expressed in terms of accomplishment and creative gesture, in love and artistic expression, in family-rearing and exploration, building of civilizations and complex structures, etc., the relationship of mind to matter begins to clarify. Values and focused intent, *held within* and expressed in any combination of life's potential undertakings and accomplishments, manifest their innate essence in the overall flow of personally encountered events and relationships. Collectively, all inner elements combine to produce mass events, with each life fitting neatly into the whole picture.

In terms of process, while unlimited potentialities stretch forward from this moment for possible outcomes, only precisely that set of events do indeed unfold that fulfill specific inner propensities of each individual, each group (seen collectively) and mankind as a whole.

So mind and matter, if fallaciously regarded as isolated elements, if seen out of each other's context and explored microscopically, seem separate, irreconcilable. But in the flow of a single life, each individual produces distinct patterns – patterns playing out in material consequence, always reflective of the overall content of mind of the individual experiencer. So mind and matter are *united*, not simply at the immediate level, with some leverage of action incited by rational regard, but in an overall flow that emerges on any scale from inner design. The apparent two are *One*, seen only at different phases of their ongoing, ever flowing cycle.

To illustrate, I might liken that flow to music.

In the now moment that consciousness occupies, music would be reduced to a single, current tone. The emotional content of music, however, manifests in its movement, employing diverse tones (at mathematically established frequencies), variances of tempo, volume and tonal quality to weave touching, arousing, annoying and other experiential effects into its expression. And that expression plays out in a dynamic display during which the mind follows the sound track, adding on the current tonal expression to those encountered just prior. The composer's statement can be a 2-minute song of love or rejection projected by voice and guitar, a 45-minute symphony accented by a 100-piece orchestra, or a 3-hour opera depicting grand tragedy or uproarious comedy by a grand troupe of performers. In any of those instances, the intended emotional impact is built by the composer into a musical structure that communicates inner value through **continuity** of a series of notes and chords.

Life is very much like those musical compositions.

The inner mind, a vast collection of complex values, personal propensities, absorbed conditioning, cultural orientations, etc., is equivalent to the composer. At any moment the psyche is assembling a composition for display, preparing its interwoven parts to manifest into life events, practicing them in dream sessions, then unfurling relationships and plots involving other performers, thus presenting the masterpiece. The work emerges into reality, playing, just as music does, with continuity as positive, rewarding events mix with disappointing, painful ones to fulfill the initial (but ever evolving) complex of inner propensities.

So, while each conscious entity exists only in the now moment, reality unfolds continuously, embodying meaning within depth in apparent time.

Seen with clarity for what it is, reality encompasses mind and matter in a flowing Oneness. They are simply two aspects of that Singularity, appearing in latent then realized forms, incorporating the current broad collection of values that comprise the Self.

Point Ten: Ideas and Thinking

So, What Do You Think?

Much of philosophers' regard for reality and the Self breaks down into basic ways of regarding them, weighted according to individual disposition. For some, direct examination of the universe was necessary to decipher its workings, a path leading – from about 1600 onward – to empiricism. For others, with an approach rooted long before that, sensory capabilities were too limited and the mind too easily fooled to rely on direct examination; they looked to *reason* as the intellectual tool necessary to more clearly discern reality's function.

From early times, thinkers tended to lean toward one orientation or the other.

Plato was clearly a rationalist, for example, where the Stoics were empiricists. The German line of Idealism evolved along rational regard, while the ultimately dominating track expanded with the emergence of empirical science and establishment of a technological-oriented modern society.

Invariably, however, thinkers in both camps fell prey to preconceived notions on which their outlook rested – some absolutely, per reliance on the god-notion, others at least significantly, in their inability to shed an attribution of independent existence for matter itself.

In regarding the apparent Mind and Matter dichotomy, the question arose as to how matter could attain consciousness in order to recognize reality and its own existence within it – or alternately, how non-corporeal based consciousness could actually interact with the real world. Beyond that issue and regardless of weighting placed on real examination vs. reasoned conclusion, a focus emerges to regard ideas and the process of thinking them: whatever the process, *thinking does exist*. So, what are ideas and what is the nature of thinking?

One angle of philosophical regard generally considers that the mind has no innate ideas of and by itself, but only encounters them through experience – only in response to the world it senses, does the mind come to conclusions and formulate ideas. The other posits that the mind engenders ideas, that reason via rational focus *initiates* thinking. But between the initial Greek consideration and modern, more complex analysis lies a millennium of yet a third source of thinking, not really falling within either group: revelation.

During that long stretch from Augustine through and beyond Thomas Aquinas, when a powerful church dominated the discussion (if there was one), neither examining the real world for information nor reasoned regard of it for conclusion was held as valid. Christian thinkers deferred to church theology and dogma for truth, relying on past definitions – even when those notions had often been concocted by committee, political motive or wide-eyed religious rant. In that act, all thinking was constricted and distorted for a long age, funneled into pious offshoots of Paul's early fantasies, steeped in the tradition of ancient prophets.

For sure, efforts were made by the more curious among Christian thinkers to align somehow the base theology with Platonic or Aristotelian concepts. Although invariably facing initial resistance, often they did have an effect. Thomas Aquinas, for example, with commentaries on Aristotle, opening understanding (slightly) to some reason and expressing greater guidelines, i.e., clearer definition for previously muddled church doctrine, overcame hierarchical resistance and initial rejection to actually influence accepted canon. First spurned, he later was named a saint.

But revising fallacious thinking only changes the flavor of conceptual poison; it doesn't neutralize its effect.

Revelation **always** rests on previous definition; it is never new. It only ever fulfills anticipated glories couched on its pre-existing content.

Ideas and philosophical thinking, in effect, do the same. The mind engages an incarnation with a clean slate, much as Locke noted. But unlike his assumption, it brings full character and a wide range of specific orientations with it. So, yes, following birth and on through childhood and youth, the mind begins to fill with specific notions, knowledge from what it learns and encounters, conclusions it draws from such. But all of that background understanding will have been absorbed and subsequently formulated to fulfill the preset orientation of the psyche.

That means that ideas in whatever regard that formulate in the mind of any individual, however intelligent, however curious and sincere, fall within particular confines: the parameters of common cultural notions that, subtly absorbed and assigned validity, combine to shape thinking and the psychological orientation of the individual character.

So ideas and thinking are far from free. Indeed, they are strongly influenced by – indeed, bent in the direction of – their underlying cultural orientation, although they fit neatly around the preset mentality of the incarnating psyche.

And the unavoidable consequence of that influence is the innate limitation of *all* thinking – empirical regard from observation and rational conclusion based on reason, as well as, of course, revelation (which emerges *purely* from inner content).

So conclusions drawn from observation are anything but the purely objective engagement they are made out to be. Perception itself, as often pointed out here, is distorted by the belief structure in place, generally fixed there through early childhood and highly oriented toward commonly accepted cultural definition. So planned observation, even double-blind testing, is given to distortion, because the tests and any associated criteria – even the initial theory up for proof or refutation – all fit within the confines of the basic belief structures at their foundation.

Likewise, reasoned conjecture as to life's function rests on the undergirding of cultural explanation and language absorbed from early childhood onwards. The psyche can only draw conclusions based on its own self-image and world view – and both of those aspects of recognition rest firmly in favored cultural definitions.

So, to reiterate my unique stance in regarding the very ideas put forth here and elsewhere: I spent 25 years exhaustively sorting through my psyche for synthetic notions. I rid myself of definitions, meaningful provenance for cultural notions and a wide range of tenets for attributing meaning to existence, along with mechanisms of mind that had lodged them into place in the naïve, curious child I was when indoctrination set things into place.

When I discuss the Oneness with which life unfolds in the experience of any individual, I do so from as clear, as unfettered, undistorted and untainted a view as exists up until the very moment I write these words. For absolute certain, my view is clearer than any philosopher's, as that person takes pride in complex analysis – all of which is based on a collection of notions, stacked on each other and resting on artificial, invariably fallacious core assumptions. And I see more clearly than the scientist, who has substituted objectivity for belief, not realizing that the objective scientific view is a paradigm itself, one inherently distorting perception of this subjective reality. And I see *far* more clearly than the religionist, whose cherished beliefs form magnificent illusions at whose ethereal feet that believer grovels for forgiveness and blessing.

Thinking is the image-based interplay that serves to interface the inner with the outer. The mind can focus inward, pulling out meaning and drawing conclusions, referencing memory or accumulated values as needed – or peer outward, perceiving a complex world and making sense out of it. The act of thinking is the focal track of such attention. But the mind can also create artistic and musical variations, mechanical devices or building plans never before conceived. It can devise absolutely new things: games, exotic sub-atomic particles, jokes and tricks, gestures of empathy and kindness – or means of torture – not to be found elsewhere in the universe. So thought can be reflective of the known, recalling of the experienced, observant of the apparent – or inventive of absolutely new material.

But the *essence* ideas invariably entail is *meaning*, however grand and brilliant, however mundane and common, however devious and detrimental, however loving and caring. For whatever their value and quality-effect, meaning is principal to thought, because the very existence of consciousness, embedded in a reality of its own manifestation, bespeaks always of values incorporated in its track of being.

Ideas and thinking cannot be recognized as what they are – the critical focal point of conscious engagement of the Self – until the nature of the Self is **perceived clearly**: a timeless, multi-dimensional yet non-dimensional, psyche at once containing complex meaning, projecting intent and realizing some variation of fulfillment and negation or neutralization of its will.

So long as scientists imagine a material brain, long evolved to attain computer-like function, as perpetrating consciousness, they will wildly miss the gist of being and the nature of thought. So far as religionists picture a synthetically glorious *other* consciousness out there as big, aloof and powerful, they will remain wide-eyed and clueless as to their own integrated status of existence. As to philosophers, conjecturing on any other variation of mind/matter fusion (or confusion), they will remain boxed inside rationalized constructs fabricated from the very notions leading to its conclusion.

Ideas emerge into attention, innate to consciousness in its regard to and representative of Self, both inner and outer. Thinking is the act of harboring, honing, recalling, speculating, planning, dreaming and otherwise massaging those ideas. However complex in practice, it's that simple in process.

Philosophical Regard

Muddled Mindset

If the above review seems complex to the reader unfamiliar with philosophical regard, it gets much deeper than that. Here are a few "-isms" and "-ologies" some touched upon, from which some aspect may have crept into common thinking – along with my comments:

- **Nominalism** doesn't accept universals (Plato's forms) as existing.
  - ✓ Good point: they don't.
  - ✓ But they seem to if you accept the idea.
- **Realism** sees reality as existing independent of conceptual themes that would depict it.
  - ✓ Well and good, but it leaves the age-old problem of *what is real* and eternal debate about it. Seeing precisely what does exist is impossible so long as the

mind holds any concepts depicting it.

✓ My solution is to end the debate (really only a ping-pong match of ideas anyway), dissolve your larder of all conceptualizations, definitions and assumptions – then you'll see Reality as it is, built on meaning.

- **Conceptualism** sits between Nominalism and Realism, allowing that universals exist within the mind.

    ✓ Indeed, they do exist there, but only as ideas.

    ✓ And they're joined there by a whole circus of other ideas: gods, forces, phantoms, power sources, processes and many other seemingly causal elements.

- **Deism** sees a non-intrusive god, perceived through reason and without the elaborate trappings of beliefs, miracles and such.

    ✓ An idea is an idea, whether in shades of subtle gray or full-blown fanciful color.

    ✓ Every god ever imagined is only a conceptualization.

- **Empiricism,** one branch of **Epistemology** (which investigates knowledge in and from various veins), draws knowledge from real experience and evidence through examination of real systems – as opposed to rational conclusion.

    ✓ The Caveat: conclusions drawn are invariably tainted by previously ingrained understanding.

- **Idealism** sees the nature of reality based on ideas, as opposed to **Materialism** in which reality consists of objects.

    ✓ This theory/movement falls short in not recognizing that the material world fits together in a cohesive flow whose events and relationships constitute meaningful ideas themselves.

    ✓ Thus, Idealism only looks at superficial, individual notions, not at the complexity of value and meaning with which the mind and its manifested reality interact.

- Existential **Nihilism** looks at reality as without purpose or meaning.
  - ✓ Actually, Reality is built on meaning – it is Nihilism itself, in failing to recognize that, which lacks validity.
  - ✓ Indeed, the Nihilistic act of denying intrinsic meaning to Reality carries a certain value in the gesture itself – thus disproving its own conjecture!
- **Henotheism** involves belief in one god while accepting that others do or might exist.
  - ✓ This gesture is enormously common – a viewpoint typical to people considering themselves as monotheists. The Christian who imagines that Satan, Mary, Jesus or the Holy Spirit has independent creative power is not a monotheist.
  - ✓ One who deems fate, luck or chance to govern real outcomes is scarcely a theist at all!
- **Monolatrism** similarly is recognition of multiple gods, but worship of only one.
  - ✓ This was likely the attitude of Abraham and early Hebrews.
  - ✓ Common to the world then, people generally acknowledged neighboring gods – perhaps even worshiping them when in that region. But they looked to their own god to overpower the others.
- **Determinism** looks at... Hey, I covered that above in Fate vs. Free Will! Quiz time: do you remember what this view holds?
- **Existentialism** from the 19th century focused on the individual in philosophical consideration.
  - ✓ Well noted: becoming too abstract or ethereal, too complex and theoretical misses the point.

- ✓ But it's just as easy to miss the point when not understanding the emergence of customized experience tied directly to any individual's mindset.
- **Teleology** sees purpose in reality, intended design in its nature.
  - ✓ Easy to notice in the grand scheme of things, but camouflaged by too objective a viewpoint.
  - ✓ In reality, design is not externally imposed (as by some god), but personally stamped with qualities reflective of the perceiver's inner nature. Thus *purpose* becomes camouflaged to any adherent of an incompatible paradigm.
- **Phenomenology** looks objectively at consciousness, including reasoning, perception and emotional response.
  - ✓ As these are all results of inner complexities, one does much better delving inward into the roots as illustrated in Angle Two than to examine phenomena that manifest from those inner bases.
- **Functionalism**, with many variations, sees mental states as interactively caused by input through the senses, via behavior or from other mental states. This weighs in between **Physicalism**, which attributes mental states to brain function, and **Behaviorism**, which looks at behavior as the process itself – rather than tied to something called mind.
  - ✓ There are lots of ways of looking at consciousness; each of them appears right if conceived and elaborated upon.
  - ✓ At the basis, though, is an aware, complex Self perceiving and manifesting an experienced Reality.
- **Darwinism** generally refers to gradual, long-term evolution of species driven by a process of natural selection: small genetic changes in species occasionally

lead to superior individuals who then succeed in reproducing better than others, thus passing along the changes.

✓ Neither this process nor **Creationism**, where some god is consciously enacting change in nature, is operative here: Darwinism inaccurately describes the surface appearance and Creationism erroneously depicts the driving process.

✓ In Reality, consciousness drives change through intent, but via overall qualification – wherein qualities are imposed on Reality suitable to supporting deeply meaningful life engagement. The Earth-based ecological system evolves now in response to man's presence and his intent, mitigated by dominant levels of negating elements. It has evolved over unfathomable ages specifically to host man's evolving mentality – not spurred by a remote, grandiose deity, but by pointed intent and determination on the part of consciousness as a qualitative attribute of all individual points of being, i.e., conscious entities seeking to incarnate. (Hmmm... Not as precise as I would like, that's the most succinctly I can phrase it.)

• **Atheism** posits that there is no god.

✓ Not merely a negative standpoint, generally atheists hold science, commonly empiricism, as their basis for regard – such that the skepticism leading to jettison of a deity never seems to pry loose the scientific paradigm.

✓ Atheists are right as far as they go: there is no external god. Knowing how reality doesn't work, however, is not to be equated to understanding how it does.

• **Agnosticism** questions whether certainty can ever be

attained about the existence of a god.

✓ Based on conventional thinking, this is as truthful and valid a point as can be made. Rather than fantasize or draw faulty conclusions, it admits to an unknown position.

✓ However, the life process illustrated extensively here, when engaged sincerely for improvement in various aspects of real life, clearly reveals that no external, manipulating force exists. But that awareness results from shedding conceptualizations that cloud the view, not from further rationalization or paradigm-building.

- **Criticism** stems from people who negatively judge somebody else's point of view when it differs from their own.

  ✓ And this is the one "-ism" in which I have the least interest!

  ✓ My clear view of functional integration between Consciousness and Reality is based on elimination of distorting notions. People who might ever criticize my message will have based their intellectual perspectives on some set of personally held beliefs and definitions, generally invisible to them – but from which they derive their understanding.

  ✓ So my disinterest in engaging criticism stems not from an aloof nature or conviction of my unerring rightness, but from a very pedestrian recognition of life's flow supported by a null set of accepted philosophical tenets.

The plethora of philosophical movements, views, subsets, variations, etc., can boggle the mind. But the mind buys into its favored notions, whatever they are. Believe them and they'll seem true. Stick an "-ism" on the end, overlay stratum after stratum of logical argument to enhance sophistication, and they seem ever more noteworthy.

But all philosophical conjecture, including religion and science, consists only of ideas. And in the end, those ideas don't enhance perception of how life works, but only mask it.

Your Heritage

While the journeyed course through these fascinating ideas is rather complex, the conclusion is remarkably simple: you exist as a conscious entity, constantly manifesting its own nature into real events and relationships.

Regardless of how you see yourself, rationalize or philosophize complex notions about reality, nurture synthetic beliefs concerning causality, or dedicate yourself to glorious gods, your total mindset becomes woven into an experienced reality. The only factors keeping you from clearly perceiving that Self/Reality interactive Oneness are the myriad of notions you hold that depict or imply some other process. And those, deeply founded in cultural traditions, language and behavior, rest – some overt, many quite subtle – within your own mindset.

From religious notions, you inherited ideas of personal powerlessness. You learned that a big, powerful creator god out there makes things happen: he created you and everything else, and you'd better acknowledge him or you are in big, eternal trouble. Hosting that archaic fantasy, your mindset will be plagued with doubt and feelings of helplessness. And that shakiness rests heavily not only on ideas you absorbed, but on nurturing and treatment from birth onward.

From scientific conceptual roots, your heritage incorporates personal insignificance. While science, empirical regard of reality, emerged much later than religion, its insidious function within your mind and life is similar. Instead of projecting creative power out to a god or gods, it attributes causality to a wide range of real-world forces and sources. Your personal power, within the scientific paradigm, is limited to your ability to manipulate the real world – for only action taken is deemed able to push things toward fulfillment of your intent.

But science, by its core tenet of acknowledging only the universe of matter as real, ignores the timeless conscious nature you encapsulate. In the act, accepting science renders you moot, temporal, insignificant by scale within a vast universe – and personally powerless.

Cultural notions, including recognized value of the common man, democratic ideas, personal inventiveness and free speech were injected by greater-thinking philosophers along the way into the mix you inherited as a mindset. Details of how that happened, and who among the worthy and courageous thinkers introduced what ideas, I could only touch upon. But those ideas mixed with truly archaic notions of fate and luck as forces out there dictating your life track, as unavoidable processes out of your realm of control, could only temper debilitation of religious and scientific notions. And that concoction, rolled into your mindset, renders you powerless, a hopeful but doubting bit player in your own life.

The gist of my review of those ideas stands simple: you see the world and yourself through lenses fabricated through the ages. Dimmed by superstitious attributions from ancient times, distorted by conceptualizations and expert connotations, dirtied by hidden, fallacious assumptions and cracked by blatant claims of miracle, mystical mystery and unquestionable thus unquestioned (yet invalid) truth, those lenses only serve to grossly warp your perception.

Freed of the lenses, a process involving dedication and

insight, you see life as a forum for engaging a wide range of creative activities and expressive outlets, a meaningful, exciting and stimulating venture in which *you can succeed* with health, love and satisfaction. Choosing to undertake that process, to delve inward to rectify a host of fallacious ideas and jettison a glut of distorted tenets, you can surpass the greatest of visionaries and thinkers in man's history.

They – and I – have helped point the way for your journey, but you alone can clear yourself a path.

THE END OF TEXT

But Not of Meaning

Who wouldn't love to sit down with Jesus or Gautama to chat for a couple hours – quiz them for what they really meant? Who wouldn't jump at the opportunity to discuss life with Meister Eckhart, with John Locke or Plato, submit some questions to Zoroaster, have a casual beer with Immanuel Kant or Nietzsche? Some extraordinary visionaries have passed this way, and a few brilliant thinkers – indeed, all too few.

Or maybe not...

Maybe just the right number. For if you have grasped the gist of what I've conveyed in these passages, you don't need to quiz those who have gone before, nor seek great perspectives from contemporaries, however highly touted, however popular and revered. You will have surpassed them.

Life, in its unfolding process, is really, really simple. You need only see that process, for the most intimate grasp of *what really is* requires no elaborate workshops, expensive retreats or courses, esoteric abilities or occult talents. The only barriers inhibiting Clear Awareness are false notions parading as truths, dimming your awareness, not elevating your rational comprehension.

We've covered a lot here: looking at life, then exploring the psyche in great depth.

And we've reviewed the greatest thinkers and visionaries in western traditions, examining their ideas, what they meant, how they influenced our cultural notions – and where they misconstrued reality. Some ideas you hold as truths came from them; many others you harbor at this very moment lie rooted in ancient myth, archaic definitions and more modern fallacy.

I've spent the greatest portion of my life clearing away conceptual debris handed me as truth, culling out phony notions, clearing away limiting, negating inner elements. And I've spent a significant portion now assembling my inner perspectives and critiquing the messages of others so that I can hand you as insightful an accounting as has ever been compiled.

If you have comprehended it, you realize that by far the most important phase of your journey toward understanding life and your own psyche is inward.

Your personal acceptance of these perspectives carries considerable benefit. But delving inward, personally and unremittingly, to remove restrictive mind-elements so that you can see clearly what you might now philosophically accept as truth – now *that* venture gets you much farther: to  where you see *yourself* as the "Prime Mover", the one and only cause – and without effort orient that creative power to beneficial fulfillment of intent.

What remains is simply to proceed. While the text of my message ends here, the meaning lies now fertile in your psyche, to be nurtured, implemented, expanded upon **and ultimately shared** with others who seek to understand the psyche and manifest reality.

All my best...

SELECT BIBLIOGRAPHY

J. L. Ackrill (editor), *A New Aristotle Reader*, Princeton University Press, 1987

Arthur Cotterell and Rachel Storm, *The Ultimate Encyclopedia of Mythology*, Anness Publishing, Ltd., 2007

John Cottingham, Robert Stoothoff and Dugald Murdoch (translators), *Descartes: Selected Philosophical Writings*, Cambridge University Press, 1988

Eerdmans' Handbook to The World's Religions, Lion Publishing, 1982

S. E. Frost, Jr. Ph.D., *Basic Teachings of the Great Philosophers*, Doubleday, 1962

The Holy Bible, New York International Bible Society, 1973 – 1978

Ted Honderich (editor), *The Oxford Guide to Philosophy*, Oxford University Press, 2005

Michael Jordan, *Encyclopedia of Gods*, R. R. Donnelley & Sons, 1993

Stephen Law, *The Great Philosophers*, Quercus Publishing, 2007

Leslie M. LeCron, *Self-Hypnotism: The Technique and Its Use in Daily Living*, Signet, 1970

Bryan Magee, *The Story of Philosophy*, Dorling Kindersley, 2001

Chris Rohrman, *A World of Ideas*, Ballantine Books, 1999

Samuel Enoch Stumpf, *Socrates to Sartre: A History of Philosophy*, McGraw-Hill, 1966

Various entries: Stanford Encyclopedia of Philosophy, www.stanford.edu

Various entries: Wikipedia, www.wikipedia.com

BOOKS

O is a symbol of the world, of oneness and unity. In different cultures it also means the "eye," symbolizing knowledge and insight. We aim to publish books that are accessible, constructive and that challenge accepted opinion, both that of academia and the "moral majority."

Our books are available in all good English language bookstores worldwide. If you don't see the book on the shelves ask the bookstore to order it for you, quoting the ISBN number and title. Alternatively you can order online (all major online retail sites carry our titles) or contact the distributor in the relevant country, listed on the copyright page.

See our website **www.o-books.net** for a full list of over 500 titles, growing by 100 a year.

And tune in to myspiritradio.com for our book review radio show, hosted by June-Elleni Laine, where you can listen to the authors discussing their books.

mySpiritRadio